Black Folks and Christian Liberty

Be Christian. Be Black. Be Culturally and Socially Free!

Rev. Walter Arthur McCray

A work in the Black Light Fellowship Series

◉ **Black Light Fellowship**

2859 W. WILCOX ST. • CHICAGO, IL 60612
POST OFFICE BOX 5369 • CHICAGO, IL 60680

(312) 722-1441

ISBN: 0-933176-00-7 Black Light Fellowship Series
ISBN: 0-933176-08-2 Volume 1
LC#: 78-71258

I would like to acknowledge the "grass roots" Black financial supporters who served as Initiators in the propagation of this work. Ecclesiastes 11:1ff.

Cover design by Ronald Maney, Chicago, IL.

A special thanks is due to brother Ronald Maney for his creative artistry. Hebrews 6:10.

The Cover design is the artist's conceptual rendition of the overall message of this study: Addressing the Black mind, three biblical principles, when made concrete within the Black psyche, enlighten the comprehending and discretionary faculties of searching Black folks, properly focusing and liberating them in their Black Christian cultural and social expressions.

Typesetting and Layout by Hieroglyphics Ink., Chicago, Illinois.

Special thanks to Chaga and Jaribu. We appreciated your guidance, tedious labor, and understanding patience with joy.

Printed in the United States of America.

TABLE OF CONTENTS

101218

Preface to the Second Edition

The times have changed, but the message is still relevant! Such is the reward of having written a publication for Black Christian young adults that was based on principles concerning social and cultural "questionable issues." Since the message was not a "Yes"/"No" message, but one which challenged young adults on the basis of biblical principles to think through the issues for themselves, the message still speaks to this generation as it did when the volume first appeared in 1979.

Black Folks and Christian Liberty is needed just as much today as it was when first published. Many Christian young adults still are grappling with what it means to be culturally and socially free. Pastors and teachers in Black congregations are yet pressed with providing answers for their young adults that are biblically-centered, freeing and responsible. The questions being raised are still hot:

Is it a sin for a Christian to dance?

Is it good for Black Christians to date or marry white?

Is a Christian permitted to drink wine as Jesus did?

Are reading horoscopes, going by your sign, and following astrology wrong?

Should a child of God play cards, shoot pool, or play table games using dice?

Is it unChristian to engage in recreation on Sundays or religious holidays?

Does the Bible say a Christian should not smoke?

Is not a Christian free to dress in any fashion that he or she chooses?

Should a Black person wear his/her hair natural?

Is it right for a Christian to strive to be Black in a white society or school?

What kinds of "changes" should a Black person have to go through in order to become a Christian?

Should Black students leave the Black Church because some people say that it is out of date and out of touch with what's happening?

Is it "worldly" for a Christian to be concerned about things like politics, racism, injustice, poverty, joblessness, mis-education, etc.?

In what way is it really possible for a Christian's entire life to become spiritual?

Black Folks and Christian Liberty is still timely. Though, for example, some of the references made to popular culture in the culturo-social profile of young Black Americans (pp. 139ff.) may be dated, the overall subject matter of the book and the way it is treated is pertinent and fresh. We believe our reading audience is able to transcend the dated materials and can still gain much benefit from this message as it presently stands. The principles explored should ring clear despite their social context.

The popular demand for Black Folks and Christian Liberty is also current. Many people have sought (in vain!) to secure a copy of its initial printing. The requests for the book are about as current as the issues being raised. We would hope that the issuing of this second edition would satisfy the longings of those who desire to explore the depths of this important subject.

Be Christian, be Black, be culturally and socially free!

Black Light Fellowship
Rev. Walter Arthur McCray
September 1987

Dedications

A belated birthday present to my Lord and Liberator Jesus Christ.
I hope you like it!

To my longsuffering and persevering dearest, Thelma, who conscientiously yeilded her freedom and rights to time, tenderness, and enjoyments so that I might compose and prepare these pages. Thank you also for the invaluable administrative assistance which you sacrificially rendered for this cause.

To all those blessed black believers who have graciously seen fit to make sure that my wife and I have a roof over our heads, a meal on our table, and some clothes on our backs. We have appreciated your support over the previous months. The Lord bless you. Titus 3:14 Galatians 6:6-10.

To all the young black Christian learners, male and female, between the change and challenge of education and actualization, who are "pressin' to please the Lord *in everything.*" I trust that you'll find some answers.

Meeting the Author

As a minister of the gospel of Jesus Christ, Rev. Walter Arthur McCray preaches, teaches, works and provides servant-leadership in the Black Christian community. He and his wife Thelma reside in Chicago, IL.

The author is the founder and director of Black Light Fellowship, a publishing and seminar conducting business/ministry. He has written several books important for espousing a biblical viewpoint for Black people. These include Toward a Wholistic Liberation of Black People (1979,); Solid: Nine Vital Lessons on Saving The Black Marriage (1981); How To Stick Together During Times of Tension (1983); A Rationale for Black Christian Literature (1985); and Reaching and Teaching Black Young Adults (1986).

Presently, Rev. McCray serves as the Editor/writer of both Direction and Young Adult Today, Sunday School quarterlies published by Urban Ministries, Inc. In addition, he is the current Chairperson of the National Black Christian Students Conference, and National Secretary of the National Black Evangelical Association.

A portion of the author's ministry involves his serving as the Junior Church pastor at his home Church, the First Baptist Congregational Church, and as pastor of the Parkview Worship Service, a Sunday evening ministry to senior citizens. He also conducts various seminars. One of the seminars in which McCray specializes is "The Black Presence in the Bible." This seminar provides a detailed study of the many Black African people mentioned throughout the Scripture.

Rev. McCray feels called by the Lord to do his personal share in discipling Black people into what he terms "Christ-centered Black nationhood." Such a conviction he impassionately pursues. His vocation objective is to develop a wholistic curriculum of biblical Christian Black education through which Black American people may be strengthened, and to share the message in this material with as many people as possible.

Foreword

I have had the privilege of knowing Walter McCray for seven years—first when he was a student and I a counselor at Trinity College, and in later years as a colleague and co-laborer in the National Black Christian Students Conference (NBCSC). I have watched his growth and skills development with admiration and respect for his desire to serve the Lord and his willingness to depend wholly upon the Lord and let Him use him in whatever way God chooses. One way God has used him is through calling him to conceptualize and live out the principles of the Black Light philosophy, which is described in the Appendix. Another important way is through the exercise of his considerable Biblical expositional and preaching skills. He exhibited these abilities in the delineation of NBCSC objectives in a book called, *Toward The Holistic Liberation of Black People: Its Meaning as Expressed in the Objectives of the National Black Christian Students Conference.*

What Walter has written here fills a void for Black youth. Just recently, at our 1978 NBCSC, several college students were grappling with the question of how their Black cultural heritage can be congruent with their Christian convictions since their prior Christian teaching had conditioned them to condemn as sinful much that is cultural and social in the Black tradition.

In the midst of a liberation theory for Black survival, this book highlights important dimensions of the meaning of Christian liberty. "If the Son makes you free, you shall be free indeed." Through the exposition of the Scriptures, Walter clearly and practically expounds *principles* for deciding what is pleasing to God as we walk with Him in holiness and submission to His will. He takes familiar passages and makes them fresh in their meaning and application to Black young people (as well as others). Here, there is the wedding of being Christian and Black in a healthy and provocative manner.

The casual reader can certainly gain much from merely reading this book, but most benefit would come from following the example of the Bereans, who "...listened to the message with great eagerness, and everyday they studied the Scriptures to see if what Paul said was really true" (Acts 17:11, Today's English Version). I commend this book to you as an aid in contemplating God's truth and in living out God's principles of holiness.

Ruth Lewis Bentley, Ph.D.
October 31, 1978

iv

Preface

"Should a Christian dance or go to discos?"
"Is it good for black Christians to date or marry white?"
"Is a Christian permitted to drink wine? (Jesus did!)"
"Is it okay for a Christian to read his horoscope and follow astrology?"
"What's wrong with playing cards, shooting pool, or playing bingo?"
"Is it unChristian to play sports, to go to picnics on Sundays or
religious holidays?"
"Who says that a Christian shouldn't smoke? The Bible doesn't!"
"Isn't a Christian free to dress in the way that he feels like dressing?"
"Should black folks wear their hair *natural*?"
"Should black folks really be so concerned about these "petty" things
in the light of racism, injustice, poverty, joblessness, mis-
education, fratricide, genocide and the like?"
"How many changes is it necessary for black folks to go through
when they become Christians?"
"Should a Christian strive to be black in a white society? School?"
"Should black youths leave the black church because some people say
that it is out of date and out of touch with their lives?"

Questions such as these are uppermost in the minds of many young blacks, and young black Christians in our day. Many of these questions are not new. They have been asked before. But today's *"Meism"* philosophy of black youth has given rise to lifestyles which pose a serious challenge to so-called "traditional" Christian ethics, values, and standards. Thus, Black Christians are faced with the task of coming up with a word and way for our black youths—a word and way that reflects both our accountability before the Lord and our utmost responsibility to this young black generation.

Through my black experience in the Black Church, in the black community, as a student in a white Christian college setting, and in my interaction with black youths, I came to the resolve that there needed to be a definitive message addressed to young blacks that attempted to deal with the nature of such questions as posed above. For from my personal observation and quest, I found that most of the material and messages which dealt with this subject—the subject of "Questionable Issues"— were either (1) unbiblically, and therefore unwisely, "Yes" or "No" in nature; or were (2) "good thinking," but thinking without an overall basis nor a diverse handle, and was therefore limited, incapable of being reproduced, and fostering a "Christian *Meism*"; or (3) dealt with these things as a side issue, and therefore relegated them to the status of "unimportant."

v

A detailed study of this subject was needed.

Therefore, in the face of these inadequate materials and messages of dealing with "Christian Liberty," and out of a conviction that there was *indeed* a word and way from the Lord for black folks, I engaged myself in this project. Hence, here it is!

This volume is unashamedly and unapologetically *black*; not merely in authorship, but moreover in perspective, and in the audience of my mind. Rather than being extensive, it is intensive. Its underlying assumptions are that black people have *special needs*, that the Lord is concerned about black folks in a *particular way*, and that he therefore has a *unique message* for them. This volume is also *Christian*. It attempts to deal with "questionable issues" in a way that is Christ-centered. It deals with the genuine, but forgotten, teaching of "Christian Liberty." It teaches liberty, freedom—*not license, nor leagalism.* And thus of necessity, it deals with Christian *principles.*

In this writing I have attempted to set forth the implications of the principles of Christian Liberty in a black culturo-social context. By doing so I have endeavored to fill the quest of young black Christians for "Blackspirituality" or, to say it another way, the quest for how black Christians are supposed to be, think, and live in the midst of this white and our black society.

The chapter patterns for this writing—which has been over two personally transforming years in the making—usually follow the headings of *Elucidation* and *Concretization*. Under the former heading I seek to interpret the biblical passages—mainly from the books of *1 Corinthians* and *Romans*—which deal with the subject. In doing so, I have endeavored to fully take into account the some 2000 years and 8000 miles which separate our culture from the culture of first-century Christianity. Under the latter heading I have systematically drawn principles from the biblical explanation, and have sought to show their pertinence to the black experience.

Following each chapter is a set of questions and suggestions which should prove beneficial in aiding reception of the chapter contents. They can be used both by groups and for individual study. Some personal notes and materials for deeper study are included in the appendices.

Though this work is primarily geared toward black college age students, it can also be appreciated by high school students and young adults alike. I trust that our black churches, homes, and Christian groups find occasion to give due consideration to what is written on these pages, for I see this work as an answer to the call of many black Christians to supply the dearth in Black Christian Educational models and materials. I further trust that this work will free up black Christians to concentrate on the "weightier" matters of the faith which are facing us in these dire days. These are those matters pertaining to discipling black people into "Christocentric Black-Ethnicism."

Not all of one's questions may be answered as a result of reading this book. Nevertheless, I do believe that young black Christians (and other blacks too) will disserve themselves by neglecting the contents of these pages. With this in mind, I commend to you its thorough reading.

A special gratefulness is expressed to my wife, Thelma Lowe McCray, for her presence, assistance, as well as her encouraging support in the preparation of this manuscript for publication. Thanks is also due to Dr. Ruth Lewis Bentley, Chairperson of the National Black Christian Students Conference, for her editorial assistance.

And also, thanks to you. For inasmuch as this work is personally published as an act of commitment to the black community, and as a means of developing a self-supporting financial base—your purchasing of it is a step toward achieving these goals.

The "Black Light Fellowship Series" means that, if the Lord wills, there is more coming!

The Lord Bless You!
Rev. Walter Arthur McCray

Chicago, Illinois
August 1978

Acknowledgements

"The Scripture quotations in this publication are from the Revised Standard Version of the Bible, copyrighted 1946, 1952, © 1971, 1973 by the Division of Christian Education of the National Council of the Churches of Christ in the U.S.A., and used by permission."

The author is appreciative of Third World Press, 7524 S. Cottage Grove, Chicago, Illinois 60619, for granting permission to use quotes taken from two of their publications: *Enemies: The Clash of Races,* Haki R. Madhubuti (Don L. Lee), 1978, and *Home Is A Dirty Street,* Eugene Perkins, 1975.

The author is very grateful to Val Gray Ward, founder/director of the KUUMBA Workshop, 2222 S. Michigan, Chicago, III. 60616, for permission to use *Principles For Creativity and Liberation.*

PRESSING THE NEED—Chapter 1

A PERTURBING PROBLEM

One day when I was in college, I was playing a game of pool in the student union with some of my friends. We were enjoying ourselves and having a good time. As the game was progressing, I happened to look into the hallway and found staring at me what appeared to be a female set of bewildered white eyes seeming to ask, "What in the world are you doing? How can such a 'good Christian' like you be playing such a contemptible game like that?" Hurriedly those eyes turned away and scurried down the hallway, never speaking a word.

As we went on to finish that game of pool, that *good* game of pool, a few unsettling questions began to plague my mind. What had that white young lady been thinking? Did I blow my Christian "reputation"? Should I stop playing this game? Is the Lord satisfied with what I am doing? What right did those white eyes have to question my activities? Questions like these and many more were working on my mind as I was working on that game. How should I react?

The school that I went to was a Christian college; predominantly white—with a handful of us black students. Moreover, there were diverse social elements represented on the campus, though it was predominantly middle class. In some other circumstance, I would have probably written the onlooker off, enjoyed the game, and not thought twice about it. I grew up with a pool table at the social center which I, and many other black children, attended in our part of the West Side of Chicago. It was an enjoyable game and provided good recreation. But in this particular circumstance at a white Christian college, questions about the rightness and wrongness, goodness and badness, of my activity were raised. And the questions were raised on three levels:

First, was this game of pool sinful for me as a *Christian*? Second, wasn't I merely experiencing a *cultural* difference? and Third, didn't I have the right to enjoy the *social* activities of my own choosing?

Because of these questions, I had to grapple with those "bewildered white eyes," and come to a solution. I needed a solution that would preserve the integrity of:

1. my Christian convictions, for this is what I believed;
2. my Black culture, for it is the outgrowth of my ethnicity, and I was born, and am black; and
3. my social choices, for this is my personal privilege.

And just as I had to grapple with this particular problem (meaningless to some, pertinent to others), I reason that many black Christian young people must deal with similar problems in their lives as well.

WHAT ARE THE ISSUES?

We need not argue as black Christians whether a person should or should not lie, steal, covet, murder, fornicate, envy, or the like. The Bible clearly condemns such activities (Gal. 5:19-21, Eph. 5:3-6). We should likewise condemn them, as well as pray for those who practice them, and encourage them to be liberated from them. We must not waste our time debating if people should or should not be loving, kind, patient, meek, humble, bold, courageous, rejoicing, forgiving, and the like. The Bible clearly justifies these good and godly qualities, and teaches that Christians ought to live them (Col. 3:12-14, Phil. 2:1-4, Acts 4:23-31). We are obligated to live them, and must encourage others to do the same.

There are, however, some issues which the Bible is silent on, or is not very explicit about. These are the things which many young people must diligently search their souls and their Lord about. They must search concerning the rightness or wrongness, and goodness or badness of these issues. What further complicates our dealing with these areas of life is the fact that Christians differ in opinions concerning them. Some Christians think that certain of these things are right. Others think that they are wrong. What are these things? They are such things as dancing, listening to "secular" music (soul, blues, jazz, rock, etc.), going to festivals, parties, and discos; attending movies, watching T.V. (especially crime, violence, sex, and soap operas), and listening to the radio. They are things like dating, inter-racial dating and marriage, using contraceptives, kissing, and petting. These issues concern playing cards, using table games with dice, playing dominoes, and shootin' pool. They have to do with the way people dress; length and style of dresses and skirts, what kinds of swim suits and swim trunks; bisexual and unisexual clothes; wearing suit coats and ties on Sunday mornin'; and shoes—how many inches? Also, women wearing pants or hot pants, halters and tube tops, and men wearing tight pants. And then there are the hairstyles, the braids, the rollers, the process, for women? for men?, the beards; and also the cosmetics, make-up, and jewelry: a lot, a little, or none? All these things fit into this category, and yet the list is in no way complete. Is it good or bad to study the zodiac, follow astrology, and live your horoscope? How about smoking cigarettes and weed, chewing tobacco, dippin' snuff, drinking wine; using drugs, pills, stimulants and depressants; or let's say sleeping pills, aspirins, cold tablets, medicines, cough syrup, and doctor's advice? And then there are things like gambling, playing bingo, the lottery, raffles, or supermarket contests and store games. Should a Christian participate or abstain? And should a Christian engage in sports or recreation on Sundays or religious holidays? And how about eating pork, being a vegetarian, using health foods, and drinking distilled water? How far do you go? What about superstitions: rabbit feet, walking under ladders, hanging horseshoes, avoiding black cats, wearing good luck charms or crosses around the neck? And then there's yoga, and biorhythm, meditation and palm reading, and reading period. Should you shy away from certain reading materials? And is it okay to use the contemporary slang and "ghetto" language, or does a Christian have a "new" talk? And on, and on, and on, and on . . . .

Christians young and old, male and female, good and bad, know that discussing many of these things usually brings on heated debates. Tempers rise, and eyes buck, and voices change, and arguments, and opinions, and "I don't care what you think anyway's," and "I stopped going to that church becauses'," and "I quit runnin' with her's," and "It's yo thang, do what you wanna do's," and we see the good, the bad, and the ugly!

These are those things.

We Must Have Answers

There are no easy or necessarily pat answers in regard to these things. Even though there are some Bible passages that deal with, and touch on some of them, many Christians are still perplexed about the posture which they should adopt towards them. There are still questions in the back of the minds of people. To Christians of past ages these things were known as "adiaphora."[1] I have chosen to refer to these sort of things as "questionable areas (or issues)" of living. To some they are known as "gray areas." Others refer to them as "neutral." Yet still, many Christians and churches have either dubbed a lot of them altogether sinful and wrong, or, on the other hand, have embraced many of them under the umbrella of "It's your own business."

If we as black Christians want to be made *whole,* then we must make some attempt to honestly deal with these areas of life. We must deal with them in such a way that is both pleasing to the Lord, and beneficial to all involved.

I think that there are three main areas of need which compel us to find answers, *principles* for ourselves, in dealing with this subject. A principle is a "general and fundamental truth which may be used in deciding conduct or choice."[2] The three areas of need are (as referred to above): Christian, cultural, and social.

A. Christian

First, we need some principles of guidance to help us in these areas because we are Christian, and Christians are principled people. Whatever anyone else does or says, we who are Christians must be true to the Lord to whom we belong and whom we serve. And though other folks may, "do it because it works," or, as they say, "I do it because I like it," we as Christians must never succumb to this baneful attitude toward the things of life. We must be ever searching out and trying to live the best good that we know. "We make it our aim to please him" (2 Cor. 5:9).

We have good principles as Christians. But not only are they good, they are also unchanging. And since they are unchanging, they are capable of being applied to many different circumstances and activities of life. For instance, the principle of children being subject to, and

3

respectful of their parents will never change. It is the same for each person, at every place, at every time. However, how this subjection and respect is worked out in each particular home may be different. For example, in a particular case it may be disrespecting to his parents for their child to stay out after 1:00 a.m. In another case, the parents are dishonored if their child stays out after dark! But in each case the principle remains the same: "Children, obey your parents in the Lord, for this is right" (Eph. 6:1).

Another reason why we need some principles of guidance to help us in the questionable areas of living is because we as Christians, and especially younger Christians, need to begin to concentrate on matters that are germane to our faith, rather than concentrate on things that are peripheral. Much good time is wasted talking about such things as dancing, movies, ways of dressing, etc., while other more important things get neglected. I'm not saying that these questionable issues are not important, for they are. Matter of fact, one can usually check out whether or not they are really committed to the Lord *in all things* by gauging his attitude toward such things as these. Nevertheless, it still remains true that there are "weightier" matters of the faith such as blackness, restoring lost identity, liberation from all kinds of oppressions, promoting justice and righteousness, healing broken homes and relationships, redeeming precious minds being wasted in schools, alleviating poverty, finding jobs and decent housing, healing the sick; delivering the demon possessed, alcoholics, drug addicts, and pill pushers; redeeming prostitutes, pimps, homosexuals, bi-sexuals, and unwed fathers and mothers; reclaiming delinquents, criminals, and many more. Actually, the "weightier" matters of the faith for black people are increasingly being focussed in the term "survival."[3]

We as black Christians need to learn to deal with the peripherals of our faith in such a way that it will free us to become unified and committed, so that we can begin to concentrate on the more important problems facing our lives in these days.

Another reason why we need principles of guidance as Christians is because we are engaged in winning others to Christ. From my experience in evangelism, I found out that when I have testified to a person about forgiveness of sins through faith in Jesus Christ, and have encouraged them to follow Jesus as their Lord, they usually ask, "If I become a Christian will I have to give up_____?" Usually without fail they will fill in the blank with a particular questionable area or two, such as smoking, or partying, or music. And sad to say, they have often been given the impression that in order to become Christian they must first give up this thing or that thing. Some Christians have made rules and hindrances to salvation that are not given in the Bible. A crucial shift in emphasis has occurred. The shift from a person giving up himself totally to the Lord and Liberator Jesus Christ, to the emphasis of giving up two or three "bad" things.

Wouldn't it be better to teach some principles to a person so that he will know that he must earnestly ask the Lord to show him His will for his life in these particular areas of living? Isn't it true that many young people think that they must commit social suicide in order to become Christians? Don't non-Christians ask Christians, "What do you do besides go to church?" Is it right for us as Christians to impose non-biblical rules and regulations upon prospective Christians? We need principles of guidance so that we do not add any unnecessary offense to people. The teaching of "Christ crucified" is offense enough. It is *power* enough to save as well! (1 Cor. 1:21-24; Rom. 1:16).

B. Cultural

Secondly, we need some principles of guidance to help us in these areas of living because people come from different cultures. People are from different groups. And black people have a unique identity and culture of their own.

It was after our Lord was resurrected from the dead that he gave this command to his disciples, "Go therefore and make disciples of all nations,..." (cf. Mt. 28:16-20). The Greek word for nation is *ETHNOS,* from which our English word *ethnic* is derived. Therefore, Christ is in effect saying that Christians must disciple the different ethnic groups. Now the black culture is the result of our black ethnicity. So there is no better reason for finding principles for guidance and application to our own culture as blacks than this: *Christ desires for it to be done.* The Lord did not only recognize individuals, but he recognized different groups of people as well. He recognized nations as entities within themselves. He recognizes the black nation as an entity within itself, and he likewise recognizes other nations (cf. Rev. 5:9-10, 7:9-10). He desires for us to not only spread the gospel to our people, but also to be committed to our people in terms of working out that message in our own unique culture. Therefore, in essence we have a command from the Lord to disciple black folks. And discipling black folks results in Christocentric Black-Ethnicism.[5]

Although there are many diverse cultures, I believe that the Christian faith can stand the test of implementation into these different cultures. I believe that our faith can be believed and practiced in various cultures without either diluting the faith nor destroying the culture. For although the principles of the faith are unchanging, they are capable of being applied differently in different cultures. What happens can be explained in the language of John 1:1, 14: "In the beginning was the Word, and the Word was with God, and the Word was God...And the Word became flesh and dwelt among us, full of grace and truth; we have beheld his glory, glory as of the only Son from the Father." These familiar verses about the eternal Son becoming the God-Man Jesus strikes home the point. For when the Living Word—*Jesus*—becomes alive in people—say, *black people*—then the end result will be glory—that is, *a glorious black people!* The faith transforms our ethnicity and culture. It brings them to fulfillment.

Now we must be careful as black Christians not to be encroached by

5

the culture of white Christianity. It has happened, and it can continue to happen. (It seems that we so easily forget that black people are in the minority in this country, and in the minority in many Christian schools, organizations, etc. You know...it is conceivably possible for us to be imposed upon!) The "man" gives us his slightly enculturated faith; or should we say his highly segmented culture of which faith is a "luxury." And some blacks take it.

It almost goes without saying that, despite the good done, there were (and are) many injustices that were perpetruated by white "Christians" upon blacks. The credibility of white Christianity was and still is being questioned by growing numbers of blacks (and third world people also). Blacks are beginning to ask if white Christianity can suffice for an oppressed black people. And the forthcoming answers are "some," and "little," and "no!"

It seems that white Christianity has become bedfellows with the beautiful American dream; which dream would have become a nightmare had black people entered into the vision. One need only mention the hassles which black Christians undergo at white Christian institutions (the schools that claim to be producing God's *leaders* for this generation) to see that the future is not very promising at all. On these campuses black students, black ethnicity, and black culture are denied, suppressed, neglected, or labeled "unChristian." (This happens of course if the black students are together. If not, they assimilate and are "tolerated" by the whites.)[4] But, the Lord made us, and the Lord loves us. And He will give us the kinds of biblical insights into life that we need to protect ourselves from what some white folks call "Christian."

But, not only do we need to protect ourselves, we also need to be a model to others of how the Christian faith can be manifested in a particular ethnic group which is committed to the Lord. Black folks are in the spotlight of many people within and without this country. What if the people who observed us saw an illustrious "black light" shining in the name of the Lord?[6] It would have tremendous ramifications. But as long as we seek to emulate others (whites or whomever) in the faith which we have, then all the folks who look at us will only see a "duplicate" of what others have. We must ask the Lord to help us as black Christians to be pioneering and creative in developing from the Word of God fresh, new principles for living in this changing and challenging age.

C. *Social*

Last, but not least, the third reason why I believe that we need some principles of guidance in dealing with the questionable areas of life is because of the social makeup of the black culture. There are a diversity of social forms within the black culture. Black people are not all the same. All blacks do not have the same tastes. All black folks do not participate in the same kinds of activities. Therefore, as Christian Blacks, we need comprehensive and concrete principles that will enable us to critique from a Christian perspective our own different social forms. Then we will be able to openly and effectively speak to our own lifestyles. If this comes about, then the Lord will not only speak an inter-cultural message through us, but also have an intra-cultural message for us. Matter of fact, the intra-cultural message is of first importance. For if we do not get it together as black people, then we forfeit the right to speak in the name of the Lord to anyone else. We lose by "default."

Principles will also help us to unite as Christians for a concerted witness to our community. There are a number of prominent black denominations, as well as numerous churches. The denominations have their own concepts of what is socially acceptable and not acceptable. Churches have their own lists of "do's and don'ts". No one church or denomination is necessarily right or wrong. Principles that would emphasize *ways of thinking,* rather than rules which specifically condemned or promoted certain social activities (in the questionable area), would be a major factor in uniting the Christians.

Principles that govern our ways of thinking would not only free us from unnecessary rules and regulations, but would also free our minds to be creative. A principle will take a person where rules and regulations cannot. For example, principles are able to constrain a person from doing things which are not specifically labeled "taboo," but which things in the long run might prove detrimental to the person's overall welfare anyhow. Or, principles can liberate a person so that he can think about new kinds of social activities and affairs which can profitably be enjoyed. And we black Christians need to begin to provide creative alternatives for those who feel that their present social activities are not meeting their needs.

Summary & Conclusion

As has been said above, I feel that A. there is a great need for principles of guidance, in questionable areas of living, for those Christians who are concerned about being made whole in the name of Jesus Christ. And B. the need is threefold: Christian, cultural, and social.

In the following pages I will attempt to set forth three foundational principles that speak to the subject of questionable issues, illuminate them in their biblical and historical context, and then suggest ways of implementing them into one's lifestyle. I trust that many questions will be cleared up, and that there will be some good answers provided for, first of all, that unsettled black mind, and then, if need be, for those "bewildered white eyes."

Understanding What Has Been Taught

1. What was the incident in the author's experience which provoked thoughts about the subject of Christian liberty?

2. What is the difference between a questionable issue and a non-questionable issue?

3. What ten or twenty questionable issues mentioned in this chapter can you recall?

4. What is a "principle"?

5. What are two reasons why we need principles as Christians?

6. What are two reasons why we need principles in our Black culture?

7. What are two reasons why we need principles because of the social makeup of the Black culture?

Responding To And Applying What Has Been Learned

Questions

1. Have you ever been faced with an incident similar to the one mentioned at the beginning of this chapter? How did you respond?

2. What questionable areas can you think of which are not in the list given in this chapter?

3. What are some other "weighter" matters which black people face?

4. What problems in the questionable area are you facing at your school?

5. Do you fellowship with Christians from other denominations? Why? Why not?

Suggestions

Individual

1. Try isolating three questionable areas, relevant to yourself, to center on when studying this book.

Group

1. Poll your group using a questionnaire to see where each one stands on several questionable issues.

2. See if your group can determine some of your "unwritten" (or written) church rules about questionable areas of living.

EMPLOYING THREE PRINCIPLES—
Chapter 2

1 Corinthians 6:12

"All things are lawful for me," but not all things are helpful. "All things are lawful for me," but I will not be enslaved by anything.

1 Corinthians 10:23

"All things are lawful," but not all things are helpful. "All things are lawful," but not all things build up.

PARTICULARIZING OUR COMMON PROBLEMS

Sometimes we think that the problems which we face in our day are unique to us. We often tend to think that our problems have newly come about in our generation. We would like to feel that they are special and original. Well, to a certain extent our particular problems *are* unique to us—inasmuch as *we* are experiencing them for the first time. However, to a large extent, our problems are basically the same as the problems which many others have faced in their own lives. There is something about our testings that is "common to man" (1 Cor. 10:13). Yet, after we have affirmed that all folks' problems are essentially similar, we must then hasten on to particularize the problems of different people. We can and must particularize the difficulties which people face for two reasons.

First, although people experience similar problems, the circumstances and times under which these problems are faced are almost never the same. For instance, all people know to some extent what it means to suffer. But when a person considers the type of suffering in slavery which black folks in North America experienced, then he will most certainly conclude that this composite and complex type of suffering is hard to be found among any other people.[1] Therefore, black people have experienced a rare and particular kind of suffering.

Secondly, we must particularize the kinds of problems which people have faced because this causes us to find accurate solutions to those problems. In order for solutions to problems to be helpful, they must be very direct. For example, suppose a person has the problem of a headache. Well, there is a general solution for most people with a headache—take an aspirin. But what if this person's headache is the result of bad eyes? Then he had better get some eyeglasses before he goes blind! However, if the headache is a result of tension caused by guilt from sinning, then neither glasses nor aspirin will be useful. The person will have to deal with the problems of sin. Then he will have a lasting solution to his guilt, sin, and subsequently, his headache.

Or, following through on the example of suffering in slavery of black people, we can surely say that the present predicaments of black people in America is a vivid witness to the fact that our problem (being a continuously oppressed and suffering nation) has never been sufficiently particularized so as to alleviate our plight. Despite the tokenisms of guilt-ridden whites, the honest concerns of well-meaning whites, and the remarkable gains of dedicated blacks, we still have a long way to go for liberation.[2]

"Now what," you may ask, "does all this have to do with questionable areas of living?" Simply this, that some 1900 years ago the first-century Christians faced and handled problems which are similar to our own. These Christians had questionable areas of living for which they had to find solutions. And for these areas of living they *did* find solutions. *And furthermore, if we as black people take the principles of their solutions, and apply these principles to our own problems—keeping in mind our own unique and different black cultural and social context—then I believe that we will be well on our way toward securing some lasting answers for the black people of this generation in the area of questionable issues.*

WHAT WERE THE PROBLEMS OF THE FIRST-CENTURY CHRISTIANS?

Some of the problems which the early Christians had to face centered around their pre-Christian lifestyle. Before, let's say, Jojo got saved he used to visit the pagan temples. There he used to worship idols and offer up sacrifices to his favored god—much like the Jews who offered up sacrifices to the Lord at the temple in Jerusalem.

Since all of the sacrificial meat from say his pig, sheep, or bull was not eaten during the service, the priest would then serve some of the remainder at a cultic meal that was held in the temple at a later time. Frequently, the priest sold some of the meat back to the worshipper to take home, or he sold some of it to the retail merchants to place it on sale at the meat market.

One day Jojo got saved. And because he was saved he began to go to the Bible study at his church. At the Bible study class Jojo came to learn that an idol did not mean anything at all. It was merely a piece of wood or stone or metal. And it did not have any real power of its own. He learned that there was only one true God, who had made the world and everything in it. This new knowledge impressed Jojo very much. And it began to affect the way he looked at things in the pagan temples. Now when he went to the temple (by special invitation from a friend, or to enjoy the cultic meal) he did not take the sacrifices seriously. Instead he considered that his being at the temple set a good social example. It even afforded him an opportunity to witness for the Lord. This was especially true since he had been delivered from his false conceptions about idols and gods.

Jojo continued to eat meat that had been offered to idols. But he gave it no value as having been sacrificed to a god. He now gave thanks to the Lord for that meat (cf. 1 Tim. 4:3-5). Whenever he went shopping at the market place, or was invited over to someone's home for dinner, he could enjoy the food which was served with a new enthusiasm. He now knew that all things came from the Lord. The Lord had put him in his right mind. He had a whole new outlook on life. This freed Jojo from his former "superstitions." He gave praise to the Lord for what had happened.

Jojo had a friend named Tony. Jojo and Tony had run together before they got saved. But Tony did not get saved until about a year after Jojo. Now when Tony met the Lord, his life took a different turn than Jojo's life.

Tony used to go to the pagan temples just like Jojo. He also used to offer up sacrifices to his favorite god who was Isis. As much as he could, Tony paid allegiance and worship to his god. He also used to stay for the cultic meal in the temple. And when he was able, he bought meat at the market place which had been offered in sacrifice to idols.

But when Tony got saved he left everything behind. Anything that had to do with those pagan temples, idols, and sacrifices he dropped cold. He gave up his old way of life. He quit going to the temple. He stopped visiting with the sacred prostitutes who were a part of the pagan religious system. He even gave up eating meat that had been offered to idols. He would eat other meats and foods, but he wouldn't touch idol-meat at all.

When Tony went shopping, or was invited out to dinner, he would always inquire as to where the food being served had come from. He wanted to know so that he could avoid that "infected" unchristian meat. Tony now considered himself liberated by the Lord. Since he was now saved, he wanted to stay saved. He did not want anything whatsoever to tempt him to return to that idol-temple bondage. So he would leave any and all idol-meat alone. He considered that anything which had been sacrificed to some other "god" was not fitting for a Christian. Tony was trying the best that he could to live a clean life. And he personally felt that he was doing pretty good, considering he was only a one month old Christian.

To look at the lives of both Jojo and Tony one might say that they both were setting fairly good examples. Both were trying to please the Lord. Both had made substantial changes in their thinking concerning their temple experience. But as time went on Tony and Jojo began to have some conflicts. They began to realize that they were not getting along as well as they could be.

One day Jojo and Tony happened to meet together at the meat market. Jojo ordered the best cut of beef that the butcher could find. The butcher brought out some fine looking steaks. He said that the steaks were fresh from the sacrifices at the temple of Serapis. Jojo didn't mind at all that the meat had been offered in sacrifice. He was glad to get some fresh meat. So he eargerly paid for his purchase.

Meanwhile, Jojo had begun to pick up some negative vibes from brother Tony, who was becoming a bit irritated at Jojo for buying that idol-meat. Jojo then turned to Tony and invited him over to his home for some fellowship. Brother Tony gave Jojo a hard "No thank you!" And in the process, Tony also let him know that since he had become a Christian he had given up eating food offered to idols. He also suggested that brother Jojo might be slipping in the faith.

With that insinuation Jojo got very uptight. He accused Tony of acting "uppity" and trying to be a super saint. This wasn't the first time that Tony had come out of his bag on Jojo. He had done the same thing last week at a community get together. At that occassion Tony had gone around trying to warn the brothers and sisters that some of the food that was being served had been offered in sacrifice to idols. He almost upset the whole happening. Everybody became real disturbed with his conduct.

By this time both Jojo and Tony were turning bitter. Tony had also become somewhat pensive about standing around the market place. He didn't want anyone to see him with Jojo and his purchase of sacrifced meat. Jojo was angry. But with more people gathering around, they both decided to cool it and go their separate ways.

On their way home, each of them tried to think back on how the argument had started in the first place. They both reasoned, "Over some food; some meat." This meat used to be a common everyday thing to both of them. But since they had become Christians it now took on a new meaning. If they proved unable to find a solution to this problem, then they were not going to be friends for much longer. What would they do?

Such was one of the thorny problems which the early Christians had to face. How would they resolve it? The solution might have far reaching repercussions for the Christian community. And yet, this issue of eating idol-meat was not the only issue involved in the problem. Besides being a place to offer sacrifices, the pagan temples were also the scene of public and social festivities. If Tony completely turned his back on the temple, his social life might go down the drain. He might even be considered an unpatriotic citizen. The temples were also an avenue of climbing up the commercial ladder. The trade guild members made use of the temple provisions. And Tony would be making a bad business investment by avoiding the temples.

On the other hand, people did indeed come to the temples in order to worship idols. And they did visit with the temple prostitutes. Would Jojo want to continually be in such an environment? Surely it would have a bad effect upon him in the long run. People could not read his mind. So unless he told them so, they would not know that the idols and the prostitution really meant nothing to him. He might be mistaken for being a hypocrite. But still, the pagan temples were not totally bad. For instance, all the poor people could come to the temples for a free banquet. The hungry could fill themselves up on that sacrificed meat. And should the poor brothers and sisters refuse to eat meat that had been offered in sacrifice? Especially since their church wasn't helping them out a whole lot? (cf. 1 Cor. 11:17-22).

These were the problems which the early Christians had to deal with. What would be the solution to these dilemmas? Could a yes/no answer suffice? Could these Christians, who held different beliefs, continue to be at peace with one another, and at the same time feel that they were living lifestyles that were pleasing to the Lord? Or would their problems begin to infect the Christian community (the place where the problems started originally) with bitter animosity? Would the church be stifled in growth by such problems?

CAN THE LORD HELP US?

Surely we face similar problems today; only we face them in our own unique setting. Is the Lord able to help us as black Christians to get it together? Can he give us the answers that will unite us so that we will be able to direct our energies into furthering our total liberation[3] in the name of Jesus, or will we continue to major in minors? Can he reconcile the alienated Christians of our community so that we can give a concerted witness to the Lord Jesus Christ so that many blacks who are lost may be saved? Or will we be polarized and fragmented? Can the Lord provide an atmosphere among black students on college campuses that will enable them to deal with the more important problems and challenges of their particular schools rather than quibble over non-essentials? I believe that the Lord can help us. He helped the first-century Christians with their problems. He can do the same for us today. Let's see if we can discover some of His answers.

TWO IMPORTANT BIBLE PASSAGES THAT DEAL WITH QUESTIONABLE ISSUES

I don't think that it was by coincidence that the Lord used Paul, a Jew who became the apostle to the Gentiles, to give help to the first-century Christians in the problem of questionable issues. Within Paul's writings, there are two passages of particular interest that can help us in our study and illumination of three principles that deal with questionable areas of living. They are 1 Corinthians 8:1-11:1 and Romans 14:1-15:13. Both of these passages deal primarily with the subject of Christian convictions in the area of Christian liberty.[4] As well as these two extended passages, there are also some other verses on the subject.[5]

Elucidation

THREE PERTINENT PRINCIPLES

The three principles which I believe are foundational for providing answers for the questionable areas of living are given in the book of 1 Corinthians. They are:

1. " 'All things are lawful for me,' but not all things are *helpful*" (1 Cor. 6:12a).
2. " 'All things are lawful for me,' but I will not be *enslaved by anything*" (1 Cor. 6:12b).
3. " 'All things are lawful,' but not all things *build up*" (1 Cor. 10:23b). (All emphases mine.)

13

From these three sentences we can learn several things. The Corinthian Christians had a key saying which they used in order to justify living in the way that they alone wanted to live. They said, "All things are lawful for me." These Christian were prone to a philosophy which was to be later called *gnosticism*. Gnosticism, a philosophy or religion, centered around gaining knowledge (Gk. *GNŌSIS*); especially gaining esoteric knowledge and elite secrets of spiritual things. Its followers held that the mind and soul were more important than the body; because, to them, immaterial things were more important than material things. Actually, matter and the body (in which their soul was imprisoned or entombed) were considered evil, and, therefore, were a hindrance to their gaining salvation. Salvation was synonymous with getting spiritual knowledge about the origin of the world and evil, thus attaining purification and immortality. They also sought to acquire knowledge in order to gain power as well as come to know future secrets. They felt that their calling was to understand and explain the universe. They conceived that the world was ruled and governed by certain aeons, that is, intermediary beings and powers that emanated from the Godhead and served varied functions. This philosophy was a mixture of Greek, Oriental, Jewish, and Christian thought. It came to full bloom in the 2nd century A.D., when it became a chief rival to Christianity. Suffice it further to say that their systems of thought, coming from contemporary philosophy, mythology, or astrology, were far more intricate and complex than is explained here. It was mind boggling.6

The tendencies of the Corinthians toward this philosophy of gnosticism led to two extremely opposite reactions. Some of the Corinthians became ascetic, and others became libertine. An ascetic is a "person who leads of life of contemplation and rigorous self-denial for religious purposes." A libertine is a "person who leads an unrestrained, immoral life." He is licentious. Both of these groups felt that the body was evil. So whether they suppressed and denied their bodily appetites, or gave themselves over to unrestrained indulgence, they felt that what they did profited their souls.

Therefore, we have this statement (most likely coming from the libertines) that says, "All things are lawful for me." Their philosophy had become predominant over their faith. They reasoned that since they had become Christians, they were absolutely free in their personal and social lives. They had become a law unto themselves with no outside constraints. They said, "All things are lawful for me! *Period!*" They did what they wanted to do. It was their own thing.

It is interesting to note that Paul does not attempt to deny their freedom in Christ. Paul agrees with them that "All things are lawful," all things are permitted. Paul, however, modifies this principle for them. He tells and proves to them that whatever they do must be 1. helpful for them; 2. freeing to them; and 3. strengthening for others involved.

14

Concretization

What are we able to learn from the verses of 1 Cor. 6:12 and 1 Cor. 10:23? *First, we can learn that there is truly such a thing as Christian liberty. Second, we can learn that there are three principles which we must deal with as we live out our Christian liberty. And third, these principles have multiple applications within their own limitation.*

CHRISTIAN LIBERTY—A VALID TEACHING OF THE BIBLE

Now, about the validity of Christian liberty; it is without a doubt that once a person becomes a Christian he is then set free by Christ. We are not here talking about freedom from the penalty of sin (Rom. 6:23), nor are we talking about freedom from the power of sin (Rom. 8:2,11; Jn. 8:31-36). We are not even talking about freedom from the law as a means of salvation (Rom. 8:3-4; Gal. 2:15-16). *When we speak of Christian liberty, we are talking about the freedom which Christ gives to believers which allows them to participate in, and enjoy the things of life which are not condemned in the Word of God. We are talking about the freedom to live as one pleases under no law except the law of God with its sole restrictions and demands upon our lives. This is the Christian liberty we are talking about. And this is the undisputed freedom which is given by the Lord to each and every Christian.*

Paul says, "All things are lawful." He says in Gal. 5:1a "For freedom Christ has set us free." And in Gal. 5:13a he says, "For you were called to freedom." The apostle Peter says, "Live as free men" (1 Pet. 2:16). There are several key words in 1 Corinthians that express the believer's freedom in Christ. They are: "right", 8:9; 9:4,5,6,12,15; "liberty", 10:29; "free", 9:1,19; and "lawful", 6:12; 10:23.[7] There is truly such a thing as Christian liberty. And since there is, there are some definite implications for each Christian.

First, no Christian should allow himself to be involuntarily put into a situation which denies and/or supresses his freedom in Christ. The thing I want to emphasize here is involuntary suppression of liberty. Christian liberty is the prerogative of each individual Christian. And in order for it to remain Christian liberty, it must be righteously maintained. A Christian should not let an individual or a group usurp his freedom in the Lord. When a Christian voluntarily yields his freedom it is between himself and the Lord. When a Christian apathetically sits by and watches his liberty being taken away, it is a sin against the Lord.

Second, no believer must respond toward other Christians in such a way as though Christian liberty did not exist. Since Christian liberty is valid, then we need to learn to respect others as they exercise their freedom. To coerce others, either authoritatively or psychologically, to conform to our own standards of living is injustice. We must do all that we can to provide a conducive context for our brothers and sisters to exercise their liberty. And we must also honor their convictions.

MODIFYING OUR LIBERTY

The second things which we can learn from our two verses is that *there are three principles which must modify our Christian liberty.* We must ask ourselves three particular questions about the questionable areas of living. When we are about to engage in a given action or activity we must first ask ourselves:

A. *Is it helpful?*[8] (1 Cor. 6:12a). Is it advantageous, expedient, profitable, beneficial? The things which we do must be more than just "convenient." They must be useful.

B. *Is my freedom being preserved?*[8] (1 Cor. 6:12b). Am I being mastered by this thing? Am I being enslaved? Is this thing exercising authority over my life? Is it freeing? We must not enter into things which become habit forming or addictive. We must have no other "gods" nor idols in our lives.

C. *Does it build up my neighbor?*[8] (1 Cor. 10:23b). Does it edify, encourage, and strengthen others? Is it constructive? We must choose to do those things which are advantageous to the spiritual growth of other Christians; and are also advantageous to the well-being of non-Christians.

It is good to know that we can *employ* these principles. We can make them work for us. And I believe that they *will* work for us. For they are the Word of the Lord. I have seen them work in my own life, and also in the lives of others. And I am convinced that they can work for any honest Christian who will put them to work. Would you like to employ them?

We must learn to modify our freedom as Christians by examining each aspect of our lives with these three principles. The first-century Christians were not to hold to an absolute freedom. They subjected their freedom to the thought patterns of these three principles. Paul, who said, "For freedom Christ has set us free;" said also, "stand fast therefore, and do not submit again to a yoke of slavery." He affirmed, "For you were called to freedom, brethen;" and hastened on to say, "only do not use your freedom as an opportunity for the flesh, but through love be servants of one another." Peter said, "Live as free men," and then added, "yet without using your freedom as a pretext for evil; but live as servants of God" (Gal. 5:1,13; 1 Pet. 2:16). We must learn to qualify our freedom.

MAKING MULTIPLE APPLICATIONS WITHIN A STRICT LIMITATION

The early Christians had principles to guide them when practicing their Christian liberty. And since they did have these principles, they were able to use them in many different areas of life, for these principles dealt with "*all* things." These are the principles which were applied to the problem of eating meat offered to idols, and going to banquets in the idol temples (1 Cor. 8:1-13; 10:14-11:1). But not only were these principles applied to those needful areas, they were also applied to the areas of lawsuits among Christians (1 Cor. 6:1-12), to fornication (1 Cor. 6:13-20), to marriage (1 Cor. 7:1-40), to finances (1 Cor. 9:1-18; 1 Thess. 2:5-10; 2 Thess. 3:6-13), to evangelism (1 Cor. 9:19-23), to worshiping

(1 Cor. 12,14), to observing special holy days (Rom. 14:5-6a; Gal. 4:9-10), to drinking wine (Rom. 14:17-21; Col. 2:16), to vegetarianism (Rom. 14:1-4), and probably to many other areas of life as well.[9]

The above instances show that these principles can be applied to various aspects of our lives. Paul gets at this when he says, "So, whether you eat or drink, or *whatever you do,* do all to the glory of God" (1 Cor. 10:31). He says in another place, that "it is right not to eat meat or drink wine, or *do anything* that makes your brother stumble" (Rom. 14:21). (All emphases mine.) Since the application of these principles is broad, we can find many areas in our lives where they can and should be applied. We must come to understand the principles which the early Christians made use of, and guide our lives by them. The answers which the Lord provided for them are good enough for us as well.

Though these principles can be applied to many different areas of life, they do however have a strict limitation. Their application is limited to "questionable areas of living." When the Lord has explicitly spoken on a subject, then a person cannot apply these principles to those areas of living. These principles deal with areas of *opinions, thoughts, persuasions,* and *conscience* (Rom. 14:1, 14,23; 1 Cor. 8:10; 10:25-29). They don't pertain to areas of living where the Lord has given clear commands and teaching. We will stress this point in the next chapter. But it deserves mention here because we are prone to apply these Scriptures to areas where they should not be applied. It is not only possible for us to misinterpret the Bible, we can also misapply it. We will come to find out how the Corinthian Christians did this very thing.

Summary & Conclusion

I have tried to teach four things in this chapter. I have tried to show that, A. in our own unique context, we have the same kinds of problems in our lives (regarding questionable issues) which the first-century Christians had in their lives. B. The teaching of Christian liberty is a genuine Christian teaching. C. There are three principles which must modify our Christian liberty. And D. The principles of Christian liberty have multiple applications within their own limitation.

It is my earnest prayer that as you begin to realize the value of these principles of Christian liberty that you will respond to them positively by employing them in your own lifestyle. With this in mind, we can go on to the following chapters where we will "put some meat on the hamhock bone" of these three principles by considering how they are explained in the books of 1 Corinthians and Romans, and, at the same time, by observing how they were employed in the lives of the early Christians.[10]

Understanding What Has Been Taught

1. What are the two reasons why problems must be particularized?
2. How did Jojo's thinking change when he became saved?
3. How did Tony's thinking change when he became saved?
4. What were some of the issues involved in dealing with pagan-temples?
5. What are the two major Bible passages which talk about Christian liberty?
6. What three or four things can you recall about the teaching of Gnosticism?
7. How did the beginnings of this teaching affect the Corinthians?
8. What is Christian liberty?
9. What are the three principles of Christian liberty?
10. What is the strict limitation to the application of the principles of Christian liberty?

Responding To And Applying What Has Been Learned

Questions

1. When was the first time you learned about Christian liberty?
2. Have you ever gotten into an argument about a questionable area of living? For what reasons?
3. Before hearing of these three principles, what was your means of determining what you should or should not do?

Suggestions

Individual

1. Examine five aspects of your lifestyle by using the three principles.

Group

1. Act out a contemporary "Jojo & Tony" scene at a group activity. Then discuss the issues involved. This is good for consciousness raising.

SEARCHING THE BIBLE—Chapter 3

1 Corinthians 6:1-20

When one of you has a grievance against a brother, does he dare go to law before the unrighteous instead of the saints? Do you not know that the saints will judge the world? And if the world is to be judged by you, are you incompetent to try trivial cases? Do you not know that we are to judge angels? How much more matters pertaining to this life! If then you have such cases, why do you lay them before those who are least esteemed by the church? I say this to your shame. Can it be that there is no man among you wise enough to decide between members of the brotherhood, but brother goes to law against brother, and that before unbelievers?

To have lawsuits at all with one another is defeat for you. Why not rather suffer wrong? Why not rather be defrauded? But you yourselves wrong and defraud, and that even your own brethen.

Do you not know that the unrighteous will not inherit the kingdom of God? Do not be deceived; neither the immoral, nor idolaters, nor adulterers, nor sexual perverts, nor thieves, nor the greedy, nor drunkards, nor revilers, nor robbers will inherit the kingdom of God. And such were some of you. But you were washed, you were sanctified, you were justified in the name of the Lord Jesus Christ and in the Spirit of our God.

"All things are lawful for me," but not all things are helpful. "All things are lawful for me," but I will not be enslaved by anything. "Food is meant for the stomach and the stomach for food"—and God will destroy both one and the other. The body is not meant for immorality, but for the Lord, and the Lord for the body. And God raised the Lord and will also raise us up by his power. Do you know that your bodies are members of Christ? Shall I therefore take the members of Christ and make them members of a prostitute? Never! Do you not know that he who joins himself to a prostitute becomes one body with her? For, as it is written, "The two shall become one flesh." But he who is united to the Lord becomes one spirit with him. Shun immorality. Every other sin which a man commits is outside the body; but the immoral man sins against his own body. Do you not know that your body is a temple of the Holy Spirit within you, which you have from God? You are not your own; you were bought with a price. So glorify God in your body.

A. The Problem of Lawsuits Among Christians Tried by Non-Christians, 1-12a
   1. The Problem Itself
   2. Paul's Solution to the Problem
      a) Showing Alarm
      b) Saints Can Arbitrate
   3. Paul's Conclusion to the Problem
      a) A Warning
      b) A Reminder
      c) What's Helpful
B. The Problem of Fornication, 12b-20
   1. The Problem Itself
      a) Environment
      b) Philosophy
   2. Paul's Solution to the Problem
      a) God Will Resurrect The Body
      b) God Owns The Body
   3. Paul's Conclusion to the Problem
      a) Flee Immorality
      b) Preserve Freedom

Some years ago, at an early age in my life, I and another person were talking with a Christian leader whom we knew fairly well. As the casual conversation took place in our home, this Christian leader reached into his coat pocket and pulled out a pint of Gordon's gin. As he began to pour and drink of this which (I afterward learned) was his favorite pastime, I recall a word of justification being spoken on behalf of this behavior. I was reminded that Paul told Timothy to "use a little wine for thy stomach's sake." As I reflect back on this occasion, it occurs to me that Paul said "wine" not gin. And furthermore, I don't remember any complaints about gastric irregularities either. Nor do I remember this person taking only a "little" of his pint. I am afraid that this Christian leader (who in no way typifies the many reputable leaders which I knew then and know now) was somewhat off base—like in left field!

Jesus said to the Sadducees, "You are wrong, because *you know neither the Scriptures* nor the power of God" (Mt. 22:29). (Emphasis mine.) How often are we led astray by being ignorant of what the Bible really says! I mentioned in the previous chapter that we have a tendency to misapply Scripture. We try to put things into the area of Christian liberty that do not belong there. I am convinced that we must test each questionable area by the Bible to see if it truly fits into the area of Christian liberty. As we examine the 6th Chapter of 1 Corinthians, we will come to see how the Corinthian Christians misapplied Scripture. They therefore participated in some supposed questionable activities which they thought that their Christian liberty allowed.

Elucidation

The two activities which the Corinthians thought could be governed by Christian liberty were, *A. Lawsuits among Christians tried by non-Christians, 1 Cor. 6:1-12a; and B. Fornication, 1 Cor. 6:12b-20.* They thought that it was okay for one Christian to sue another one in the pagan courts. They also felt that fornication, that is visiting with a prostitute in an idol temple, was not prohibited by the Lord. They did both of these things under the "auspices" of Christian liberty.

Paul had to set them straight on these matters. He showed the Corinthians that these two areas of living were not areas where Christian liberty should or ought to be exercised. By illuminating Bible themes that have a bearing on these two situations, he taught them that these actions were wrong. Let's see how Paul handled these problems.

A. The Problem of Lawsuits Among Christians Tried by Non-Christians, 1-12a

As we look at this first passage, we will consider, first, the problem itself; second, Paul's solution; and third, his conclusion.

1. *We can notice three things about the problem of lawsuits.* First, there was wrongness and defrauding that occurred among the Christians (6,7,8). We don't know the exact nature or specific details about the problem. Nevertheless, it did appear to be something major.

Second, the grievances which resulted from the wronging and defrauding needed to be heard by a third party who would then determine a just and equitable solution (1,4,5). The Christians involved were evidently not able to settle the problem by themselves.

Third, instead of taking the case to the church for a solution, or taking it to another Christian for counsel, the debating Christians took the matter to the civil authorities, the unbelievers (1,5,6).

2. In looking at *Paul's solution* to the problem we can observe three things. *First, he expresses his alarm; second, he teaches them that they can arbitrate their own problems; and thrid, he says that suffering wrong is a better alternative than going to the court of unbelievers.*

Paul expresses his alarm that the Christians would go to unbelievers in order to have their grievances settled. He said, "When one of you has a grievance against a brother, does he dare go to law before the unrighteous instead of the saints?" (1, cf. 5,6).

Paul shows the Corinthians that this method of settling problems with one another is inconsistent with the role that the Lord has prepared for the saints. If they had known the Christian teachings which depicted the saints as judges, then they would have been able to claim guidance for themselves in handling this problem. They would have been able to *arbitrate* their own problems. Notice the phrase, "Do you not know" in verses 2 and 3, which emphasizes this point. (This phrase will also be used several other times in this chapter).

Paul let the Corinthians know that they would judge the world. He said,

"Do you not know that the saints will judge the world? And if the world is to be judged by you, are you incompetent to try trivial cases?" (2). Next, Paul let them know that they would judge angels. He said to them, "Do you not know that we are to judge angels? How much more, matters pertaining to this life!" (3). This seems to be Paul's argument: since Christians will be used of God (in the Day of Judgement) to decide issues of great importance, why can not they practice this wisdom and authority right now? Therefore, Paul implied that the saints should have courts to decide trivial cases, and matters pertaining to this life, between members of the brotherhood (1-3, 5).[1]

Paul furthermore lets the Corinthians know that even if the believers have no legal system of their own whereby they can settle their own disputes, that there is still a better alternative than taking one another to court before unbelievers. They can choose to *suffer*. Paul said to them, "Why not rather suffer wrong? Why not rather be defrauded?" (7b; cf. 1 Pet. 3:8-17ff.).

3. *Paul concludes his remarks on this subject by giving the Corinthians a warning and a reminder, and by emphasizing that they should do what is helpful.*

Paul points out to the Corinthians that whenever there is wronging and defrauding in their relationships, that this behaviour is the sin of unrighteousness.[2] And he *warns* them that the "unrighteous will not inherit the kingdom of God" (cf. 7-10).

The next thing that Paul does is to *remind* the Corinthians that the Lord had made a definite change in their lives. He says in verse 11 (after stating a number of sins): "And such were some of you. But you were washed, you were sanctified, you were justified in the name of the Lord Jesus Christ and in the Spirit of our God." In this verse Paul seems to be suggesting that the Corinthians were showing tendencies of going back into their pre-conversion lifestyle. He reminds them that the Lord had wrought miraculous transformations in their conduct. They were a "new creation" (cf. 2 Cor. 5:17) because of their relationship to Jesus. And this change should affect the way in which they treat one another.

Verse 6:12a seems to be Paul's conclusion to all that he has said. It reads, " 'All things are lawful for me,' but not all things are helpful." He lets the Corinthians know that it is not beneficial to have non-Christians settle disputes between Christians. The city of Corinth made provisions, even good provisions, for settling disputes among its citizens.[3] Nevertheless, no matter how "lawful" this judicial system proved to be, it was not *helpful* for Christians to take to it their disagreements with one another.[4]

B. *The Problem of Fornication, 12b-20*

As we approach this second passage, we will follow the same pattern we followed for the first one: *first, the problem itself; second, Paul's solution; and third, his conclusion.*

1. *In looking at the problem of fornication we will discuss the immoral environment of Corinth and the philosophy which aggravated the problem among the Christians.*

The people of the city of Corinth had a problem with immorality. At one time, prior to 146 B.C., there were over 1,000 religious prostitutes in the temple of Aphrodite.[5] This *immoral atmosphere* had a major influence on the Christian community in the city. Some of these Christians thought that fornication (as well as other sexual sins suggested by the Greek word *PORNEŌ*, from which we get the English word *pornography*) was a good activity in which to participate.

The Corinthians' basic *philosophy,* leaning toward gnosticism, led them to treat their bodies in any way which they preferred. Therefore, for instance, whatever they ate would not matter to them. Even if they overate, they were not troubled in the least. One of their slogans was, "food is meant for the stomach and the stomach for food" (13a). They could even get drunk without its disturbing their conscience (cf. 1 Cor. 11:21). This attitude not only affected their eating and drinking, but it also extended into the area of fornication, immorality.

They tolerated incest—a man living with his father's wife; living with his own step-mother (1 Cor. 5:1-13). Just as they reasoned that food was meant for the stomach and the stomach for food, they would also reason that the body was meant for immorality, and immorality was meant for the body. To be sure, some of them had been delivered from their past sins, sexual sins notwithstanding (6:9-11). But it seems as though their leanings toward gnosticism provided them with a new "freedom" to get back into some old habits. So they felt free to fornicate (visit with an idol-temple prostitute) at will. They even considered that fornication was a blessing from the Lord to be enjoyed in this passing lifetime along with other physical blessings. These Christians were becoming yoked to sexual sins.

2. *In Paul's solution to this problem he shows the Corinthians that, one, God will resurrect their bodies, and, two, that God owns their bodies.* Just as in the case of the lawsuits, Paul handles this situation by stating what the Scripture has to say about this problem.

In answer to their persuasion that immorality is for the body and the body for immorality, Paul let them know that this slogan was not true. He told them that the body is meant "for the Lord, and the Lord for the body" (13). These Christians thought that the body would be destroyed just as the stomach and food would one day be destroyed. But Paul made a distinction between those things which are temporary and transient functions of the body, and the body as a whole. The body in this context includes the entire personality, and, moreover, is eternal. Paul therefore spoke of the resurrection of our Lord, and reminded the Corinthians that *they will be resurrected* just as Jesus was resurrected. He said, "And God raised the Lord and will also raise us up by his power" (14). Christians will live forever in what Paul later calls a "spiritual body" (1 Cor. 15:44).

Paul does not stop at this point. He proceeds to illumine their understanding by bringing to their attention truths which have a bearing on the subject of fornication; which truths they must take into consideration when dealing with this activity. Here again, the phrase "Do you not know" (15,16,19) is a starting point. The truths which Paul makes known to the Corinthians suggests that *God owns their bodies.*

The Corinthians were ignorant of some important Christian teachings. They did not know that 1) their bodies were members of Christ (15; cf. Rom. 12:4-5; 1 Cor. 12:27); they did not know that 2) the person who joined himself to a prostitute became one body with her (16; cf. Gen. 2:24; Mt. 19:4-6; Mk. 10:6-8); they did not know that 3) their bodies were the temple of the Holy Spirit (19; cf. Jn. 14:16-17; 2:21); and, they did not know that 4) they had been bought with a price (20; cf. Acts 20:28; 1 Cor. 7:23).

If the Corinthian Christians had followed through on the implications of this teaching which Paul gave to them, then they would 1) not have taken the members of Christ and made them members of a prostitute (15); 2) not have become one with a prostitute (16-17); 3) not have defiled their bodies, their temples (18-19); and they would 4) have begun to glorify God in their bodies (19b-20).

3. *Paul concludes this problem by instructing the Corinthians to run from immorality and to preserve their freedom.*

Paul's basic answer to the Corinthians is for them to *run from sexual immorality* (18; cf. 1 Thess. 4:3). The verb in this sentence means to "continue to run." Paul considered fornication an enslaving sin. He said, "Every other sin which a man commits is outside the body; but, the immoral man sins against his own body" (18). Even though gluttony, drunkenness, sadism, and suicide may hurt the body, fornication is the only sin that arises from within the body. And even though another person is involved in the act, the basic purpose of fornication is the satisfaction of one's own body. Moreover, the consequences of fornication run directly against the very nature and purpose of the body which is to glorify God. It is no wonder that sexual immorality is not as easily dealt with as are other sins. In the words of a good Christian mother on the issue of lusts: "The Lord has shown me that you just can't shake that sin off like you can other sins."

Paul said, " 'All things are lawful for me,' but I will not be enslaved by anything" (6:12b). He didn't want the Corinthians to lose their Christian liberty by participating in the habit forming activity of sexual immorality. He said, therefore, *"You are not your own; you were bought with a price. So glorify God in your body"* (19b-20; Emphasis mine.). If the Corinthians would come to fully realize that they were purchased by God, then they would begin to understand that they owe their complete allegiance to Him alone, their Lord (cf. 1 Pet. 1:17-19).

Concretization

In this passage of 1 Cor. 6, we have seen how the Corinthians thought that the problem of lawsuits among Christians tried by unbelievers, and the problem of fornication both came under the umbrella of Christian liberty. We also saw how Paul overcame their wrong conception by exposing them to Christian teachings that had a bearing upon these two activities.

We can learn two lessons about Christian liberty from our study of the passage of 1 Cor. 6:1-20. We can learn that, *first, we are prone to have tendencies of license; and second, there may be Bible passages which have a bearing upon a particular supposed questionable area of living.*

A. *Just like the Corinthians, we are also prone to have tendencies of license.* We *can* be libertine, because people are lawless. We naturally "go astray." We do our own thing. And even after a person gets saved, he still oftentimes must struggle to do the Lord's will. There is not an automatic change. The Christian still maintains his old nature against which the Spirit of God engages in battle (Rom. 7:7ff; Gal. 5:16ff). Victory only comes as a person reckons himself dead to sin, and then yields himself to God (Rom. 6:1ff.).

Our proneness to license is often complicated by a misunderstanding about freedom from the law. Some Christians reason that they are not saved by the works of the law. And this is true. "For no human being will be justified in his sight by works of the law, since through the law comes knowledge of sin" (Rom. 3:20; cf. Rom. 4:5). They further reason that since they are not saved by works, but through grace, that they are not obligated to keep the law. And this is also true. "For Christ is the end of the law, that every one who has faith may be justified" (Rom. 10:4; cf. Gal. 3:24). *But* they are misled because they confuse keeping the law as a means of salvation, and keeping the law as a means of holiness; as a means of pleasing the Lord. Keeping the law as a means of salvation is a curse and ends in eternal death. "For all who rely on works of the law are under a curse; for it is written, 'Cursed be every one who does not abide by all things written in the book of the law, and do them'." (Gal. 3:10). But keeping the law as a means of being holy is a good thing. "So the law is holy, and the commandment is holy and just and good" (Rom. 7:12; cf. Rom. 8:4). Matter of fact, because Christians are under the law of Christ, which is love, then we will do much more than what the law requires. "Owe no one anything, except to love one another; for he who loves his neighbor has fulfilled the law. The commandments, 'You shall not commit adultery, You shall not kill, You shall not steal, You shall not covet,' and any other commandment, are summed up in this sentence, 'You shall love your neighbour as yourself.' Love does no wrong to a neighbour; therefore love is the fulfilling of the law" (Rom. 13:8-10; cf. Gal. 5:14).

Jesus himself said, "Think not that I have come to abolish the law and the prophets; I have come not to abolish them but to fulfill them" (Mt. 5:17ff). The Lord came in order to give us power so that we are able to fulfill the law. We do not keep the law in order to be put right in the sight of God and to be accepted by Him. We keep the law because we *are* put right with God, and thus the law becomes our "standard of conduct." If one reads the Lord's teaching about murder and adultery in the Sermon on the Mount, they should readily see that the Lord expects his followers to bring the law into completion, fulfillment, by their lifestyle (Mt. 5:21ff.; 27ff.).

I have taken the time to say these things about the law for this reason. As a result of the misunderstanding which some Christians have about keeping the law, they "pervert the grace of our God into licentiousness and deny our only Master and Lord, Jesus Christ" (Jd. 4). They think that because a person is not saved by the law, but by *grace throught faith* (Eph. 2:8-9), that they therefore have the legal freedom to break God's law and not suffer the consequences for doing it. They believe that they are "gettin' into heaven anyhow." They believe that if they confess the sins which they are about to commit that God will forgive them, and that everything will be "cool." Suffice it to say that people with this kind of thinking and attitude have learned erroneous teachings, are seriously deluded, and may not be born again in the first place.

Paul says in Rom. 8:6-17, in so many words, that a person who knows the Lord has a *desire* to please Him, and *is able* to please him, because God has made all the necessary provisions. A person who is really changed, who is really being transformed, "can't help themselves" as far as wanting to please the Lord is concerned. "But," nevertheless, "God's firm foundation stands, bearing this seal: 'The Lord knows those who are his,' and, 'Let every one who names the name of the Lord depart from iniquity'." (2 Tim. 2:19).

Now if a person who is a Christian has a wrong concept about freedom from the law, surely they also are going to have just as bad, or worse conception about Christian liberty. Let me repeat, *people are prone to put things into the area of Christian liberty that do not belong there.* The spirit of the times and of our communities, which calls folks to live the way in which they alone desire to live, has infected our Christian consciousness. The world translated "licentiousness" In Jd. 4, Gal. 5:19 and Eph. 4:19 means "excess," "absence of restraint," "libertine." This spirit has infected us. Therefore, it should not despairingly alarm us when we see people who appear to have no restraints in their actions and activities. For we can be sure that they have already taken off the restraints *in their own minds.* This brings us to the next thing which we can learn from this passage.

B. We can learn from this passage that *there may be Bible passages which have a bearing upon a particular supposed questionable area of living.* If we look back at our passage, we will notice that Paul asked the Corinthians no less than six times whether or not they *know* something (2,3,9,15,16,19). Paul appeals to their minds, their intelligence. More specifically, he appeals to their intelligence of the Scriptures. The word "know" as used in these verses means "to have seen or perceived." It frequently means to have a "fullness of knowledge."[6] Paul is speaking to the Corinthians about what they should have *obviously known.* They should have "had it down pat," or "uptight."

Many times if we have some questions about some particular activity and our involvement in it, we would do well to reflect upon Bible passages of which we already have a good understanding. For instance, sometimes a young person may feel that they can participate in a certain activity, but his parents will not permit him to do this activity. When this happens, then this particular questionable area is no longer in the realm of liberty for that young person. The Bible verses which talk about parental authority must be applied to this situation.

The same principle also holds true when a person is under the authority, not only of parents, but also a school, a church, an employer, the government, etc. For example, a school may have certain rules and restrictions which the students are obligated to obey by virtue of their applying and being admitted to that particular school. Now suppose a student, after attending this school for some time, comes to feel that some of the rules and restrictions are not good and ought to be changed. Being the nature of institutions not to change very quickly, the student takes it upon himself to flaunt the rules and restrictions which he does not agree with. Now even though this student may be right in feeling that the Lord allows him to exercise his Christian liberty, I believe that he will be wrong in feeling that the Lord also allows him to break the rules of the school. A primary rule of Scripture is to be subject to authority.

"Wait a minute," you may be saying. "Suppose the rules are *wrong*?" Well, let us be reminded that here we are not talking about right and wrong things. We are talking about questionable areas of living—things that are neither necessarily right or wrong within themselves. We are talking about things that are not explicitly written about within the Scriptures. And a school has its right to set its own standards for its own students.

Now when the leaders of a school, or of any administration, step out of their bounds and began to legislate in areas where they ought not to legislate, then we are obligated to "obey God rather than men," just as the Apostles did (Acts 5:29). However, it is wrong for a Christian to flaunt restrictions merely because the restrictions run against the grain of his own particular *tastes*. In disobeying authority we must be very careful to make sure that it is not a questionable area that is involved, but one that is explicitly right or wrong. And when we do feel obligated, for conscience sake, to set a particular restriction to the side, we must never do it clandestinely, hoping not to get caught in the process. Instead, we must do it openly and be willing to suffer for it patiently as a Christian ought (1 Pet. 2:13-23; 3:13-17; 4:12-19). We must not use our freedom as a "pretext for evil" (1 Pet. 2:16).

The principles of Christian liberty do not usurp the authorities in one's life. Certain wishes which an employer or pastor may desire may not be in line with our own particular tastes or style. Nevertheless, if we serve under the leadership of these people, then we should do all that we can in order to honor their wishes.

Sometimes rules and restrictions are outdated. Sometimes they do not sufficiently take into account the needs and desires of the people for whom they were made. Black Christians who attend predominantly white Christian colleges will most likely have to face such situations. I would recommend that these black students meet together with one another, formulate their feelings and thoughts, and then deliberate with the administration about the matters. Often the administrator's eyes must be opened to the vicissitudes of life and experiences which black students undergo.

Sometimes the Bible does indeed speak to a supposed questionable area of living. And we as Christians must have knowledge of the Scriptures in order to determine whether something is or is not governed by Christian liberty. This is the prerequisite to applying the three principles to any activity or action. For example, a person might think that eating pork is wrong. But when they study such passages as Mk. 7:19, Acts 10:9-16, and 1 Tim. 4:3-5, then they will come to find out that "everything created by God is good." Or on the other hand, a person may think that borrowing money and getting loans is the "American" way of doing things. They may feel that it is a Christian's privilege to get into the mainstream of buying on credit. But when such passages as Prov. 6:1-5; 22:7; Ps. 37:25-26; Lk. 6:30-31; and Mt. 5:42 are considered, then they will begin to think twice about borrowing large sums of money. They will also be challenged to give to the needy, rather than lend to them.

In order to know what the Scripture says, we must be willing to search through the Bible for ourselves. It is not enough to hear "good preachin' " on Sunday morning, nor is it enough to attend Bible Class during the week. In order to be satisfied and helped each Christian must learn to study the Bible for himself. Unless you are willing to consistently study the Bible on your own, then even the benefits of reading this book will eventually fade out! We must seriously search the Bible in order to receive direction for living.

Searching the Bible involves indept study. This is how we should study in order to get the meat and deep teachings of the Lord. Many of our difficulties in dealing with the questionable areas of life—and other areas of life as well—come about because there is no serious indepth study of the Word of God. Many of us tend to be biblically shallow. So, for example, even when we try to have a decent conversation on a Christian subject, usually a few familiar Bible verses come up, and then everyone else pools their ignorance. Our souls are lean. The prophet Isaiah said, *"Hearken diligently to me,* and eat what is good, and delight yourselves in fatness. *Incline your ear,* and come to me; *hear,* that your soul may live" (Is. 55:2b-3b; Emphasis mine.). There is no substitute for knowing in an indepth way what the Bible has to say about life.[7]

Searching the Bible also involves *inbreadth* study. Sometimes Christians get stuck in a rut about a particular problem because they have not read widely within the Scriptures. There are certain Bible personalities which some of us have never even heard about. Certain Bible books do not even exist to us. Relevant Christian teachings have escaped our concentration. All this occurs because we have not read broadly within the Scriptures. An hour of Bible reading each day would not hurt anyone. Indepth and inbreadth study of the Bible is especially important in dealing with the questionable areas of living. Because, if a person has not learned the rules, then how can he possibly deal with the exceptions?!

Sometimes we are willfully ignorant of the Lord's will. The Scriptures say, "Therefore do not be foolish, but understand what the will of the Lord is" (Eph. 5:17). At the age when your black mind is being challenged and expanded by the institutions of learning; at the time when you are seeking to get a diploma, and seeking to go on to perfect your learning and learning abilities; shouldn't you at the same time match or surpass this knowledge that you receive in the schools with the knowledge that you can receive from studying God's Word? Shouldn't a Christian young person know—and know very well—what the Lord has to say about life? Right On!!! "The Lord gives wisdom, from his mouth come knowledge and understanding; he stores up sound wisdom for the upright" (Prov. 2:6-7a). We must know "What thus saith the Lord."

Paul asked the Corinthians, "Do you not know?" The Lord asks us the same thing. We must *know* what the Scriptures say. For whatever is in our minds are the things we will most likely find ourselves doing. We should spend time formulating our convictions as well as thinking through the implications of what we have studied in the Word. We must do this just as Paul encouraged the Corinthians to do this. And above all, we must be *willing to do* what the Bible teaches. For that is the only way that we can have a good understanding of the things of God. For "The fear of the Lord is the beginning of wisdom; a good understanding have all those *who practise it*" (Ps. 111:10a; Emphasis mine.).

Summary & A Word of Caution & Conclusion

We have learned two lessons from 1 Cor. 6:1-19. A. We have learned that it is possible for us to have the tendency of libertines. And B. We have learned that there may be Bible passages which bear upon a supposed area of Christian liberty. Now a word of caution is in order.

In following Paul's pattern in dealing with the two problems at Corinth, I believe that we are permitted to do one thing, and are prohibited from doing another. First, *we are permitted* to search the Scriptures just as Paul did in order to come to our own conclusions about a particular questionable activity. We can conclude that something is or is not beneficial. And we can conclude that something is or is not mastering. We are able to draw these conclusions just as Paul did (1 Cor. 6:12).

Second, *we are prohibited* from applying our own conclusions to everyone else's problems. Paul was able to bring the Corinthians, by principle, to the knowledge that what they were doing was sinful. And since Paul concluded that these practices were sinful for them, then these same practices are just as sinful for us today. Lawsuits among Christians tried by unbelievers, and sexual immorality are wrong. Paul was speaking from his apostolic authority, and writing inspired words from the Lord (cf. 2 Pet. 3:1ff.; 2 Tim. 3:16-17; Rom. 16:25-26; and Gal. 1:1). What Paul wrote became law to be accepted and obeyed by each and every Christian.

However, after we ourselves have studied the Scriptures for ourselves about a particular matter, and have subsequently been satisfied within ourselves by the answers we have received from the Lord, then the best that we can do is to *persuade* others to follow our example. We cannot say, "Because this is wrong for me, everyone else must also feel that it is wrong." Neither can we have the attitude that "Because I feel that this is right, it is also on the up and up for all my peers." What we discover in the Scriptures for ourselves (pertaining to questionable issues) becomes only principle, not law. It becomes a personal conviction and not a public commandment.

In this chapter I have tried to show that we as Christians must know the Scriptures in order to determine if something is or is not truly questionable. We are required to do this before we begin to apply the three principles of Christian liberty to our various actions and activities. We must fight our proneness to be libertine. We have looked at how Paul enlightened the Corinthians when they thought that they were permitted to participate in lawsuits among Christians tried by non-Christians, and also to participate in fornication. Paul broadened their intelligence of the Scriptures in order to show them that these actions were wrong.

In the next three chapters we will move on to see how the three principles, which we studied in chapter two, were applied to various problems which the Christians faced in their own day. We will begin with the most important principle, that of edification: the principle that puts others above self.

Understanding What Has Been Taught

1. What did the Corinthians think about the activities of lawsuits and and fornication?

2. What kind of lawsuits did Paul prohibit?

3. What action did Paul suggest for a solution to the problem of lawsuits?

4. What temple in the city of Corinth fed fuel to the Corinthian's immorality? Why?

5. Why did the Corinthians believe that they were allowed to fornicate?

6. What was Paul's conclusion to this problem?

Responding To And Applying What Has Been Learned

Questions

1. When did you come to learn that fornication was sinful? How did this knowledge change your life?

2. What was your previous understanding about being "free from the law"?

3. Do you respect the desires of the people to whom you are responsible? Why? Why not?

4. How much do you study the Scriptures, and what is your method?

5. Have you ever tried to enforce as law your own convictions upon others? If so, what happened?

6. How good is your power of persuasion? Do you try to convince others to follow your own example?

Suggestions

  Individual

1. Isolate several questionable areas to determine whether or not the Bible has anything to say about them.

2. Begin a Bible study time, or improve a study time which you already have going.

  Group

1. Have a meeting around the topic: "How to Study the Bible."

2. Start a library of basic Bible study helps for your group.

BUILDING YOUR NEIGHBOR—
Chapter 4

1 Corinthians 10:23b

"All things are lawful," but not all things build up.

What think ye of Jesus the Son of God? *Would he put others first?* Let's see.

Matthew 17:24-27

When they came to Capernaum the collectors of the half-shekel tax went up to Peter and said, "Does not your teacher pay the tax?" He said, "yes." And when he came home, Jesus spoke to him first, saying, "What do you think, Simon? From whom do kings of the earth take toll or tribute? From their sons or from others?" And when he said, "from others," Jesus said to him, "Then the sons are free. However, not to give offence to them, go to the sea and cast a hook, and take the first fish that comes up, and when you open its mouth you will find a shekel; take that and give it to them for me and for yourself".

Would *God* put others first? *Certainly!*

Though Jesus was inside the house away from what was going on outside, He was nevertheless already on top of the situation when Peter came inside to get the tax-money. Peter knew that Jesus had always paid his temple taxes faithfully. He expected Jesus to do as usual. But before Peter could open his mouth to say a word, Jesus already had an answer for him. By using a simple everyday example, Jesus brought Peter to the understanding that he is not obligated to pay the temple tax. Jesus said that the tax-collectors have no right to ask him to pay taxes on his Father's house, the temple. I would imagine that by this time Peter began to feel a little uneasy, somewhat unsettled. But instead of Jesus "toughing it out" (and at the same time leaving Peter holding the bag) by sending Peter back to the tax-collectors empty handed with a staunch "No Way!", he paradoxically directs Peter how to go and get the tax-money. And Peter is instructed to not only pay the taxes of Jesus, but also to pay his own taxes. *Jesus yielded his rights.* The Son of God who was "greater than the temple" set aside his personal freedom. He set aside, if you please, his "Christian liberty," and paid his tax.

Why would our almighty, our all powerful, Lord Jesus do such a humiliating thing? Why? "Not to give offence to them." Jesus did not want them to become "ensnared"[1] in sin about his actions. Sure, Jesus' conclusions about the matter of paying the temple-tax were true and right. But the tax-collectors did not understand Him. Their thoughts about Jesus would have become all fouled up if the Lord had refused to pay. But since he did not want to offend them, he paid the tax anyhow. Jesus wanted to help people, not hinder them. He wanted to free them, not ensnare them. Jesus desired to edify, not to destroy; to build up, not to tear down.

Just as our Lord and Liberator was concerned about building his neighbor, so likewise we must have the same concern. Jesus would say to each one of us "Build Your Neighbor." A person can choose between two different lifestyles: one of helping people, and the other of hurting them. There is very little middle ground. As someone has so aptly put it, "If you are not a part of the solution, you are a part of the problem." We must be very careful to build up others. For " 'All things are lawful,' but not all things build up" (1 Cor. 10:23b).

Christians must be very sure to do the right kind of building. For there is an inspection day coming. There will be a testing day, the "Day of the Lord." Listen to the sobering words of Paul:

> According to the grace of God given to me, like a skilled master builder I laid a foundation, and another man is building upon it. Let each man take care how he builds upon it. For no other foundation can any one lay than that which is laid, which is Jesus Christ. Now if any one builds on the foundation with gold, silver, precious stones, wood, hay, straw—each man's work will become manifest; for the Day will disclose it, because it will be revealed with fire, and the fire will test what sort of work each one has done. If the work which any man has built on the foundation survives, he will receive a reward. If any man's work is burned up, he will suffer loss, though he himself will be saved, but only as through fire (1 Cor. 3:10-15).

God's fiery judgment will test if we have done the true, right, and good things which make the lives of other people better. If we have failed to build up others properly, then we will suffer loss. It will be just like a person who, suddenly awakening from sleep at the frightening alarm of fire, starts desperately running through his blazing home trying to reach safety, but only barely escaping being intensely burned to death in the raging flames! Paul says that "he shall suffer loss."

Each of us must ask ourselves, "In what way am I building my neighbor? What will be the outcome of my words, actions, activities, and acquaintances, on the lives of others?" From chapter two we can recall the problem which arose between Jojo and Tony. The problem arose because Jojo felt that he was free to eat meat which had been sacrificed to idols, and Tony felt that he could not eat this meat. What were these two Christians to do if they were to get along? Would it be right for Jojo to continue to eat the meat even though Tony felt that this was sinful? Would it be right for Tony to want Jojo to give up eating idol-meat forever, even though Jojo could honestly give thanks to the Lord for his new freedom? What should be done?

33

Considering our own situation, should one Christian participate in raffles and similar contests when another one doesn't think that this is proper for Christians? Should one Christian attend discos when another one thinks this is wrong? Should a Christian young lady wear mini-skirts and dresses when another one thinks that this is not right to do? Should a young man wear an open shirt to church when the pastor believes that a tie and coat are in order? Should one Christian denounce horoscopes, when another one feels that he is daily guided by them? Should one believer limit himself to only G and PG rated movies because another Christian feels that R and X rated movies are entirely bad without question?

We are in a similar kind of predicament that the first-century Christians had to face, and the kinds of decisions which we make in regards to these questionable issues of living will determine if we build our neighbor or destroy him. I think that we will be able to find some help in studying 1 Cor. 8:1-13. We will be able to learn how Paul handled the problem of eating meat sacrificed to idols. And once we learn to think as he does, then we will be able to govern our own lives in such a way as to build up others. Let's see what Paul has to say.

1 Corinthians 8:1-13

Now concerning food offered to idols: we know that "all of us possess knowledge." "Knowledge" puffs up, but love builds up. If any one imagines that he knows something, he does not yet know as he ought to know. But if one loves God, one is known by him.

Hence, as to the eating of food offered to idols, we know that "an idol has no real existence," and that "there is no God but one." For although there may be so-called gods in heaven or on earth—as indeed there are many "gods" and man "lords"—yet for us there is one God, the Father, from whom are all things and for whom we exist, and one Lord, Jesus Christ, through whom are all things and through whom we exist.

However, not all possess this knowledge. But some, through being hitherto accustomed to idols, eat food as really offered to an idol; and their conscience, being weak, is defiled. Food will not commend us to God. We are no worse off if we do not eat, and no better off if we do. Only take care lest this liberty of yours somehow become a stumbling block to the weak. For if any one sees you, a man of knowledge, at table in an idol's temple, might he not be encouraged, if his conscience is weak, to eat food offered to idols? And so by your knowledge this weak man is destroyed, the brother for whom Christ died. Thus, sinning against your brethen and wounding their conscience when it is weak, you sin against Christ. Therefore, if food is a cause of my brother's falling, I will never eat meat, lest I cause my brother to fall.

A. A Perfect Preface, 1-3
   1. A Closed Case
   2. The Emptiness of "knowledge," 1a, 2
   3. The Effects of Love, 1b, 3
B. A. Proper Perspective, 4-13
   1. The Reality of God, 4-6
      a) An Idol is Nothing, 4a, 5
      b) God is Everything, 4b, 6
   2. The Reasoning of People, 7-13
      a) They Hold Differing Convictions, 7-8
      b) They Draw Depthless and Damaging Conclusions, 9-13
         1) The Depthlessness, 9-10
         2) The Damage, 11-13

Elucidation

This chapter is the first of three consecutive chapters in 1 Corinthians which deal with the subject "food offered to idols." It can be divided into two main parts. *The first part, verses 1-3, are a preface to the subject. And in the second part, verses 4-13, Paul seeks to give the Corinthians a proper perspective on the subject.*

A. *A Perfect Preface,* 1-3

From Paul's initial remarks on the subject of food offered to idols we are able to learn three things. *First, the Corinthians thought the subject was a closed case; second, Paul showed them that their "knowledge" was empty, 1a, 2; and third, he revealed to them the effects of love, 1b, 3.*

1. First, we are able to learn that there were some people in Corinth who thought that they already had a good understanding of the problem. They would say, "all of us possess knowledge." They felt that they had come to a complete knowledge on the subject. As Paul puts it, they had come to *know something.* They believed that they had a good grasp on the matters at hand. When the letter was written to Paul from this church asking questions about the different problems (cf. 7:1), they probably expressed their opinion that it was not necessary to consult Paul about the issue. Or, at least, they had expressed that the libertarian position, which they were leaning toward, was substantially correct. They were content with their own way of thinking. *So as far as they were concerned, the matter was settled; the issue was closed.*

2. Secondly, we learn from verses 1a, 2 that Paul told these Christians that the kind of understanding which they claimed to have was inadequate in dealing with the problem. In effect, Paul told them that *their "knowledge" was empty.* He said " 'knowledge' puffs up" (1a).

Because of their tendencies toward gnosticism, the Corinthians became inflated within their own minds. They became preoccupied with their own intelligence. They were so to speak "know-it-alls." From time to time all of us come to cross the irritating path of a know-it-all. A know-it-all doesn't necessarily annoy people because he doesn't tell the truth. He doesn't get on folks nerves because he knows answers to many different problems. He is bothersome becaues he is preoccupied with ramroding what he knows. He shares more than enough facts. He gives answers to questions people do not ask. He is not sensitive to the needs and feelings of others. He is sort of aloof from personableness. Some of the Corinthians were this way. They were self-conceited and self-opinionated. No one could tell them a thing. And in it all they were superficial.

Many of the Corinthians knew the facts about God. They prided themselves in the highest knowledge. But they took the facts which they had learned about God out of the context of everyday living. They wanted the substance of pure knowledge, but all they got was emptiness. They believed that they possessed the truth. But Paul had to tell them that "If any one imagines that he knows something, he does not yet know as he ought to know" (2).

They took knowledge out of its proper relationship to other virtues of life—especially the virtue of love. One wonders whether the knowledge which they claimed to have was true *knowledge* at all! Are facts taken out of context, and lived out of context true? Can it be said that facts which are not in a proper proportion to other facts are true? Hardly not! Even though some of the Corinthians knew about God, they did not *know* him. To their shame Paul said, "some have no knowledge of God" (1 Cor. 15:34b). They were claiming and holding to a knowledge of God, but they did not know Him in experience. They did not know as they should have known. They did not comprehend the situation as well as they thought they did. Their knowledge was off. They were empty. And the major evidence which showed that they were off in their thinking was the fact that they did not have love. This brings us to the third point which we can learn from our preface.

3. Thirdly,Paul shows the Corinthians that *they were lacking the quality of love. He chooses to show this to them by emphasizing the effects, or results of love.* This love produces results in relationship to both people and God.

Paul reminded them that "love builds up" (1b). Love edifies. Love strengthens. In spite of the fact that the Corinthians knew some things about food offered to idols, they did not have the kind of relationship to one another that was healthy and helpful. A true knowledge would have led them to love one another. Since they did not have this kind of knowledge, they were tearing down one another. There were factions and strife among the members of the church at Corinth (See 1 Cor. 1:10ff; 11:17ff.). The problem of food offered to idols only proved to serve as another indication of their meager love for one another. It is no wonder that in the letter of Paul to this church we have some of the most profound teaching on love (1 Cor. 13). The Corinthians could have made more progress as saints if they would have had love for each other. They would have been a blessing to one another.

Not only were they lacking love for one another, they were also lacking love for God. They were overly concerned about learning about

God instead of loving him. So Paul told them that "if one loves God, one is known by him" (3). Paul wanted them to understand that anyone who has a proper relationship to God is not so much overwhelmed with what he knows about God, as much as he is secure in the truth that God knows him. "The Lord knows those who are his" (2 Tim. 2:19b).

The Christians at Corinth needed some security, some assurance in their relationship to the Lord. Paul revealed to them that they would get this assurance by loving God, rather than trying to figure Him out and putting him into their own intellectual mold.

In these first three verses, Paul has given his justification for addressing the subject of food offered to idols. His two reasons were that the "knowledge" of the Corinthians was empty, and that they needed love which would produce the effects of edification and assurance. In the following verses he will help his readers to get a good perception of the real issues involved in the problem. Let's see what he goes on to say.

B. *A Proper Perspective*, 4-13

In these verses Paul attempts to give his readers a proper perspective on two things. *First, he wants them to understand the reality of God, verses 4-6, and then understand the reasoning of people, verses 7-13.*

1. In verses 4-6, Paul begins to get down to the "nitty gritty" of the problem. He gets down to the *"eating"* of food offered to idols. In this paragraph he will magnify the reality of God by showing first, *that an idol is nothing (4a, 5), and second, that God is everything (4b, 6).*

As was said earlier, there were some Christians at Corinth who felt that eating food offered to idols was a sinful practice. Because of their background and pre-conversion experience, they made a clean-cut break with idol-food. Paul wanted these Christians to know that, contrary to their understanding, an "idol has no real existence" (4). He wanted them to understand that a piece of wood is a piece of wood, nothing more. A stone is a stone. Even though people may worship and give reverence to many so-called gods and lords in heaven and on earth, nevertheless, these "gods" and "lords" are not alive. They are not real. They are as dead as a "Do' nail."

People may indeed worship the sun, moon, planets, and stars. People can also worship stone, wood, silver and gold. But all these idols are vain. They have no life. There may be replicas and images of the "gods" of the air, water, fire, light, love, war, sex, planting, harvest, and so on and so forth. But, an idol is nothing.

It should be noted that in 1 Cor. 10:20ff. Paul will deal with this subject of idolatry from a different perspective. There he will deal with the reality and forces behind idolatry. But in this chapter he deals with the idol itself. He would agree with the Psalm writer who says,

Our God is in the heavens; he does whatever he pleases. Their idols are silver and gold, the work of men's hands. They have mouths, but do not speak; eyes, but do not see. They have ears, but do not hear; noses, but do not smell. They have hands, but do not feel; feet, but do not walk; and they do not make a sound in their throat. Those who make them are like them; so are all who trust in them (Ps. 115:3-8).

Paul wants to be very sure that his readers apprehend that an idol is nothing.

Paul doesn't stop at the negative talk about idols when trying to affirm the reality of God. He goes on to the positive and testifies about how real God is. In verse 4, he says that "there is no God but one." He wants the Christians to know very well that there is only one being whom believers recognize as supreme. And he wants his readers to be sure that they recognize the one to whom he is referring. So he identifies this one God as the "Father" (6).

God is the Father of our Lord and Liberator Jesus Christ (Eph. 1:3). He is the Father "from whom every family in heaven and on earth is named" (Eph. 3:15). He is "Our Father" (Mt. 6:9) by virtue of the fact that he birthed us and bought us into his family (Jn. 1:11-13; Gal. 4:4-7). He is the one supreme God, and besides him there is none other (Is. 43:11; 44:6,8; 45:5-6,21).

Paul further identified the one God as he is seen in the person of the "Lord Jesus Christ" (6). The one Lord of Christians is Jesus Christ. He is the Jesus of Nazareth, the lowly carpenter (Mt. 13:55; 21:11). He is the one who was anointed "with the Holy Spirit and with power...he went about doing good and healing all that were oppressed by the devil, for God was with him" (Acts 10:38). He is the Christ, the "Anointed One," chosen and sent by God to be our Lord and Liberator. This is our one God; our one Lord.

Paul goes on to describe the attributes and works of our God. Of the Father he says:
1) "from whom are all things"—He is *Creator* (Gen. 1:1).
2) "for whom we exist"—He is *Jealous* (Ex. 34:14).

Of the Lord he says:
1) "through whom are all things—He is the *Agent in Creation* (Jn. 1:3; Heb. 1:2).
2) "through whom we exist"—He is the *Regenerator* (Eph. 2:5).

What is Paul trying to get at by saying these things? I think that he is saying that God is real! *God is everything!* For an idol cannot create from nothing. An idol cannot be jealous for our allegiance. An idol cannot regenerate a person. Only God alone can do these things. Hence he is everything.

Some of the Corinthians already knew these truths. Paul wanted them *all* to be sure about these things. He wanted them *all* to have a proper perspective about the reality of God. He wanted those Christians who had ceased to eat food offered to idols, because they thought that an idol had a real existence, to understand that this belief was erroneous and binding. Since an idol is nothing, then meat offered that idol is nothing also. Based on this understanding of God and idols, Paul would agree with those who felt that there was nothing wrong with eating idol-food.

Knowing these things would free the Christians at Corinth to enjoy eating whatever kind of meat they desired. They could freely partake with the assurance that their partaking did not displease the Lord. Their proper understanding of the Lord enabled them to consider all kinds of meats and foods "kosher."

Now although a proper perspective in regard to the reality of God settled the fact that it was not wrong to eat meat that had been offered to idols, this answer was not enough in itself to satisfy the entire problem. For the Christians had to still live with and relate to one another. So in verses 7-13 Paul hastens on to help Corinthians to gain a proper perspective on the matter as it relates to the reasoning of people.

2. Paul wanted the Corinthians to know that the thoughts which arise in the minds of people are very important. *We can identify two points which Paul makes about the reasoning of people. First, they hold differing convictions (7-8), and second, they draw depthless and damaging conclusions (9-13).*

Paul begins the paragraph of verses 7-8 by saying, "However, not all possess this knowledge" (7). Immediately after Paul sets the believers straight in their thinking about God and idols, he then forcefully says "now everyone does not know what I have just told you." Paul recognized different levels of awareness among Christians. The Corinthians were saying *"we* know," and *"All* of us possess knowledge" (1,4; Emphasis mine.) Paul says "no, *we all don't know."*

Paul was saying in effect that there were some in Corinth who, although they could acknowledge that certain teachings were true, nevertheless had not personally interacted with what they knew. So to speak, they knew it in their heads, but not in their hearts. These Christians were violating their own convictions. Paul said, "But some, through being hitherto accustomed to idols, eat food as really offered to an "idol" (7b). These particular Christians once had the experience of worshiping idols.[2] Their pre-Christian lives were idolatrous. They were accustomed to eating sacrificial food. They were accustomed to smelling the vapor of meat through which they communed with their god. They lived among idolatry and they practiced idolatry. It was their way of life.

When these people became saved, they put away idolatry from their lives. Their gut feeling told them that an idol was real. They felt that idols were in themselves spiritual beings and forces. Furthermore, in their hearts they felt that eating idol meat was wrong, unclean, sinful. But they began to eat it anyhow. They jumped on the bandwagon and ate idol-food just as many of the others did at Corinth. They ate the meat, and ate it while even believing it was sacred meat with a special religious value. They ate the food even though they believed that the idol was real. Why would these Christians do such a thing? Maybe because they had deep needs to be accepted by others. Probably because of peer pressure.

Paul said that the conscience's of these Christians were "weak" (7). This weakness meant that they could not handle such a close association with those things from which the Lord had delievered them. They wanted to be free in their minds from their past ways of thinking, but somehow they could not at that time get up over that hump. They could assent to the fact that "an idol has no real existence." They could say "Amen!" to the truth that "there is no God but one." But at this stage of their spiritual maturation, their consciences had not been entirely cleansed from their old ways of thinking. When someone would mention idol-meat, a flashing red light would appear in their minds. Their experience can be described in the words of Rom. 14:14 where Paul said, "I know and am persuaded in the Lord Jesus that nothing is unclean in itself; *but it is unclean for any one who thinks it unclean."* (Emphasis mine.)

Deep down and underneath, these Christians felt that idol-food was unclean. Only the Lord knew how long it would take them to get over this feeling. In the meantime, by continuing to eat idol-meat instead of abstaining, they were defiling their conscience's (7). Defile (*MOLUNŌ*) as used here means to "besmear," "to smear thoroughly, as with mud or filth," "to befoul." Suffice it to say that they were messing up their consciences. Instead of waiting on the Lord to thoroughly purge their minds, they were making it much harder for themselves. They were getting to the point where they would eventually become callous to sin. If they had reached this point then not even a caution light, much less a red one, would appear in their minds. They defiled their consciences because they violated their own convictions.

Paul helped the Christians at Corinth to understand that people hold differing convictions. He wanted them to know that even though some among their members were apparently having a good time eating idol-food, underneath they were ruining their lives. "He who has doubts is condemned, if he eats, because he does not act from faith; for whatever does not proceed from faith is sin" (Rom. 14:23).

The next thing which Paul does is to show the proper place of food. He says, "Food will not commend us to God. We are no worse off if we do not eat, and no better off if we do" (8). The libertines probably used this saying to justify doing whatever they wanted to do. Since they felt that eating food would not determine a person's relationship to God, they then reasoned that it did not matter if a Christian (including one who had been accustomed to idols) ate food that had been sacrificed to idols. But by using this saying, Paul most likely had another purpose in mind than that of confirming the libertines in their own erroneous way of thinking.

I believe that Paul wanted to show the brothers with the weak consciences that they need not feel pressured into eating idol-food. Some of the brothers with weak consciences probably felt that they were spiritually immature in not wanting to eat idol-meat. Paul assures these brothers that if they refrain, for conscience sake, from eating food offered to idols, that this action would in no way affect their relationship to God. He would say to them: "The kingdom of God is not food and drink but righteousness and peace and joy in the Holy Spirit" (Rom. 14:17).

The next thing which Paul wants his readers to understand about the reasoning of people is that *they draw depthless and damaging conclusions.* Some of those at Corinth were shallow in their understanding. And because they were this way, they incurred some personal damage to their lives. So Paul wanted those who felt free about eating idol-food to be on their guard for people who do not draw good and helpful conclusions. Let's examine what he says in verses 9-13.

Paul said in verses 9 and 10: "Only take care lest this liberty of yours somehow become a stumbling block to the weak. For if any one sees you, a man of knowledge, at table in an idol's temple, might he not be encouraged, if his conscience is weak to eat food offered to idols?" Though it was not necessarily sinful to eat idol-food, it could nonetheless become a stumbling block to the weak.

A Christian could be in an idol's temple having a meal. This meal might have been an official ceremony, a trade guild affair, a public festival, or just an everyday practice.[3] This Christian would be in the banquet hall enjoying himself. Then, along would come a weak brother (most likely a newer Christian) who just happened to *look* into the open banquet hall and saw his brother, "a man of knowledge," in the temple enjoying himself eating the food that had been sacrificed to idols. The weak brother, who had been accustomed to idols, would reason that if the man of knowledge could eat idol-food, so could he. In a turn of speech Paul says that the weak brother would be encouraged, would be "built up,"[4] to eat food offered to idols! The weak brother would go in and join the man of knowledge, but only to his own detriment.

In doing this, *the weak brother would have come to some unsound, depthless conclusions.* First of all, he would have acted merely on what he "saw." He probably would not have reflected on the different experiences or backgrounds between himself and the man of knowledge. Or, he would not have reflected on the different way in which the Lord was working in their separate lives. He merely would "see" that the man of knowledge was having a good time. And because of what he *saw* he desired to join the man of knowledge, not even considering that there were differences in their convictions.

The second immature conclusion which the weak brother might come to would be in reasoning that a person could be a Christian and at the same time participate in idolatry. Paul seems to be saying that there would be an actual compromise taking place. To eat idol-food at home with a weak conscience is bad. To eat idol-food at a temple with a weak conscience is worse. For not only was the meat in these shrines dedicated to a particular god, the entire occasion itself was dedicated to the deity. There would be a natural danger that the weak brother would begin to take the best of both Christianity and idolatry. He would believe that they could exist side by side. These are the kinds of conclusions which he might draw from merely *seeing* the man of knowledge in an idol-temple.

As a result of the weak brother's bad conclusions, there were some *damaging results* that would occur, (11-13). Paul wanted the man of knowledge to know that by exercising his liberty in public, that he could possibly become a "stumbling block to the weak" (9). A stumbling block, (*PROSKOMMA*), is "something on which a person may dash his foot." The man of knowledge would have tripped a Christian who was trying to walk worthy of his calling (cf. Eph. 4:1).

The group of words which Paul uses to describe what happens to the weak brother is quite sobering. He is *destroyed;* the brothers (Christian community) are *sinned against;* their already weak conscience is *wounded;* and the brother is made to *fall.*[5] The weak brother will end up being no use to God and no use to others. His life will spoil.

Paul wants the man of knowledge to know that the Lord also enters into the picture. Destroying a brother is directly contrary to the work of Christ (11). Christ died in order to give life, and to give it in all its fulness (Jn. 10:10). But when the man of knowledge becomes a stumbling block, he "destroys the work of God" (Rom. 14:15, 20). He tears down the work of our Lord's sacrificial death. But not only is Christ's death robbed of its results in the brother's life, the man of knowledge sins against Christ himself (12). By being a stumbling block to another, the man of knowledge puts himself at odds with the Lord. He breaks his own fellowship with Christ.

Passage Summary & Conclusion

In summary of this passage, Paul gave a proper perspective to the Corinthians about the reality of God and the reasoning of people. In verses 4-6 he showed them that it was permissable for them to eat food offered to idols because an idol is nothing and God is everything. In verses 7-12 he taught them that people have different convictions because of their past experiences. He also taught them that people come to depthless and damaging conclusions based on what they "see." And because of their shallow understanding they participate in activities which for them are wrong; and thus they spiritually degenerate.

There is one verse I did not comment on, but chose to save it for last. *This is verse 13. It provides a very fitting conclusion.* In it, Paul says, "Therefore, if food is a cause of my brother's falling, I will never eat meat, lest I cause my brother to fall." Paul did not want to leave the Corinthians in any doubt about what he himself would do if he were in their situation. It is interesting to note that Paul did not tell them what they ought to do. Instead, he emphatically stated his own principles. "...*I* will never eat meat..." said Paul.[6] (Emphasis mine.)

One can hear the principle of 1 Cor. 10:23b ringing in his ears: " 'All things are lawful,' but not all things build up." The love which Paul expounded in verses 1-3 is now seen working in his own life for the benefit of his brothers.

Concretization

I believe that we can learn at least six lessons from our study of 1 Cor. 8:1-13 that will help us to deal with Christian liberty as it pertains to building our neighbor. *First, we must be open to accepting the counsel of others concerning questionable areas of living. Second, Christian liberty involves edifying. Third, when dealing with questionable areas, it is equally important to properly understand both God and people. Fourth, a person's spiritual progress may be at stake dependent upon how we deal with questionable areas of living. Fifth, our own lives may be at stake if we unnecessarily offend others in the area of Christian liberty. And sixth, each Christian must come to definite resolves concerning edifying.*

A. *We must be open to accepting the counsel of others concerning questionable areas of living.* We learned from verses 1-3 that some of the Christians at Corinth thought that they knew all that there was to know about the problem at hand. But they were sadly mistaken. Continuing in their own path would have surely brought destruction to their lives because they were sinning against the Lord (cf. 1 Cor. 11:30-32). Even though they didn't realize it, they needed the instructions of Paul.

It is dangerous for Christian young people to think that they themselves have all the answers they need to know about dealing with questionable areas of living. When a person closes himself off from the advice of others, he is headed for trouble. Listen to the words of wise king Solomon: "Where there is no guidance, a people falls; but in abundance of counsellors there is safety" (Prov. 11:14). "The way of a fool is right in his own eyes, but a wise man listens to advice" (Prov. 12:15). (See also Prov. 15:22; 20:18; 24:5-6.)

In dealing with questionable areas, oftentimes a special wisdom is needed. Many of the older saints—those preachers, deacons, and mothers—who have walked faithfully with the Lord over the years can offer good advice. More than not they have keen insights on what the Scripture teaches. This, coupled with years of experiences, is a wealth of wisdom.

We must be open, as much as possible, to what we can learn from other Christians. We must especially be open to the counsel of our preachers and leaders. For the Lord has put them over us so that they can guide us (Heb. 13:17).

B. *Christian liberty involves edifying.* The major theme of 1 Cor. 8 is edification. In verse 1, Paul said that "love builds up." In verse 10, in a turn of speech, he said that a brother can be "encouraged," or *built up* to do what for him would be sinful. The converse would be that this brother could be built up to do what was righteous. And in unfaltering language he states that his own personal policy is, in essence, to edify (13).

Building others is an essential element of the Christian experience. Consider these verses: "Therefore encourage one another and *build one another up,* just as you are doing" (1 Thess. 5:11); "Let no evil talk come out of your mouths, but only such as is good for *edifying,* as fits the occasion, that it may impart grace to those who hear" (Eph. 4:29; cf. also 4:12, 16). And specifically on the subject of Christian liberty: "Let us then pursue what makes for peace and for *mutual upbuilding"* (Rom. 14:19); "let each of us please his neighbour for his good, to *edify* him"

(Rom. 15:2) (All emphases mine.). The Lord calls us to have a lifestyle that is productive and positive; a lifestyle that helps and strengthens others. This is an aspect of Christian liberty. He wants us to build our neighbor.

C. We can learn from this chapter that *when dealing with questionable areas, it is equally important to properly understand both God and people.* The "weak" at Corinth did not have a clear understanding about God, so they felt that eating idol-food was sinful. The "men of knowledge" at Corinth did not properly perceive what was happening in the minds of the brothers with the weak consciences. As a result, they were not very cautious about their actions and were causing some of the weak brothers to be ruined.

When we properly understand God, it is freeing. For when we become increasingly aware of the Lord, then many *unnecessary* rules and restrictions cease to carry a major importance in our lives. We begin to concentrate more upon our relating to the Lord. The writer of Hebrews hits on this when he says, "Do not be led away by diverse and strange teachings; for it is well that the heart be strengthened by grace, not by foods, which have not benefited their adherents" (Heb. 13:9).

One sabbath day, Jesus and his disciples were walking through some grain fields. The disciples were hungry so they began to pluck the grain, rub it in their hands, and eat it as they walked. Now according to certain laws which the Pharisees enforced upon the people, the disciples should not have been doing this on the sabbath day. According to their laws the disciples were working on the sabbath by plucking and rubbing this grain in their hands. And since they were working on the sabbath they were sinning. And to add insult to injury, the disciples were enjoying their sin! They were *eating* the grain!

The Pharisees then came to Jesus and asked him why the disciples were doing wrong. Jesus told the Pharisees that they did not know their Bible very well. For if they had known their Bible, they would have known that the disciples were merely following in the steps of king David and of the priests in the temple. They too had broken the law and profaned the sabbath, but they were guiltless (1 Sam 21:1-6; Lev 24:5-9; Num. 28:9-10). Matter of fact, Jesus told the Pharisees that they did not even know what real mercy was all about. They had condemned the guiltless. I'm sure that it really got to the Pharisees when Jesus said, "The sabbath was made for man, not man for the sabbath; so the Son of man is lord even of the sabbath" (Mt. 12:1-8; Mk. 2:23-28).

This incident shows that the Pharisees were bound by their own petty restrictions because they did not properly understand the Lord. The disciples were free because they *walked* with the Lord. We can likewise be free.

When we properly understand people we become more considerate of them. People come from diverse backgrounds. The social climate in the black community is very diversified. Contrary to a typical white opinion, we are not "all the same." Our home situations are different one from another. The places that we go vary. The things which we do change from street to street, school to school, church to church, etc. We have different opportunities for learning God's Word. Some of our churches have well established Sunday Schools. Other churches have no Sunday School at all. Some young people have few good leaders who take a personal interest in their lives. Other young people enjoy the benefits of committed adults who spend time with them inside and outside of the church. Our experiences as black young people and young adults are different. Our opportunities for learning the Lord and his ways are different. We all grow up under an oppressive society that afflicts us with suffering and injustice. But our own individual experiences of living tend to be many and complex. Because of this, it is important, even imperative that we understand one another.

We must properly perceive at what stage our brothers and sisters are at in their spiritual development. We must ask ourselves, "How well does he know the Bible? The Lord? How quickly does he grasp spiritual truths? What are her convictions? What kind of life did the Lord save her from? Was it rough and tough? What things from his past experience might prove to be a "weight" to his further development? These are the kinds of questions to which we must have answers if we are going to make a sincere and honest attempt to understand people. This will be an aid in the effective use of our Christian liberty.

D. The fourth thing which we can learn from our study of this chapter is that *a person's spiritual progress may be at stake dependent upon how we deal with questionable areas of living.* The man of knowledge became a stumbling block to the brother with a weak conscience. Paul said, "Do not, for the sake of food, destroy the work of God. Everything is indeed clean, but it is wrong for any one to make others fall by what he eats; it is right not to eat meat or drink wine or do anything that makes your brother stumble" (Rom. 14:20-21).

Each Christian is a witness. It is up to each one to determine what kind of witness he will be—bad or good. If we are a bad witness then we are causing others to stumble. Once when I was at a barber shop I was speaking with a man (let's say Bud) about the Lord. As Bud talked about his relationship to the Lord he mentioned an incident that occurred in his past. He mentioned how a professed Christian, a church leader, had tried to get him to drive a young lady to a certain place and drop her off. The leader thought that Bud was not aware of what was going down. However, Bud was up on what was happening. So he refused to transport the young lady. Bud ended up saying that a wrong Christian leader is the cause of many people being brought down.

This incident happened early in Bud's Christian experience. At the time he was a member of a church and was going on with the Lord. Now Bud is not going to church. He is not living in a way that is fully pleasing to the Lord. I asked Bud if this incident with the Christian leader had been a turning point in his degenerating Christian experience. Bud said no. But I sort of believe that it was; at least to some extent. Because, for some reason or another, this incident was very vivid in Bud's mind. And as he reminisced about his Christian experience it came to the surface.

Now whether or not this incident in Bud's life led to his falling out of fellowship with the Lord, it is an undebatable fact that church leaders must be above reproach (cf. 1 Tim. 3:2ff., 8ff.; Tit. 1:7ff.). I wonder how many "has beens" have been made to stumble because their leaders let them down? Christians have a tremendous affect upon the lives of others; this is especially so for those of us who are Christian leaders. And the people we tend to influence the most are new Christians; young converts. The older Christians tend to be more stable; either in the Lord, or in the "games that Christians play." The recent convert is looking for the Way. They are sincerely trying to please the Lord. They can be easily turned off by "seeing" something that doesn't look right. They can be ruined by seeing you read questionable literature; hearing you listen to questionable music; watching you participate in questionable activities. Christian beware!

The Christian people with whom you associate may be coming to discover and participate in full Christian liberty. If so, then I think that it would be well for you to come to a good understanding of the lives and past experiences of any new group members, so as not to offend them. And if some new group members have stopped associating with your group, you might want to get in touch with them in order to find out the problem. It may be that they are offended. And one more thing, there may be some regular members of your group who participate in your activities, but who are being torn up on the inside. They may be silent, but souring. An open rap session, evaluating your group's activities, may be a good eye opener to some brewing problems. Let's not cause others to stumble.

E. The fifth thing which we can learn from this chapter is that *our own lives may be at stake if we unnecessarily offend others in the area of Christian liberty.* By sinning against his brothers, the man of knowledge sinned against Christ (8:12). When a person sins against Christ and does not deal with that sin, they suffer for it. In 1 Cor. 11:30 Paul told the Corinthians that they were experiencing the consequences of their sin against their brothers and the Lord's table. Some were "weak and ill," and some "died."

Your Christian liberty may not only be hurting others, but also may be hurting the Lord. The church is the body of the Lord (cf. Eph. 1:22). Therefore when we sin against the body, we sin against the Head. God lives in the Church. He wants the Church to be useful to him. If another person is wiped out by our own actions, God is affected. Paul has a stern warning for anyone who sins against the Lord's Church: "Do you not know that you are God's temple and that God's Spirit dwells in you? *If any one destroys God's temple, God will destroy him.* For God's temple is holy, and that temple you are" (1 Cor. 3:16-17; Emphasis mine.).

If you happen to know that some of your actions and activities are causing spiritual degeneration in the lives of others, it may be well for you to stop. To be sure, some of our actions as Christians are inherently offensive to those who are nominal Christians, or not Christians at all.

46

This is inherently so because of our relationship to Christ. But some of our actions and activities are questionable, and if they offend we must make amends.

I once knew a Christian lady who was dating an unchurched man. She was said to be a good Christian lady and a faithful church member. Besides the unequal yoke, she happened to be married. Her husband knew of the relationship but nevertheless did not become overtly concerned. One weekend while sitting at home, I heard a news report over the radio. It was about a gas leak in an apartment. The gas had killed two or three people. This Christian lady was one of them. The man that she had been dating took it very hard. One day as he passed by, his eyes red from crying, I remember thinking, "The Lord took her away because she was destroying his Church." When I think about this incident, I wonder just how many tears had filled the eyes of Jesus because this Christian lady was living in open adultery?

I wonder how many tears fill the eyes of Jesus when he sees us abusing our liberty in utter disregard to the spiritual welfare of others? For example, a Christian is free to wear halters, tubetops, hotpants, etc. But is it edifying to the many young men with whom you are daily in contact? To be sure, wearing halters, tubetops, hotpants, etc., may not seem as bad as adultery (which is not in the least an area of liberty). But if they provoke adultery in a man's heart, if they offend a brother, or even another sister (like one who is sincerely concerned about her man's fidelity in a day of lewdness and "tippin' ") then they are just the same as adultery—*sin.* It is dangerous to sin against the Lord by offending his church. We're liable to be destroyed. In order to avoid the Lord's judgment, we must consistently examine our actions and activities to see if they are offensive to others.

F.   The sixth and final lesson which we can learn from this passage of Scripture is that *each Christian must come to definite resolves concerning edifying.* Paul concluded that his own principle concerning food sacrificed to idols would be this: "if food is a cause of my brother's falling, I will never eat meat, lest I cause my brother to fall" (1 Cor. 8:13). He was very emphatic in this statement.[7] He had made up his mind that his life would be a blessing to others, even if it meant depriving himself until he died.

In Rom. 14:13b Paul said, *"Decide* never to put a stumbling block or hindrance in the way of a brother." (Emphasis mine.) We must settle it in our own minds that we will not be offensive to people. One time, during my high school years, I and a few other Christians were playing cards at one of our friend's home. The friend had some visitors in her home at this time. As we were sitting around the table, the subject came up that we were Christians. All of a sudden, the vistor turned to me and asked, "You are a Christian, and you play cards?" As I recall, we attempted to explain that there was nothing wrong with playing cards and tried to leave the matter at that. I can still feel that funny feeling coming all over me. We finished playing that game, but what a struggle it was.

After I returned home from our friendly visit and afternoon

recreational activity, I and the Lord had a talk. I am quite sure that I haven't played a card game since that day. I had made up my mind. Now, you can be quite certain that I am not saying that each Christian must give up card playing altogether. The decision which I made was between myself and the Lord alone. But I am saying that each Christian must make a firm decision that he will do only those things which will edify. We must *decide* never to offend a person.

There are many Christians who have not come to this mind set. They are going to "do they thang" anyhow. May the Lord help us. Then there are those who don't decide either way. They don't decide to edify, nor do they decide to destroy. They hang loose all the time. They play two ends against the middle. These Christians will most likely become confused in their thinking. When the time comes when they do find it necessary to decide, they will probably find out that their wills and minds have reaped the weakness and confusion of sowing indecisiveness.

I think that black brothers ought to consider what it means to edify in their dating patterns. We must ask ourselves, "Is it edifying for me, a black brother, to date a white young lady on my campus? When there are more black sisters than black brothers at my school? When there are not enough black *Christian* brothers for the sisters, period? When the sisters are way away from home, home-church, and home-friends? When she gets discouraged and lonely, and begins to internalize negative feelings about her black self? Is this inter-racial dating edifying to my black sisters?"[8] We ought to seriously consider the ramifications of our actions and then come to some definite resolves.

When we become resolute about edifying, it will free us to exercise our liberty. A person who refuses to yield his rights when something he does offends another may be conceding that he is bound by this particular activity. When we become resolute about edifying, then I believe that the Lord will know how we will respond to a given situation. We won't be fickle. Therefore he won't have to use extreme measures in persuading us to set aside our rights when they prove to be damaging to another.

Summary & Conclusion

In summarizing the implications of this passage, 1 Cor. 8:1-13, which included both a preface to and a perspective on the subject of food offered to idols, we have learned six lessons. A. We must be open to accepting the counsel of others concerning questionable areas of living. B. Christian liberty involves edifying. C. When dealing with questionable areas, it is equally important to properly understand both God and people. D. A person's spiritual progress may be at stake dependent upon how we deal with questionable areas of living. E. Our own lives may be at stake if we unnecessarily offend others in the area of Christian liberty. F. Each Christian must come to definite resolves concerning edifying.

Throughout this chapter I have tried to stress that the Lord wants you to "Build Your Neighbor." I trust that the message has been effective.

Having read this chapter, there now may be some questions which were raised in your mind. One question you may be asking yourself is this, "Do I have to give up everything? Forever?" Well, in Chapter 8 I'll try to answer this question for you. Thanks for sticking with what I consider to be one of the most important chapters.

Understanding What Has Been Taught

1. How do we know that Jesus yielded his rights?

2. What two things did Paul stress in his preface to the subject of "meat offered to idols?"

3. Of what two things did Paul give the Corinthians a proper perspective?

4. Based on the fact that an "idol is nothing" and "God is everything," what were the Christians free to do?

5. What preconversion practive had some of the Corinthian Christians been "accustomed" to?

6. What kind of conclusions did the "weak" draw?

7. Describe these conclusions and their affects.

8. What was Paul's personal conclusion to the problem expressed in 1 Corinthians 8?

Responding To And Applying What Has Been Learned

Questions

1. When was the last time that you secured counsel from a trusted friend about a questionable issue? Was the advice profitable?

2. Are you engaged in anything that is "destroying" someone's life? Why? Why not? What should be your response to this knowledge?

3. What have you learned from your "walk" with the Lord that has freed you to enjoy your liberty?

4. Do you understand the background and convictions of your two closest friends? If so, how has this information affected the way in which you relate to them?

5. Have you ever unnecessarily and/or necessarily offended someone? Why? What was the outcome?

6. Has the Lord ever gotten on your case because you offended someone? Did you change? How?

7. What are your feelings about coming to definite resolves about edifying? Have you ever yielded your rights in order to edify someone?

Suggestions

Individual

1. Secure someone that you trust for counseling purposes.

2. Take a few hours to thoroughly talk with a new member of your Christian group so that he doesn't get tripped up by what he "sees."

Group

1. Have a rap time where everyone shares their pre-Christian lifestyle, as well as their present convictions.

2. Make definite plans to visit all delinquent group members to find out why they are not regulars.

HELPING YOUR *SELF*—Chapter 5

1 Corinthians 6:12a

"All things are lawful for me," but not all things are helpful.

1 Corinthians 9:1-18

Am I not free? Am I not an Apostle? Have I not seen Jesus our Lord? Are not you my workmanship in the Lord? If to others I am not an apostle, at least I am to you; for you are the seal of my apostleship in the Lord.

This is my defence to those who would examine me. Do we not have the right to our food and drink? Do we not have the right to be accompanied by a wife,[1] as the other apostles and the brothers of the Lord and Cephas? Or is it only Barnabas and I who have no right to refrain from working for a living? Who serves as a soldier at his own expense? Who plants a vineyard without eating any of its fruit? Who tends a flock without getting some of the milk?

Do I say this on human authority? Does not the law say the same? For it is written in the law of Moses, "You shall not muzzle an ox when it is treading out the grain." Is it for oxen that God is concerned? Does he not speak entirely for our sake? It was written for our sake, because the ploughman should plough in hope and the thresher thresh in hope of a share in the crop. If we have sown spiritual good among you, is it too much if we reap your material benefits? If others share this rightful claim upon you, do not we still more?

Nevertheless, we have not made use of this right, but we endure anything rather than put an obstacle in the way of the gospel of Christ. Do you not know that those who are employed in the temple service get their food from the temple, and those who serve at the altar share in the sacrificial offerings? In the same way, the Lord commanded that those who proclaim the gospel should get their living by the gospel.

But I have made no use of any of these rights, nor am I writing this to secure any such provision. For I would rather die than have any one deprive me of my ground for boasting. For if I preach the gospel, that gives me no ground for boasting. For necessity is laid upon me. Woe to me if I do not preach the gospel! For if I do this of my own will, I have a reward; but if not of my own will, I am entrusted with a commission. What then is my reward? Just this: that in my preaching I may make the gospel free of charge, not making full use of my right in the gospel.

My father used to be a cigar smoker. As far back as I can remember he always smoked. Often I would run up to the corner store in order to buy him two or three El Productos or La Palinas. Sometimes he even wanted some White Owls. Usually on special occasions and holidays he would receive gift boxes of his favorite smokes from different family members. He enjoyed smoking.

Since my father was getting up in age, he had to begin to deal with his failing health. Once, after returning from a medical examination, I remember him telling me what the doctor had said about his smoking. The doctor had advised him that it would be dangerous for him to stop smoking since he had been doing it for such a long time. The doctor had said that the cigars were useful in calming his nerves and easing his tensions. To this advice my father gave his welcomed assent.

Much of the tension my father was experiencing occurred because of his concern for his children. Our mother died when we were quite young (2, 4, & 7yrs.). So my father assumed the responsibility of being both "mother and father" for us. He had been struggling many years for his children. And at this time in his life, after his retirement, he was still holding down a job at 79. He was trying to make a way for us, and he was seeking to rear us in the best way that he knew how. His smoking served to help him in his burdening task.

But one day something happened while my father was sitting on the front porch smoking one of his favorites. He had drawn a puff and then immediately had felt a catch within his chest. He also became somewhat dizzy. It was a not a heart attack, nor a major respiratory illness. It was merely a difficulty in breathing. It was a short breath. He told me that he took a stern look at that cigar, blew one more puff, and then, taking the cigar from his mouth, threw it down into the front yard. And that was it. He told me that he hasn't smoked a cigar—or anything else—since that hour. And furthermore, he said that he is satisfied about it.

It has been well over seven years (at the time of this writing) since that day—the day when my father had come to the point that the doctor's advice and his favorite pastime did not matter any more. It had become a matter of "life and breath." Now whether my father knew it or not, a principle was taking place in his life: " 'All things are lawfull for me,' but *not all things are helpful*" (1 Cor. 6:12a). The Bible doesn't explicitly condemn cigar smoking. It is "lawful." But for my father, he had come to the place where he gave up smoking because he realized that it was no longer "helpful." And this is what this chapter is all about: *helping your self.*

Christian liberty involves doing those things which are helpful; beneficial. In the eighth chapter of 1 Corinthians we noticed how Paul told the Christians that he would yield his rights if it would edify someone else. He had determined not to eat meat if it would cause his brother to fall (1 Cor. 8:13). In the ninth chapter, Paul turns to his personal everyday living. From his own personal experiences he will give the Corinthians an insight into how he is applying the principles of Christian liberty to his own life. Paul will show them that he has been willing to yield his rights so that it might *help* himself as well as help the gospel.

Elucidation

The theme of chapter 9, verses 1-18, is Paul's *support* for his ministry; or, more accurately his *sacrificed support.* In everyday language it concerns his pay for preaching. Paul saw fit to forego his right of support because doing this would prove helpful. The verses can be divided into three sections: A. The Basis and Nature of his Support (1-6); B. The Defense for and Denial of the Support (7-15); and C. The Restriction and Reward of Sacrifice (16-18). Let's see why Paul considered it helpful to yield his pay.

A. *The Basis and Nature of The Support,* 1-6.

Some of the Christians at Corinth were questioning Paul's authority as an apostle. The verses of 2 Corinthians 10-13 are an extended passage dealing with his authority. The "superlative" and "false" apostles in 2 Cor. 11:5,13 may have been the leaders of this challenge to Paul. Some of the members of the church at Corinth chimed along with the push against him. As a result, they had begun to "examine" him (9:3).

The reasoning of those who were trying to undercut Paul probably went something like this. They would reason that although Paul claimed to be a genuine apostle, he did not act like one. To them Paul was too strict on himself. He was not like the other apostles. He did not take or enjoy the benefits of being an apostle. He did not fit in very well; he was strange and austere. Paul might have even been accused of not giving himself fully to the ministry, since he had to hold down a second job. From this reasoning, the examiners tended to conclude that Paul was not a real apostle, and therefore, they did not need to submit to his authority.

1. Paul begins his argument to those who questioned his practices and authority by affirming his freedom and rights, as an apostle. This is the *basis* of his support. Paul told them that he was "free" (1) just like any other Christian. He said that he was an "apostle" just like the other apostles. They had seen the Lord Jesus during his earthly ministry (cf. Acts 1:21). Paul had seen Jesus when he (Paul) was on the road going

to Damascus (Acts 9:1ff.; 26:16; 1 Cor. 15:8-10). Jesus had commissioned Paul to be an apostle (Acts 9:15-16; Gal. 1:1). Futhermore, Paul told the Corinthians that they were his "workmanship in the Lord" (1). He had "planted" the church, and had laid the "foundation" (1 Cor. 3:6,10). He was their "father" (1Cor. 4:15). He was the first one to come all the way to them with the gospel (2 Cor. 10:14; Acts 8:1-11). By Paul himself, "The signs of a true apostle were performed among [them] in all patience, with signs and wonders and mighty works" (2 Cor. 12:12). Even if Paul was not an apostle to others he was one to the church at Corinth. For they were the "seal" of his apostleship in the Lord (2). They were the stamp on his deed. They themselves were his "letter of recommendation" (2 Cor. 3:2-3). Paul was indeed an apostle. And thus, his apostleship became the basis for his support.

2. Now Paul goes on to explain the *nature* of his rights. That is, he defends (3) the kinds of rights which he has. In verse four, Paul says that he has a right[2] to his "food and drink." This means that he has a right to daily necessities. The church should make sure that he has his everyday provisions. Even if he choses to eat idol-food, it is still his right to have his meals provided free of charge.

Paul said that he also had a right to have a "wife"[3] (5). If he needed a wife to accompany him on his journeys he was permitted to marry. The other apostles, the brothers of the Lord, and Peter were all using this right. They were married. So Paul had a right to do the same. There was no commandment which forbade him from exercising this right. He could have left the state of celibacy, and it would have been no one's business but his own. This was his right.

Paul went on to say that he and Barnabas had a right to be supported exclusively by the church without holding down a second job. They had a right "to refrain from working for a living" (6). Now, there were probably some people at Corinth (ascetics?) who felt that physical work was good, honorable, needful, and obligatory. They probably felt that Paul was doing what was fitting and proper by having another job. They would have desired for him to continue in this pattern, the same which he had practiced while in Thessalonica (a place where he had evangelized sometime before coming to Corinth, Acts 17:1ff.). There he had worked night and day in order not to be a burden to the people (1 Thess. 2:9; 2 Thess. 3:7-8; cf. Acts 20:33ff.). Paul was therefore getting it from both sides. Some thought that he was too stringent in the use of his freedom. They, therefore, reasoned that he was not a true apostle at all. Others thought that he had no right not to work. They felt that it was his Christian duty to hold down a second job. Despite the press, Paul affirmed both his apostleship and his right to be supported by the church. This was his position and his right.

B. *The Defense for and Denial of Support, 7-15*

In verses 1-6, Paul has stated his position (as being a free apostle), and the right which comes from that positon (that of support for his work). He now proceeds to give several reasons why the Corinthians are

55

obligated to support him. And then, in the same breath, he also explains why he yields his right and thus does not accept that support.

1. Paul gives ten reasons in verses 7-12a, 13-14 which *defend his right* to be supported by the Church at Corinth. He draws the first three reasons from "human authority" or, according to man's reasoning (8a).

A *soldier* gets paid for his work in the army (7a). If nothing else, he receives his regular supplies; if not, the army would fall apart.

A *vineyard planter* eats the grapes which he grows (7b). This is especially true when living in an agrarian culture where people live off the crops they produce.

A *shepherd* drinks the milk which his own flock produces (7c). It would be unwise if he got his milk from somewhere else.

The next reason, defending Paul's right, is drawn from what the law says; that is, "the law of Moses" (9).

An *ox* is to be free to eat while it is working. "You shall not muzzle an ox when it is treading out the grain" (9; cf. Dt. 25:4 and context). God is concerned about oxen, even as he is concerned about all of his creation (Mt. 6:26-30; Rom. 8:19ff.). And if God is so concerned about feeding an animal, how much more is he concerned about feeding a person? His apostles? (10a; cf. 1 Tim. 5:17-18).

The next three reasons for Paul's support reflect common experiences.

The *ploughman* should plough in hope (10b). The reason he gets the ground ready for planting is because he believes that what he plants will grow and ultimately there will be a crop.

The *thresher* threshes in hope of a share of the crop (10b). The reason he does what is necessary to get the grain or seed from the plant is because he believes that he will receive part of the finished product.

When something is *sown,* something is also *reaped* (11-12). Paul was saying that he and his companions sowed spiritual good among the Corinthians. That is, they preached and taught to them the gospel. It would only be natural therefore for them to receive (reap) material benefits from the church. Sowing and reaping go together. Matter of fact, Paul said that he and his company should have reaped more from the Corinthians than any of their other teachers. Paul and his companions had been their primary teachers (2).

The next two reasons defending Paul's right to support come from commonly accepted religious practices.

Those who are employed in the temple service get their food from the temple (13a). It was the common practice that the people who officiated in the temple, whether the pagan or Jewish temple, got their food from what the people brought into the temple to sacrifice. And likewise,

Those who serve at the altar receive a part of the sacrifices (13b). The meat was proportionately shared with those who constantly sat beside the altar waiting on the worshippers.

The last reason that Paul espouses in the defense of his rights forms the pinnacle of his defense. Even Jesus himself had something to say on the matter.

The Lord commanded that those who proclaim the gospel should get their living by the gospel (14). This is the most convincing reason why the Corinthians should support Paul. Jesus commanded this support for bearers of the gospel. He "ordained" it. He arranged it this way. This is the right way to take care of ministers of the gospel. Jesus told his disciples, "Take no gold, nor silver, nor copper in your belts, no bag for your journey, nor two tunics, nor sandles, nor a staff; *for the labourer deserves his food"* (Mt. 10:9-10). He also told them, "And remain in the same house, eating and drinking what they provide, *for the labourer deserves his wages;* do not go from house to house" (Lk. 10:7). (All emphases mine.)

These are the ten arguments which Paul uses in defense of his right to be supported by the Christians in Corinth. They are very impressive and forceful reasons. But, Paul decided to yield his right. And he gives two good reasons why he decided to deny himself his due support from the Corinthians. One reason has to do with the gospel, and the other with himself.

2. First, Paul says in verse 12b, "Nevertheless, we have not made use of this right, but we endure anything rather than put an obstacle in the way of the gospel of Christ." *This first reason for his denial has to do with the gospel.* It has to do with the "good news" that Jesus died for sinners, he was buried, he was raised on the third day, and he was seen (1 Cor. 15:1ff.).[4] Paul said in 2 Cor. 11:7-9, "Did I commit a sin in abasing myself so that you might be exalted, because I preached God's gospel without cost to you? I robbed other churches by accepting support from them in order to serve you. And when I was with you and was in want. I did not burden any one, for my needs were supplied by the brethren who came from Macedonia. So I refrained and will refrain from burdening you in any way." And in 2 Cor. 12:14-18, Paul said to the Corinthians that neither he nor Titus his companion had made use of their rights to be supported. And in 1 Cor. 4:11-12a he said, "To the present hour we hunger and thirst, we are ill-clad and buffeted and homeless, and we labour, working with our own hands" (cf. 2 Cor. 11:27). Paul and his companions did not use their right to support. Why did they take this kind of action? He said that they would endure anything—not having their daily provisions, not having a wife, not being without a second job—*edure anything, "rather than put an obstacle in the way of the gospel of Christ"* (12; Emphasis mine.).

There were probably some sinners at Corinth who would come to be saved by the preaching of the gospel. But these same people might have second thoughts about believing in the Lord if they felt that by becoming Christians they would then become burdened with the responsibility of helping to support the preachers. They would have been on the road to Christ, but then would have come face to face with a road block, an obstacle, money. So Paul decided to yield his right to support so that there would be no good excuse for the unsaved not to respond to his preaching.

Second, in verse 15 Paul gives the next reason why he yielded his right. He said, "But I have made no use of any of these rights, nor am I writing this to secure any such provision. For I would rather die than have any one deprive me of my ground for boasting."

Paul was able to boast, or glory, in the fact that he could preach the gospel "free of charge" to the Corinthians. He received some personal satisfaction, a good sense of pride, in doing this. And furthermore, he was determined that he would always have this pride. He said, "As the truth of Christ is in me, this boast of mine shall not be silenced in the regions of Achaia" (2 Cor. 11:10). He felt that it would be better for himself to die off rather than he lose this sense of self-fulfillment and self-esteem in his work.

C. *The Restriction and Reward of Sacrifice,* 16-18

Paul has adequately stated his reasons for defending and denying his rights. Now he must make a find distinction. He showed exactly in what area he is permitted to yield his right, and then he showed the reward he receives from making such a sacrifice. Let's consider these two points.

1. *First, Paul says that he cannot yield his right to preach the gospel.* He says in verse 16, "For if I preach the gospel, that gives me no ground for boasting. For necessity is laid upon me. Woe to me if I do not preach the gospel!" Paul felt that he was under constraints to preach the gospel. This was not an area of liberty as far as he was concerned. Paul had been arrested by Jesus on the Damascus road; he was "apprehended" (Phil. 3:12 A.V.). He was a "slave" of Christ (Rom. 1:1). He was obligated to preach the gospel. He had asked Jesus, "What shall I do, Lord?" and Jesus had told him to "Rise, and go into Damascus, and there you will be told all that is appointed for you to do" (Acts 22:10). So Paul said, "Woe to me if I do not preach the gospel!". He had been entrusted with a stewardship (17b). And he knew that "it is required of stewards that they be found trustworthy" (1 Cor. 4:2). He was nothing more than an "unworthy servant" (Lk. 17:10). If he would have discontinued preaching the gospel he might have had the experience of Jeremiah who said, "If I say, 'I will not mention him, or speak any more in his name,' there is in my heart as it were a burning fire shut up in my bones, and I am weary with holding it in, and I cannot" (Jer. 20:9).

Paul was restricted. He could not sacrifice his call to evangelize. He could not yield his right to preach the gospel. He had to go where Jesus wanted him to go. He had to say what Jesus wanted him to say. He had to preach "in season and out of season" (2 Tim. 4:2a).

2. Second, *Paul said that he receives a reward for his preaching.* He said in verses 17a, 18, "If I do this of my own will, I have a reward; . . . What then is my reward? Just this: that in my preaching I may make the gospel free of charge, not making full use of my right in the gospel." Paul did not have a choice in whether or not he should preach the gospel. But he did have a choice in how much he would charge for his preaching. And Paul chose to sacrifice his support. He charged the Corinthians nothing. He followed the pattern of Mt. 10:8: "Heal the sick, raise the dead, cleanse lepers, cast out demons. *You received without paying, give*

without pay." (Emphasis mine.)

Since Paul chose to sacrifice his support, he received a reward. What was his reward? It was the ability to say that he was meek (cf. Mt. 5:5); he did not use his rights completely. As far as his support for his apostleship was concerned, he was permitted to make three moves (4-6) but he chose to make none. This was his reward. It was to be able to do as Jesus had said, "It is more blessed to give than to receive" (Acts 20:34-35).

Passage Summary

We have learned several lessons through looking at this passage. We have learned that this passage teaches about one of Paul's personal experiences. He explains his own practice so that the Corinthians will be able to see that he is not asking them to do anything which he himself has not done. If he asks them to yield their right to eat idol-food (to help their weak brother), they can be sure that he has yielded his own right to, not only idol-food, but also to some other important issues.

He showed the Corinthians that he had a right to be supported as an apostle; especially since the Corinthians were indebted to him for their spiritual blessings. He told them that he had a right to be supported by the church; to have a Christian wife whom the church also supported; and to have his daily necessities, "food and drink," provided by them. His claim to these rights were not shallow. He gave ten good arguments in defense of these rights, the last argument coming from the Lord Jesus himself. But in the same breath, he told them why he had decided not to use these rights. He by-passed his rights for the sake of advancing the gospel, and to have the privilege of boasting in his work. He admitted that he could not boast because he was preaching the gospel, for he was obligated to preach. But he could boast in preaching the gospel without a "price tag." This was his reward.

Concretization

Now that we have in some measure understood Paul's financial policy toward the Corinthian Christians, we can go on to see what we can learn about Christian liberty by drawing from his experience. I think that we can learn four things from our study of 1 Cor. 9:1-18. *First, Christian liberty involves doing what is beneficial. Second, each Christian should understand the extent of his own rights and be prepared to defend those rights. Third, each Christian should be prepared to yield his rights for the sake of expedience. And fourth, each Christian must be able to distinguish between an area of liberty and an area of no-liberty.*

A. *Christian liberty involves doing what is beneficial.* Paul said " 'All things are lawful for me,' but not all things are helpful" (1 Cor. 6:12a). Those things which are helpful are the kinds of things which we must choose to do as Christians. We should do things which are profitable and useful. The Lord would say to believers, "Do those things which 'help your *self.'* "

By yielding his right to support, Paul chose a course of action which was beneficial to the gospel and to himself. Laying aside (for this point) the aspect of yielding, what must a Christian choose to do when an action or activity falls into a questionable area? He must determine whether or not that particular action or activity is helpful. There are three categories into which a questionable area may fall: good, in-between, and harmful. The Lord would have us to do those things which are good. Paul says in Phil. 4:8,9: "Finally, brethren, whatever is true, whatever is honourable, whatever is just, whatever is pure, whatever is lovely, whatever is gracious, if there is any excellence, if there is anything worthy of praise, think about these things. What you have learned and received and heard and seen in me, do; and the God of peace will be with you."

As an individual considers for himself what is beneficial or not, he might want to keep in view his own body, mind, will, emotions, conscience, etc. That is, his entire being—"spirit and soul and body" (1 Thess. 5:23-24). Our entire being is affected by what we do. Therefore, a person must consider, as best as possible, the effect which a given action or activity will have on himself as a whole. For example, as in the case of smoking, a person who smokes for nerve control will have to weigh which is most important: calmed nerves or possible throat or lung cancer, or a heart attack. Or, in the case of listening to music, a person may choose to turn up his box as loud as can be. He may like it that way. But what about his ears, his hearing? I understand that there are many folks who are ruining their ability to hear because of turning up the decibles. Is, therefore, listening to loud music helpful for that person? In the long run?

And while we are on the subject of music, we are pressed to talk about the matter of lyrics. Many young people in our day are responding to rock, funky, or disco beats and tunes, without any or little wholesome consideration on the words they are hearing.

In a matter of a few weeks, I had the privilege of meeting and talking with two black Christian Chicago D.J.'s who were concerned about the quality of music which they spin. One said that he has banned all but "positive" music from his program. The other said that he prefers to play "music with a message." Granted, one might debate about what is "positive" and what is indeed a "message," but it is refreshing to know that there are young committed black brothers who are conscientiously raising the issues, as well as setting a platform for discussion and beneficial movement in this area of the media.

In the meantime, black youths must educate themselves to listen with discernment to the top 10's and 20's. Those rhymes and that poetry, which are sweetly and/or strongly sung into our minds, but which are neither true, nor right, nor good, ought to be tuned off our dials, raised from our spindles, and taken out of our tape decks. Lyrics should prove beneficial.

When a Christian begins to consider what kinds of things are helpful to him, his mind and conscience will play an important part. Matter of fact, even the Holy Spirit speaks through the conscience of a Christian

(Rom. 9:1,2). Paul has a few things to say about the place of the mind and conscience in Christian liberty. He says, "One man esteems one day as better than another, while another man esteems all days alike. Let every one be fully convinced in his own mind" (Rom. 14:5); "I know and am persuaded in the Lord Jesus that nothing is unclean in itself" (Rom. 14:14a); "The faith that you have, keep between youself and God; happy is he who has no reason to judge himself for what he approves. But he who has doubts is condemned, if he eats, because he does not act from faith; for whatever does not proceed from faith is sin" (Rom. 14:22-23). Each person must decide for himself if a particular activity is beneficial or not. Each must be guided by his own conscience and convictions.

Between my late teens and early twenties I had to face a problem which many other black men must also face. It is called *Pseudofolliculitis barbe* (PFB),[5] and is better known as the "razor bumps." Everytime that I shaved it would become a real battle; and blood bath too! I tried Magic Shave, a safety razor, an electric razor, a double edged razor, and a straight razor. Nothing worked. Not even a lemon for aftershave!

How glad I am that the Lord brought me to my senses. He told me to quit trying to look like what some folks thought a "clean cut" preacher ought to look like. He began to impress me with the fact that I should do what was helpful to me. I decided to grow a beard. Myyyy was it good to put down that blade! No more blood, sweat, and tears! Growing a beard proved to be very beneficial for me. I'm sure that it would also be beneficial to the many other black men with similar problems. (Sometimes, I think the beard enhances my opportunities for spreading the gospel. I actually believe that because I have a beard some folks listen a little more attentively to what I have to say. You know, our street folks!)

In the past, the Lord led me to give up several things because for me they were not beneficial. Before I began to date the sister who is now my wife, the Lord led me to stop dating for the period of about two years. I felt that this is what he wanted, and what was most beneficial for me at the time. I'm glad that I did. There were a number of things which I had to learn during that period.

During my high school years the Lord led me to give up social dancing. He convinced me at that time that I was not able to handle it. And I wasn't. This proved to be another beneficial move in my life. As a result of setting aside this activity I grew much stronger in the Lord.

When we ask ourselves, "Is it helpful?" we must not only take into account our own persons, but also take into consideration our message and ministry. For instance, I gave up selling encyclopedias because it was not helpful to my ministry. As I sold encyclopedias from day to day, it began to make me look at people only in terms of their money. My values began to change. My concern for people as persons began to diminish. Some people who are salesmen would not have had to worry about this problem. But I did. So I got out of the encyclopedia business. Selling encyclopedias was not helpful for me as a person, much less as a preacher of the gospel.

For another example, take the case of inter-racial dating and marriage. A black brother will have to consider the kind of ramifications which a white young lady will have on his ministry. Not too long ago a brother was telling me about a black young preacher who had a prospering ministry. His ministry was prospering until he married a white young lady. The person with whom I was talking told me that, as far as he could tell, the black brother's ministry as it pertained to the black community, went down the drain. Granted, each person must follow his own conscience. But we must all ask ourselves, "Is it helpful?" Some brothers might think twice about inter-racial marriage if they considered the limitations which it might place on their ministry to black people. It occurs to me that any marriage has its own limiting factors. Therefore, one must consider what kind of limitations he is willing to accept and endure. My advice to those who are considering, especially inter-racial, but also intra-racial marriage, and also celibacy! is this: consider if it will be helpful to your message and ministry.

B. *Each Christian should understand the extent of his own rights and be prepared to defend those rights.* In 1 Cor. 9:4-6 Paul listed his rights in detail. He was entitled to be salaried by the church, to have his daily meals provided, and to marry a Christian lady. He knew the extent of his rights.

Christians must know the extent of their rights. Sometimes believers are ignorant of the freedoms which they have in the Lord. One day Paul and Silas exorcised a demon from a young girl. The owners, having become upset that they had lost their money-making diviner, seized Paul and Silas and dragged them to the government authorities. The authorities beat Paul and Silas with rods, and had them thrown into jail. That night, as Paul and Silas were praying and singing hymns, the Lord sent an earthquake to shake the jail and set them free. The jailer, who was about to commit suicide, was constrained by Paul and led to the Lord, along with the rest of his family, that night.

The next morning the authorities decided to let Paul and Silas go. They sent some police to the jail to give them the news. That is when Paul and Silas laid a bombshell on the authorities. Paul said, "They have beaten us publicly, uncomdemned, men who are Roman citizens, and have thrown us into prison; and do they now cast us out secretly? No! let them come themselves and take us out" (Acts 16:37). What a shock! It was even greater than the last nights's earthquake. Roman citizens were not supposed to have been treated as Paul and Silas had been treated. Roman citizens had the right of a fair trial and of undegrading forms of punishment. To these rights and more Paul and Silas were entitled, and yet they had been denied them.

When this heavy word got back to the authorities it shook them up so bad that they personally came down to the jail and apologized to Paul and Silas. They wanted to avoid any of the consequences which might have occured as a result of their ignorance and haste. They escorted Paul and Silas out of the jail house and then *begged* them to leave town peaceably. Paul and Silas did decide to leave, but only on their own terms. They first desired to take some time to visit the brothers and sisters. And then they left (Acts 16:16-40).

Paul and Silas knew the extent of their rights. And they were not afraid to defend those rights either. Just because they were Christians it did not mean that they should let other folks push them around.[6]

The Lord wants us black folks to know the extent of our rights. He desires for us to not only know our rights as Christians, but also our rights as black people created in his image, and our rights as black people who are members of this society. Sometimes we as Christians are guilty of trying to yield rights that we do not in actuality really possess. Granted we know what the Constitution, along with the other laws of the land, have to say about rights. But a lot of the laws which were made were not made with black folks in mind. They were made for white folks. I think proof of this can be found, not only in historical fact, but also in the present reality. Black folks must go through major hassles and court battles just in order to get many laws enforced on their behalf.[7] What am I saying? I am trying to say that black people don't really know in fact the rights which they have unless they put the law to the test. But to the contrary, we try to yield what we sometimes don't have.

I remember a Christian sister telling a church group about an interview which she took for a job. The interviewer "raked her over the coals." He gave her a down right hard way to go. She told us that she had started to say something about this inhumane treatment, but decided to hold her peace. She also said that the Lord was trying to teach her some lessons that day. After the interview was completed, the interviewer told his sister never to let anything upset her. (What whites have been telling blacks for a long time!) I don't know whether or not she got the job.

As she was telling us this incident, a few questions came into my mind. Should she have allowed the interviewer to send her through the third degree? What was most beneficial to her, her dignity or a job? My answer was that she should not have allowed herself to be so abused by this interviewer. She should have preserved her dignity. Now I have no doubts that God can make "the wrath of men" to praise Him (Ps. 76:10). But that is his business, not ours. Our business concerns our civil rights as responsible members of this society seeking to be gainfully employed. Our business concerns our rights as human beings made in God's image, which making dictates that we be treated with dignity and respect. And that notwithstanding job interviews either. We blacks can empathize with one another over the tight and tightening job market. It is putting the squeeze on us. But I would think twice (maybe even three or four times) about trading my dignity for the whims and frustrations of a man who offered me a two-bit job. And I pray that I would not degrade my Lord by making the trade in His name!

We as Christians must be prepared to defend our rights. We receive some of our rights just by being Christians. Other rights come from having certain positions and our subsequent work out-put, as in the case of Paul (1 Cor. 9:2,11). However, in whatever way we receive our rights we must know them and be prepared to defend them. Paul defended his rights on several different levels. He defended them on the levels of human reasoning, the law of Moses, common experience, accepted religious practices, and what the Lord had to say. If Christian liberty means anything, if it has any worth whatsoever, then it is worth defending.

C. *Each Christian should be prepared to yield his rights for the sake of expedience.* This is not the same as opportunism. Opportunism is "the policy or habit of adapting one's actions, thoughts, and utterances to circumstances, as in politics, in order to further one's immediate interests, without regard for basic principles or eventual consequences."[8] In opportunism a person sacrifices a principle. And it usually implies very selfish motives. An opportunist reneges on his convictions in order to get what the moment offers. On the other hand, expedience is a principle in itself. It does not sacrifice Christian liberty, but is in fact part of the substance of Christian liberty. Paul said, " 'All things are lawful for me,' but not all things are helpful" (1 Cor. 6:12a).

Paul yielded his rights to support in order that the Gospel and he himself would benefit. One might ask, "Well, isn't it selfish for Paul to want to have something in which to boast? Doesn't this show opportunism, or at least pride?" I might answer that when one considers what Paul gave up in order to boast, Paul does not come across very selfish at all. Because of what he gave up, he had to face death everyday (1 Cor. 15:31; 2 Cor. 11:23ff.). And there is a difference between a good pride and a bad pride. The bad pride is opposite humbleness. The good pride is opposite shame.

God fights agains the bad pride. He tries to destory it. But God helps a person who is shamed. He gives them a good pride. He gives them dignity, self-esteem, self-acceptance, etc. Paul wanted that good pride. He would have rather died than have nothing in which to glory.

There are some examples of people who yielded their rights for the sake of expedience, helpfulness. Abram (Abraham) is a good example. In Genesis 14 we can read about the four kings who fought against the five kings. Lot, Abram's nephew, was living in Sodom, one of the five kingdoms. The five kings were defeated in the battle, and Lot and his household were taken captive. News reached Abram about what had happened. So he got his own men together and went to rescue Lot. He brought Lot, his kinfolks, and their goods safely back to Sodom.

The king of Sodom went to greet Abram after the victory. All he asked Abram to give him of the spells were the people. He told Abram to keep the goods. This was Abram's reply to the king of Sodom: "I have sworn to the Lord God Most High, maker of heaven and earth, that I would not take a thread or a sandal-thong or anything that is yours, lest you should say, 'I have made Abram rich'." (Gen. 14:22-23). Abram had certain rights as conqueror on behalf of the king of Sodom. But he did not use those rights. He yielded them. The Lord had made a convenant with Abram. The Lord had promised to bless him (Gen. 12:1-3; 13:14-17). Abram was going to make sure that when he became rich, that everyone would know beyond a reasonable doubt that the Lord had done this for him. So he yielded his rights as a conqueror. It was beneficial that he did not take any of the spoils of war for himself.

Nehemiah is another good example of a person who yielded his right because it was helpful. While in Persia he received permission from king Artaxerxes to go to Jerusalem to rebuild the walls which had been destroyed by the Babylonians. As the work on the wall was progressing, some of the people came to Nehemiah with a complaint. They did not have enough food. As a result of this, some of them were forced to mortgage their houses and lands in order to buy grain. Others sold their children into slavery for this same purpose. These people were being oppressed by their own leaders, their own brothers.

Nehemiah became very angry at what was happening. He made the leaders take an oath that they would discontinue their oppressive practices, and make restitution as well. This incident gave Nehemiah an opportunity to share his own personal practices.

Although he, as governor of Judah, was allowed to collect an allowance of food from the people, he refused to accept this allowance. Even the former governors had exercised this right, but Nehemiah yielded his right. Neither did Nehemiah buy up cheap land or property. Although this opportuntiy afforded itself, he did not take it. He stuck to his work. And that wasn't all. Nehemiah also took money from his own pocket and supplied the food for over 150 people each day. He gave when he did not have to give. Even with all the money he spent for this food he said, "yet with all this I did not demand the food allowance of the governor, because the servitude was heavy upon this people. Remember for my good, O my God, all that I have done for this people" (Neh. 5:1-19). It was indeed lawful for Nehemiah to take the governor's share. But it was not helpful. So Nehemiah did not make full use of his rights. (See also Gen. 23:1ff., Ezra 8:21-23, and 2 Kings 5:1-27 for other examples of those who yielded rights.)

I personally know some black people who belong to the board of a Christian organization. Many times they have paid their own way to meetings, etc. I am sure that they have certain privileges as board members, but they have waived some of those privileges. Why? Because the organization needs the kind of commitment which they are showing. It is helpful to the organization.

It is the goal of my wife and myself to be financially self-supporting in our work. We believe that this will be an asset to the ministry which the Lord has given us to do. Until our goal is achieved, the Lord has led us to be supported by black Christians inclusively.[9] Since we made the move, it has been tremendously beneficial to my own way of thinking about ourselves and our ministry. I believe that it has also been of value in helping our black brothers and sisters to realize their responsibility to support our own Christian works (cf. 3 Jn. 5-8). We could have made full use of our rights to be supported by the Christian community at large, but we decided to yield some of our rights. This proved very helpful.

I have mostly talked about financial matters under this point. I have done this because we black Christians must resist the tendency to be bought out, or to be left floundering in our ministries when whites withdraw their support. We must learn how to yield our rights, especially in this area of finances. Moses yielded his rights, and the Lord used him to save and solidify an entire nation (Heb. 11:24-29). If we are faithful in "unrighteous mammon," then the Lord will entrust to us "true riches" (Lk. 16:11).

Howbeit, the principle of helpfulness can and ought be applied to many areas of living. And we must be willing to yield our rights for the sake of helpfulness when exercising our liberty.

D. We can learn from 1 Cor. 9:1-18 that *each Christian must be able to distinguish between an area of liberty and an area of no-liberty.* Paul did not have any liberty as to whether he should or should not preach the gospel. He was obligated to preach the gospel. He did, however, have a choice as to what he charged for his ministry (1 Cor. 9:16-18). Because Paul knew how to make good distinctions, he was the better for it.

When we make those sort of distinctions, it is better for us also. For example, a Christian may feel that it is beneficial to go to social gatherings or parties. This may be the Lord's will for them. But it is certainly not the Lord's will for a person to be involved in *wild* parties. The Scripture condemns such activities (1 Pet. 4:3-4).[10] And furthermore, "Do not be deceived: 'Bad company ruins good morals'. " (1 Cor. 15:33).

Some people drink wine. I cannot conscientiously say that the Scriptures absolutely forbid this. Christians in other parts of the world (e.g. Italy) drink wine without making any issue of it. I myself don't drink wine nor any other alcoholic beverage. And I trust that the Lord will keep me from it as long as I live. But if a person does drink wine, he'd better not get drunk. The Bible says that drunkeness is a work of the flesh. People who do such things will not inherit the kingdom of God (Gal. 5:19-21). Even though Jesus drank wine (and it was the intoxicating kind, cf. Lk. 5:37-39; 7:33-34), he never got drunk. He was never "strung out." He never had to sleep it off, or helplessly be taken home. Drinking wine *may* be an area of liberty. Drunkenness, *absolutely not.*

The new styles of clothing and hair-do's deserves comment under this point. Someone has noted that black young men are "becoming increasing feminized." To which I reply, "Ain't it the truth!" There may be liberty in the area of dress, but not in confusing the sexes. "A woman shall not wear anything that pertains to a man, nor shall a man put on a woman's garment; for whoever does these things is an abomination to the Lord your God" (Deut. 22:5).

How confusing it is when you ride the "L" or bus and can't tell if the person sitting in front of you is male or female! Young black men now have processed or straight hair, tight pants, and earrings. What a sad condition! As we walk down the street, we see young black men with pink hair rollers, or braids. May the Lord help us. The Lord did us a lot of good by giving us the wisdom to wear the natural. It hurts, and it hurts black people, to see it going out of style.

Then there is the bi-sexual clothing which either men or women can wear. All it serves to do is confuse the sexes and roles. The Lord wants black men to be black men, and black women to be black women. There is no liberty in confusing one's sex. And as Paul said, "woe" unto us if the present trend continues.

Summary & Conclusion

I have tried to stress four things which we could learn from the passage of Scripture which we have studied in this chapter. A. Christian liberty involves doing what is beneficial. B. Each Christian should understand the extent of his own rights and be prepared to defend those rights. C. Each Christian should be prepared to yield his rights for the sake of expedience. And D. Each Christian must be able to distinguish between an area of liberty and an area of no-liberty.

In this chapter we have learned some important teachings about Christian liberty by examining the personal experience of Paul. He sacrificed his due support in order to do what was beneficial. He helped his *self*. And helping your *self* is a major part of Christian liberty. " 'All things are lawful for me,' but not all things are helpful" (1 Cor. 6:12a).

At this point we have talked about two principles of liberty: one for our neighbor, edification, and one for ourselves, expedience. In the next chapter, we will talk about the principle which preserves our freedom.

Understanding What Has Been Taught

1. What was the basis of Paul's support?

2. What were the three things that composed the nature of Paul's support?

3. Name five of the ten reasons Paul gave in defense of his right to be supported.

4. For what two reasons did Paul deny himself his due support?

5. Was Paul able to yield his right to preach the gospel? Why? Why not?

6. What reward did Paul receive for yielding his right to be supported?

Responding To And Applying What Has Been Learned

Questions

1. Are you engaged in anything that is not helpful for you? Why? Why not?

2. Have you ever defended your rights? How did it make you feel?

3. What rights have you yielded because it was beneficial to your *self* and to the Lord?

4. Are you involved in any activities which force you to draw a fine line between an area of liberty and an area of no-liberty? If so, how is it coming?

Suggestions

Individual

1. Evaluate your clothing styles to see if they are beneficial in distinctifying your sex.

2. Determine if any of your actions or activities are a hindrance to your message and ministry.

Group

1. Choose to do a group activity that is beneficial to your black awareness and appreciation.

2. Discuss the idea of black Christians being and becoming financially independent of outside funds.

PRESERVING YOUR FREEDOM— Chapter 6

1 Corinthians 6:12b

"All things are lawful for me," but I will not be enslaved by anything.

1 Corinthians 9:19-27

For though I am free from all men, I have made myself a slave to all, that I might win the more. To the Jews I became as a Jew, in order to win Jews; to those under the law I became as one under the law—though not being myself under the law—that I might win those under the law. To those outside the law I became as one outside the law—not being without law toward God but under the law of Christ—that I might win those outside the law. To the weak I became weak, that I might win the weak. I have become all things to all men, that I might by all means save some. I do it all for the sake of the gospel, that I might share in its blessings.

Do you not know that in a race all the runners compete, but only one receives the prize? So run that you may obtain it. Every athlete exercises self-control in all things. They do it to receive a perishable wreath, but we an imperishable. Well, I do not run aimlessly, I do not box as one beating the air; but I pommel my body and subdue it, lest after preaching to others I myself should be disqualified.

A. The Saving Slave, 19-23[1]
   1. His Self-imposed Service, 19
   2. His Several Relationships, 20-22
      a) To The Jews, 20a
      b) To Those Under The Law, 20b
      c) To Those Outside The Law, 21
      d) To The Weak, 22a
         1) He Became Weak
            (a) The Exception Pertaining to God and the Gospel
            (b) The Exception Pertaining to People and Love
         2) He Strengthened The Weak
   3. His Share In The Gospel, 23
B. The Subduing Self-discipline, 24-27
   1. Its Motivation, 24
   2. Its Preparation, 25
   3. Its Concentration, 26-27

During the summer between my second and third years in high school I experienced a turning point in my Christian growth. It involved the sport of basketball. The first major sport which I enjoyed in my life was baseball. I liked to play it very much; probably because it was my father's joy and excitement. I began to get into basketball in the sixth grade because I wanted to play on the seventh and eighth grade team just like my brother.

I made the team in junior high school, and when I went into senior high school, I made the team there as well. During my sophomore year I played first string. I was looking forward to going out for varsity in the fall of my junior year.

During my summer vacation I would "shoot the rock" at the neighborhood court and at the boys club. By far, I was not necessarily a good player. I was average. But I wanted to get better. So I spent a considerable amount of time on the court. Actually, I ended up spending too much time. Because of this, the Lord began to deal with me about my commitment to himself. Many a time I would go home from play with a burdened conscience because I knew that I should not have been playing. I should have been studying the Word. Or sometimes I should have been praying. Other times I should have been preparing for my responsibilities as president of our Christian youth group. And then again I was missing a lot of opportunities for evangelizing. And my home life was being neglected also. A lot of times I should have just been around the house. During this period in my life, I was away from home far too much. But instead of doing these and other more important things I was playing ball—sometimes two or three hours a day. The Lord was being neglected, and his work as well. Matter of fact, I was neglecting myself. Improper meals, rest, and hygiene were sacrificed for playing a few average games. The Lord was trying to get through to me. And he finally did. He brought the thing to a head. He forcefully said, "Walter, is it going to be me or the ball?"

As I look back, I am so grateful that I had the grace to say "Lord, it's going to be you." I gave up playing ball on organized teams. When I went back to shcool that fall, I told the coach and my friends that I could not play on the team any longer. I had made a commitment to the Lord and I wanted to do his will. Basketball subsequently faded in the light of the Lord. Sure, I played and still do play some games with my friends. But basketball doesn't mean to me now what it meant to me then.

The Lord showed me that I was bound by the ball. Everytime I would pass by a court, or see a loose ball, I wanted to take a shot. I was hooked. Granted, I was free to play ball. There were no Bible teachings which prohibited me from playing the game. I was at liberty to choose my own recreation. But I was bound. I was mastered. The ball and the hoop were my lord. Paul said, " 'All things are lawful for me,' but I will not be enslaved by anything" (1 Cor. 6:12b). Could it be that something questionable has gotten you strung out? Wrapped up? Bound? if so, then maybe this chapter can be of help to you. It is all about preserving your freedom. I'm sure that we can be enlightened by considering what the

Lord wants to say to us through the verses we are about to study.

Elucidation

This passage of 1 Cor. 9:19-27 has to do with preserving Christian liberty. It contains two more of Paul's personal experiences. *One of his experiences can be entitled the Saving Slave, verses 19-23; and the other the Subduing Self-discipline, verses 24-27.* Let's see what things Paul had to tell the Corinthians about himself.

A. *The Saving Slave, 19-23*[1]

In this passage Paul will show the Corinthians how he uses his freedom to bring people to Christ. He made himself a slave to people in order to win them to the Lord. This passage can be divided into three parts, each of which characterizes the servant: *1. His Self-imposed Service (19); 2. His Several Relationships (20-22); 3. His Share in the Gospel (23).*

1. Paul opens this passage on the foundation that he is free (9:1). We saw the reason why he considered himself free. It was because of his relationship to the Lord, and his apostleship. But he was also free because of his financial policy (9:12,15). Paul was not bound by a church which, so to speak, salaried him. And even though he did at times accept the offerings of others, they in no way dictated what he should do. And if push came to shove regarding his needs being met, he did not renege on his convictions, but instead, this was his attitude: "Not that I complain of want; for I have learned, in whatever state I am, to be content. I know how to be abased, and I know how to abound; in any and all circumstances I have learned the secret of facing plenty and hunger, abundance and want. I can do all things in him who strengthens me" (Phil. 4:11-13 and see context of 10-20; 1 Cor. 4:11; 2 Cor. 11:27).

Paul was "free from all men" (9:19). But Paul did not revel in that freedom. Instead, he made himself a "slave to all." He gave *self-imposed service.* Paul made a definite act of commitment, and brought himself into bondage to all men. He did this voluntarily. He did this of his own free will. And he did it for an important reason. He said, "I have made myself a slave to all, that I might win the more" (19b). And, "I have become all things to all men, that I might by all means save some" (22b).

Paul was willing to become a slave so that others could become saved, and could make spiritual progress. We will see the extent of this radical action under the next heading. Suffice it now to say that he did what he did in the spirit of Mt. 20:25-28. There Jesus told his disciples, "You know that the rulers of the Gentiles lord it over them, and their great men exercise authority over them. It shall not be so among you; but whoever would be great among you must be your servant, and whoever would be first among you must be your slave; even as the Son of man came not to be served but to serve, and to give his life as a ransom for many." Paul also had the spirit of Jn. 10:17-18a. There Jesus said, "For this reason the Father loves me, because I lay down my life, that I may

71

take it again. *No one takes it from me, but I lay it down of my own accord."* (Emphasis mine.) Paul's choice to become a slave was a choice of his own free will. Not, though, in respect to God, but in respect to people. He was a slave of God, but he was free from men. And he of his own choosing became a slave of men.

2. Paul, in making himself a slave, *fostered several realtionships.* As we look at these relationships, we will be able to see what it meant for him to be a slave. In this passage Paul tells us about his relationship to *four different groups of people: a) To the Jews (20a); b) To those under the law (20b); c) To those outside the law (21); and d) To the weak (22).*

"To the Jews," Paul became "as a Jew" (20a). There are several indications in the book of Acts depicting how Paul did this. 1) Paul circumcised Timothy (whose father was a Greek and whose mother was a Jew), so that as they worked together in evangelism Timothy would not be an offense to the Jews (Acts 16:1-3). 2) Paul's custom was to go to the synagogue of a particular city, and to reason with the Jews about Christ, using the Scriptures (the O.T.) as his basis (Acts 17:1ff.). 3) Paul evidently took a Nazarite vow while in Corinth (Acts 18:18). 4) He also participated in the Jewish feast of Unleavened Bread (Acts 20:6). 5) At the request of James and the brothers Paul paid the expenses of four brothers who were under a Nazarite vow. He also purified himself with them (Acts 21:20-26ff.). 6) When it was beneficial, Paul would remind his audience that he was a Pharisee (Acts 23:6; 26:5). 7) When we read the messages that Paul preached to Jewish audiences, we can readily see how he accomodated himself to them. When speaking to Jews he always talked about the Old Testament Scriptures, as well as his own relationship to the Judaism of his day. Sometimes he even spoke in the Hebrew (or better, Aramaic) language to get his message across more adequately (Acts 13:14-41; 22:1-21; 26:1ff.) 8) Paul encouraged his Gentile converts to respect Jewish food and marriage laws when living among them (Acts 15:19-29; cf. Lev. 17:8-18:6ff.). 9) Moreover, Paul had a heart for his own people. This, too, enabled him to become as them. Listen to what he says: "For I am not ashamed of the gospel: it is the power of God for salvation to every one who has faith, to the Jew first and also to the Greek." "For I could wish that I myself were accursed and cut off from Christ for the sake of my brethren, my kinsmen by race." "Brethren, my heart's desire and prayer to God for them [the Jews] is that they may be saved" (Rom. 1:16; 9:3; 10:1). Paul became a slave to the Jews in order to win Jews, just as also "Christ became a servant to the circumcised," in order to save them (Rom. 15:8).

Paul said, "to those under the law I became as one under the law—though not being myself under the law—that I might win those under the law" (20b). It appears that "those under the law" are an extension of "the Jews." This category would be composed of proselytes. Paul had a relationship to proselytes.

A proselyte was a Gentile who wanted to participate in the Jewish religion. After he had undergone certain rites (for example, circumcision, purification, instruction, and sacrifice),[2] he was admitted. Paul became as one "under the law" along with them just as he did with the Jews. The law of Moses commanded that certain obligations should be met by those who became God's people. Paul would observe those obligations in the presence of "those under the law" so that he could win them to Christ.

Paul said, "To those outside the law I became as one outside the law—not being without law toward God but under the law of Christ—that I might win those outside the law" (21). "Those outside the law" are Gentiles (cf. Rom. 2:12, 14). They are described by their relationship to the Jews: whereas the Jews have the law (cf. Rom. 9:4-5) the Gentiles do not. The Gentiles do indeed have a law within their hearts (Rom. 2:14-16), but Paul is not talking about this law. He is talking about the law of Moses. This is the law that the Gentiles do not possess.

Paul had a relationship to the Gentiles. He became as a Gentile to the Gentiles. There are a number of instances where this can be observed. 1) One example of Paul's becoming as a Gentile is so obvious that we often overlook it. The name *Paul* is a Roman name. During and after the ministry to Cyprus, the apostle was no longer referred to as Saul, his Hebrew name, but instead Paul, his Roman name (Acts 13:9, 13). Since Paul was beginning to work in areas where there were mostly Gentiles, it was useful for him to use his Roman name. 2) When Paul had a Gentile audience, as in Lystra (Acts 14:15-17), and Athens (Acts 17:22-31), his content, style, and emphasis in preaching were definitely geared toward Gentiles. He does not develop a message centered around the Old Testament and Judaism. Instead he speaks about common things of life such as humanity, vanity (14:15), the Creator (14:15), nations (14:16), food and gladness (15:17), etc. He becomes relevant to the Gentiles. 3) What also helped Paul to become as a Gentile to the Gentiles was his commission by the Lord. The Lord told Ananias, "Go, for he [Paul] is a chosen instrument of mine to carry my name before the Gentiles and kings and the sons of Israel" (Acts 9:15; see also Acts 22:21; Gal. 1:15-16; 2:7-9; Eph. 3:7-8). Paul said, "Inasmuch then as I am an apostle to the Gentiles, I magnify my ministry" (Rom. 11:13b). To "those outside the law" Paul became as one "outside the law" in order to win them to Christ.

Paul said, "To the weak I became weak, that I might win the weak" (22a). Paul had a relationship to the weak. We know who the weak are. They are those who were formerly accustomed to idols. They are the weak in conscience of 1 Cor. 8:7, 11. They are also the weak of Rom. 15:1. These are they who merely had a different conviction from their brothers (cf. Rom. 14:2, 5). *Two things should be noted about Paul's relationship to the weak. First, he became weak, and second, he strengthened the weak.*

First, Paul said that *he became weak,* not *as weak.* To the Jews he became *as* a Jew. To those under the law he became *as* one under the law. To those outside the law he became *as* one outside the law. But to the weak, he *became weak.* What was Paul trying to get across by saying this? *I think that Paul was bringing out an exception in his several relationships.* Matter of fact, *Paul was bringing out a dual-exception.* In the case of the Jews and the proselytes he was saying that he could not sacrifice the truth that a person was justified by faith. And in the case of the Gentiles he was saying that he could not sacrifice the law of Christ which is love. He was obligated to love people. Let me further explain these points.

The first part of the dual-exception pertains to God and the gospel. Paul was converted to Christianity from Judaism. Therefore he could never become a Jew (in religion) again. However when Paul got saved, he never lost his ethnicity, his *nationality.* He could never give that up. He was a Hebrew, a Jew, because he was born that way. God made him that way.

Now in the case of a person being born a Jew, he was also born into a religion. He entered into a covenant with God. Therefore, he who was a Jew in nationality was also a Jew in religion. This is why Paul could say in Rom. 2:28-29, "For he is not a real Jew who is one outwardly, nor is true circumcision something external and physical. He is a Jew who is one inwardly, and real circumcision is a matter of the heart, spiritual and not literal. His praise is not from men but from God."[3] This union of nationality and religion is often hard for us to conceive whose ethnicity and culture is not wed to our religion. But it was real for the Jews (cf. Phil. 3:2-6).

So when Paul says that he became *as* a Jew, he means that he adopted some of the external forms of Judaism. Since he was a Christian, he could only go so far. An example of this action can be seen in the fact that although Paul circumcised Timothy (whose mother was a Jew and whose father was a Greek), he did not circumcise Titus (whose parents were both Greek), (Gal. 2:1, 3). If Paul would have circumcised Titus, he would have been following Judaism, and Christ would then have become of no advantage to himself nor to Titus (Gal. 5:1-3). (This point about circumcision would also apply to those "under the law.")

Paul said that though he became *as* one under the law, that he nevertheless was *not* under the law (cf. Gal. 2:14-21). Paul told the Galatian Christians that God sent forth his son "to redeem those under the law, so that we might receive adoption as sons" (Gal. 4:5). For Paul to be under the law, and not *as* under the law, would have meant that he was going back into Judaism as his main religion. And if he had done this, he would have then fallen into disfavor with God.[4] He would have been denying that God justifies people on the basis of their faith. Instead, Paul was willing to suffer persecution for not being a Jew (in religion), (Gal. 5:11; Acts 15:1ff.).

So this is the first part of the dual-exception; the part relating to God and the gospel. Paul could sacrifice anything in relating to people except the core of the gospel. In Gal. 2:5, 14, he called it "the truth of the gospel." He could never put himself in a postion where he would deny that it is by grace that God accepts a man based on his faith (Eph. 2:8-9). God justifies people (puts them right with himself) by faith (Rom. 5:1). Paul always held on to this gold nugget. He would not deny it. To deny it would have meant that he would have "spurned the Son of God, and profaned the blood of the covenant by which he was sanctified, and outraged the Spirit of grace" (Heb. 10:29). Paul would never have set aside the "truth of the gospel" in order to better relate to people.

The second part of the dual-exception pertains to people and love. Now, to the Gentiles, who did not have the law, Paul could only become *as* a Gentile. The Gentiles were converted from other religions and philosophies into Christianity. Paul could not become a Gentile. If he had done so, it would have meant that he no longer observed the law of God. He would have become lawless, for Gentiles are characterized by lawlessness. Gentiles do what *they* want to do. They do not have God's law. So "To those outside the law" Paul became "*as* one outside the law—*not being without law toward God, but under the law of Christ*" (9:21a; Emphasis mine).

Just as Paul could only go so far in relating to the Jews, he also could only go so far in relating to the Gentiles. Once he had become a Christian, he could never then become a Gentile. He never could have come into a position of lawlessness for he was involved in an intimate relationship to Christ. And thus, he would always observe, the law of Christ, *the law of love.* "For the whole law is fulfilled in one word, 'You shall love your neighbour as yourself'," (Gal. 5:14; cf. Mt. 19:19; 22:39; Rom. 13:8-10; Jms. 2:8). Paul was a slave of Christ (Rom. 1:1; 1 Cor. 7:22-23); therefore, he was obligated to love the people to whom he ministered.

This then explains the second part of this dual-exception as it pertains to people and deals with love. Once again, Paul would sacrifice anything in order to get a better hearing for the gospel—*sacrifce anything*—except love. He had an obligation to love people. Therefore he could never become "lawless" (9:21). He was always under the law of Christ, which law is love (Jn. 13:34-35; Gal. 5:14; 1 Pet. 1:22ff.; 1 Jn. 3:11; 4:21).

So, to the Jew Paul became *as* a Jew. To those under the law he became *as* one under the law. And to those outside the law he became *as* one outside the law. But to the weak, Paul *became weak.* Paul did not have to become *as* weak, for Paul was a Christian just as also the weak were Christian. He did not have to win them to Christ. Therefore, he could *become weak,* and not *as weak.* This brings us to the *second* thing which we should notice about Paul's relationship to the weak.

The second thing that we can notice about Paul's relationship to the weak is that he strengthened them. *The weak, though not needing to be saved, did need to be strengthened.* Paul has their spiritual growth in mind when he says "that I might *win* the weak" (22, Emphasis mine). Paul seeks to convert the Jews, the proselytes, and the Gentiles. But he seeks to strengthen the weak in their relationship to Christ. Whatever it takes, therefore, to strengthen the weak in their relationship to Christ, Paul is willing to do. Paul said in 1 Cor. 8:13, "Therefore, if food is a cause of my brother's falling, *I will never eat meat,* lest I cause my brother to fall" (Emphasis mine). Paul was willing to go all the way for the weak. And he *could* go all the way for them. He could pull out all the stops. He purposed to become weak (never eat meat) if that would help his brother. So he said in 2 Cor. 11:29a, "Who is weak, and I am not weak?" And if the other Christians were not willing to go all the way in winning, strengthening the weak, Paul became angry. He said, "Who is made to fall, and I am not indignant?" (2 Cor. 11:29b). To the weak, Paul became weak in order to strengthen them in the faith. He did this in the spirit of John 15:12-13 where Jesus said, "This is my commandment, that you love one another as I have loved you. Greater love has no man than this, that a man lay down his life for his friends."

Paul sums up his different relationships in verse 22b. He says , "I have become all things to all men, that I might by all means save some." Paul did what he did in order to save people for the Lord. He knew that the eternal destiny of people was at stake. He was, therefore, willing to become as they were in order to win them. He was willing to sacrifice anything if that sacrifice gave him a greater opportunity to spread the gospel.

3. The third thing which we can learn about Paul as a saving slave is that he had a *share in the gospel.* Paul says, "I do it all for the sake of the gospel, that I may share in its blessings" (23). Because Paul made the sacrifices that he did, he received a blessing.

Christians get a blessing for living for the gospel (Mk. 8:34-38; 10:29-31). Paul wanted to receive this blessing. And Paul knew that the people whom he served, if he was successful in winning them, would be right by his side getting their own share in the blessings of the gospel as well. Paul's sacrifices in order to save people were not in vain. The least that he would receive for his work would be to reap in his own life the benefit of spreading the gospel; which benefit is spiritual progress.

Passage Summary

In this passage (19-23) Paul has been unfolding another of his personal experiences. He wanted the Corinthians to know for certain that the kinds of sacrifices which he calls them to make are not foreign to himself. He shares with them how he willingly yielded his freedom in order to become a slave (19). He unfolds to them how this slavery is fleshed out in his relationship to various people: Jews, Gentiles, and Christians (20-22). He furthermore goes on to tell them why he has yielded his rights. He has done it so that others may be saved, and that he himself may receive a blessing (23). To the Corinthians, (who were prone to be libertine; who abused their freedom), this experience of Paul as a saving slave, and especially his unreserved commitment in relating to the "weak," would pierce them to their heart. Now Paul turns to his third personal example which is given in this chapter.[5]

B. *The Subduing Self-discipline,* 24-27

Paul did not want the Corinthians to think that there was no struggle to the life of Christian liberty. He wanted them to realize that if they wanted to make progress in the area of liberty, then they must be willing to pay the price of discipline. Moreover, they must discipline themselves until they master themselves. Paul accomplished this type of discipline in his own life. He said, "I pommel my body and subdue it" (9:27). In the four verses under consideration, Paul suggests that there are three aspects to subduing self-discipline. These three aspects are, *1. Its Motivation (24); 2. Its Preparation (25); and 3. Its Concentration (26-27).* In explaining these aspects of discipline Paul uses analogies from the Isthmian games, which were very familiar to the Corinthians, to aid him in getting his point across. The games were held near the city of Corinth every two years.[6]

1. What *motivates* self-discipline? Paul says a "prize." He commented, "Do you not know that in a race all the runners compete, but only one receives the prize? So run that you may obtain it" (24). At the Isthmian games, all the runners in the stadium would get together for their respective events.[7] Many would compete in the *foot race.* Plenty of the runners would start the race, and many would finish the race. But at the end of the race there would be only one victor; only one winner who would carry the palm branch; only one person who would receive "the prize."

Paul wanted the Corinthians to win the prize. Paul was not saying, by using this example, that only one Christian would be the winner. He was not even saying that only a select few would make it. What he was trying to do was purge the Corinthians of their half-heartedness. To be sure, they were indeed running in the Christian liberty race. But they had not made up their minds to win. They needed to "run in such a way" so that they would win.[8] They needed motivation. They needed urging. They needed to be convinced that they could win concerning this matter of Christian liberty. They needed the spirit of Hebrews 12:1: "Therefore, since we are surrounded by so great a cloud of witnesses, let us also lay aside every weight, and sin which clings so closely, and let us run with perseverance the race that is set before us." They needed to run in this way so that they could receive the prize.

Those who won the Isthmian games received a "perishable wreath." They received a wreath woven of withered celery or pine. Eventually, the prize would become old, dried up, and corrupted. Those who win the Christian "event" win an "imperishable" wreath. This prize will never fade or corrupt. It will be the eternal reward for those who have won in the "Christian liberty race." (See Jms. 1:12; 1 Pet. 5:4; and 2 Tim. 4:8 about the rewards of faithful believers.)

2. Paul said, "Every athlete exercises self-control in all things" (25a). By using another analogy, he wanted the Corinthians to understand that merely participating in the games, is not enough to win. A good athlete *prepares* himself before the games. In the Isthmian games, the contestants began preparing themselves about ten months in advance.

The word used in this verse for "athlete" (*AGŌNIZOMAI*) means "to contend," "to strive," "to fight." It is the same word from which we get our English word *agony.* By using this word, Paul seems to be saying that each one who really wants to win an event, each one who is willing to agonize in order to be a victor and receive a prize, will prepare himself for his event. He will "exercise self-control in all things."

In order to achieve the subduing self-discipline, the Corinthians will have to be self-controlled in every part of their lives. Every athlete who is worth his stuff goes through much preparation, much training. Sometimes it takes weeks, sometimes months, and sometimes years. But if he wants to win, he will prepare himself. He will drop bad habits, like those involving diet and rest, for example. He will drop, so to speak, "good habits." That is, he will seek to devote as much time as possible to his training. He will run a "tight ship." The Corinthians needed this kind of mind-set.

Paul wanted them to be self-controlled in all things (cf. Gal. 5:23). He wanted them to understand that their lives must not be lopsided. They must have mastery over themselves in everything, Christian liberty notwithstanding. It would not have been enough for them to major in Christian liberty while other aspects of their Christian experience were being neglected. They needed to be perfect and complete Christians (cf. Jms. 1:2-3; 2 Tim. 3:16-17).

3. The third thing which Paul says about the subduing self-discipline is that it requires *concentration.* He said, "Well, I do not run aimlessly, I do not box as one beating the air; but I pommel my body and subdue it" (26-27a). Previously, Paul has talked about "all" the runners, and then, "every" athlete. Now he talks about himself: "I." He likens himself to a runner and a boxer. Paul knew that it was possible for a runner to run around the course aimlessly. Maybe the runner did not know what was the purpose of the race. Or maybe he did not know the place of the finish line. Whatever the case, he ran uncertainly. He was unsure. He probably became an obvious spectacle to the fans. Paul also knew that a fighter could box as though he was *beating the air.* The boxers in the Isthmian games fought with studded leather on their hands and arms. A blow by an opponent would inflict grave injury. Therefore, the fighters sought to duck and dodge punches rather than stand in the middle of the ring blocking punches, or slugging it out. Paul envisioned a fighter in the middle of the ring swinging wildly. This fighter would be throwing unnecessary and useless punches. He might be desperate, but he was certainly doing no damage to his skillful opponent. In the long run, he would only be tiring himself out. And in the meantime he would probably be K.O'd.

Both the aimless runner and the unskillful boxer accomplished very little. They were no more than a humorous or pitiful exhibition of good athletic competition. Both lacked concentration. But Paul was different. He concentrated on his life. He concentrated on his self-discipline. Just like a good boxer, Paul said, "I pommel my body and subdue it" (27). Paul (literally) "gave a black eye" to his body. He "brought his body into bondage." Someone might ask, "Did Paul consider his body evil?" No, I don't think that he did. Paul's battle was against sin (Rom. 8:13; 13:14). He fought against sin. Sin makes use of the body and its members. So Paul can say in Rom. 6:13-14: "Do not yield your members to sin as instruments of wickedness, but yield yourselves to God as men who have been brought from death to life, and your members to God as instruments of righteousness. For sin will have no dominion over you, since you are not under law but under grace" (cf. also verse 19).

Paul set a good example for the Corinthians. He concentrated on his personal self-discipline. His overall objective was to maintain a subdued body; one over which he had complete control. (He also may have had some specific aims in accomplishing this objective, as suggested by the running and the boxing metaphors.) If the Corinthians were to follow in his path, they would have to look "to Jesus the pioneer and perfecter of our faith, who for the joy that was set before him endured the cross, despising the shame, and is seated at the right hand of the throne of God" (Heb. 12:2). Paul told the Corinthians how to achieve the self-discipline which gains mastery over their bodies. In order to achieve it, they must *concentrate* on it.

One last thing, Paul knew that it was possible to become "disqualified." He said, "I pommel my body and subdue it, lest after preaching to others I myself should be disqualified" (27). Could it be that an ill-prepared runner, who seeing that he could not win the race, decided to take a shortcut, or decided to interfere with another contender? Sure! Could it be that a boxer who was not in shape, and seeing that he was losing the fight, would resort to dirty tactics? Sure! Is it, therefore possible that a proclaimer of the gospel, who is not self-disciplined, can find himself slipping? Yielding to temptation? Making excuses? You'd better believe it! Would the runner be disqualified? Yes. Would the boxer be disqualified? Yes. Would the proclaimer of the gospel be rejected? Definitely! (Cf. 1 Cor. 4:4). Paul knew that it was possible for himself to become "un-approved."[9] He could have failed the test. He himself could have been disqualified for lack of self-discipline. In 2 Tim. 2:5 he said, "An athlete is not crowned unless he competes according to the rules." Paul wanted to spare himself and the Corinthians the mockery and humiliation of disqualification. (In chapter 10 he will give a vivid example of how the Hebrews were disqualified from entering the promised land.) Therefore, Paul encouraged the Corinthians to concentrate on their personal discipline until it is achieved.

Passage Summary & Conclusion

From this, the third of Paul's personal examples, we have learned about self-discipline. I believe that Paul has tried to show the Corinthians that they must preserve their liberty by being self-controlled. He wanted them to be able to yield their rights: to forego their freedoms when the situation called for it. And they would only be able to do this if they possessed subduing self-discipline. He taught the Corinthians what was involved in self-discipline. It involved a motivation—the *prize*; a preparation—*self-control in all things;* and a concentration—*not aimlessly, not beating the air.* Having this kind of self-discipline enabled Paul to conscientiously testify, "I pommel my body and subdue it." And then, at the end of verses 24-27, he warned the Corinthians that the punishment for lack of self-discipline is disqualification.

This passage ends our study of the two sections of the second half of 1 Corinthians chapter nine. Both parts dealt with preserving Christian liberty. In the first section Paul presented himself as a Saving Slave (19-23). He became all things to all men, so that by all means he could save some (22). By this passage he attempted to show the Corinthians that they should use their liberty to win others to Christ, and to help those who were saved to make spiritual progress. In the second passage, Paul gave some instructions on Subduing Self-discipline (24-27). He drew his analogies from the Isthmian games. He said that he pommeled his body and subdued it (27). I believe that he was trying to teach the Christians at Corinth that they should guard their liberty by being self-controlled in all things (25). Now, after studying these passages, we must ask ourselves...

Concretization

What can we learn from 1 Cor. 9:19-27 about Christian liberty? I think that we can learn four things. *First, Christian liberty involves preserving one's freedom. Second, each Christian should preserve his liberty in order to freely give it to others. Third, there is a restriction to liberty involved in fostering inter-personal relationships for the purpose of evangelizing. And fourth, self-discipline is a key to preserving one's liberty.*

A. *Christian liberty involves preserving one's freedom.* Paul said, " 'All things are lawful for me,' but I will not be enslaved by anything" (1 Cor. 6:12b). If Christian liberty is to remain Christian liberty, then it must be preserved. Paul realized that he had freedom in Christ, and he was determined not to lose that freedom. He was unwilling to become enslaved by anyone. If he became a slave, it would be his own doing; he would enslave himself (9:19). He would not even let his own body master him (9:27). Paul was "free" because the Lord had set him free. And Paul preserved that freedom. And the Lord expects each of us to preserve our freedom as well. He desires for us to remain free from bondage to people (1 Cor. 7:22-27) and things (2 Pet. 2:19).

At the beginning of this chapter, I made mention of an obsession I used to have with basketball. As I observe from time to time the reaction of different brothers to this game, I must conclude that many others are mastered by the game just as I was. Fights on the court, senseless arguments, and late night playing, all tend to show that some young men are mastered by the game. And, like others, Christians are included in this observation. When Christians are not trusting the Lord for victory in this area, then they can become bound just like anyone else.

When I entered into college, the Lord began to show me (through the superiority attitudes and racism of some of the white brothers in intramural sports) that it was not only with basketball that I had a problem. My problems extended to sports overall. This was not an area of my life of which the Lord enjoyed complete control. When the Lord made me aware of the problem, I began to cooperate with him in dealing with it. And the Lord began to liberate me from the problem. He is the only one who can free a person from sin. He is the only one who can help us to resolve those problems which usually take a long time to overcome. We can be thankful that Jesus said, "If you continue in my word, you are truly my disciples, and you will know the truth, and the truth will make you free." "So if the Son makes you free, you will be free indeed" (Jn. 8:31b-32, 36).

Sports are not the only thing that can bind us. Other things can rob us of our freedom as well. The Lord does not want us to enter into anything in the questionable area that may be habit forming. For example, certain drugs are addictive. The Lord, therefore, wants us to stay away from such drugs. But then, there are some legitimate drugs and medicines; things like cough syrup, aspirins, sleeping pills, etc. These "good" things can also become habit forming. We must guard ourselves so that we do not become dependent on such things. Good things can turn into bad things if we are not careful. I have heard of people who are cola-holics. They are addicted to colas! This may seem humourous, but this is just the kind of thing that Paul is talking about. The Lord wants his people to be free.

Some of us can become bound to things like records, the radio, and the T.V. A particular activity which I must stay on guard against is watching the news. I like to listen to the news. But I must never let it become my master. Many Christian women (and men!) are bound by the soap operas. If you ever happen to be downtown in the afternoon hours, stop into a department store and go to where they sell the T.V. sets. In this area there will usually be crowds of ladies gathering around the sets trying to see what is going to happen next. Some of the managers of the stores now provide seats around these viewing areas so that the people will have a place to sit. Many women are bound by these unChristian, unBlack, despairing middle class soap operas, which portray nothing less (or more!) than unfaithfulness and immorality. What a sad kind of picture to become bound by!

I used to be bound by my music—my *Christian* music. I used to get up early every morning to listen to one of the gospel music programs on one of Chicago's black radio stations. Someone might say, "But that was Christian music to which you were listening. That's okay." True, it was Christian music (most of the time). But do you know that this music actually became more important to me than my morning prayers? It became even more appealing to me than reading the Word. And the Lord had to deliver me from that program—that *Christian* program. And I am glad that he did. And I trust that the Lord will also deliver a lot of other young people who are likewise hooked on our good gospel music, at the expense of earnest praying and Bible reading.

It is possible for a young person to be bound by the clothing styles of this day and age. There are many brothers and sisters who have an obsession about keeping up with the latest styles. They spend far too much time and money on clothes. This may be because of the pressure from their peer group. Other young people go to the opposite extreme. They go around in blue jeans and sweat shirts *all the time*. This is also a prominent style. A person can be bound either way. Paul said, "I will not be enslaved by *anything*."

A young person must be careful not to be bound by a young lady, or a young man. All of us need healthy social relationships. And Christ can help us to achieve these kinds of relationships.[10] But he must be made first in everything. Wise king Solomon said, "Keep your heart with all vigilance; for from it flow the springs of life" (Prov. 4:23). A young adult must protect his/her heart. If for no other reason, so it won't get broke!

Dear black sister, please don't forsake your virtue because the black 'Christian' brothers don't act right. Despise being pimped, and let no one get your nose wide open. Don't compromise your chasity because the brothers threaten to forget about you if you don't sleep with them. Refuse to wallow in self-pity when the other sisters parade their rings and you don't have one. Tell the Devil he's a liar when he says you'll be an old maid. Hold your head up high. Be the best black woman that you can be. Trust in the Lord, and he'll be there. And he'll make a way for you; one way or another. Preserve your freedom.

What about superstitions? Well, they can bind you also. Good luck charms, rabbit feet, horseshoes, knocking on wood, crossing the fingers, etc. All these things can rob a person of their freedom. A Christian should trust in the Lord at all times. And a person gets bound by superstitions when they do not fully trust the Lord. Moreover, when a person does not trust the Lord for everything, they incur the tendency to worry, fear, fret, anger, depress, etc.

Christian liberty has to do with preserving one's freedom. If a person is not on guard, their liberty can be turned into bondage.

B. *Each Christian should preserve his liberty in order to freely yield it to others.* Paul said, "For though I am free from all men, I have made myself a slave to all, that I might win the more" (1 Cor. 9:19). Paul preserved his freedom in order to freely give it to others. He caused himself to be in "bondage" to others. He had preserved his freedom by means of his financial policy toward the Church at Corinth. Therefore, he could effectively minister to other people (as well as the Corinthians) without being under the pressure of obligation to the Corinthians.

The Lord wants us to be free to serve.[11] When I was in college, I did not want to accumulate a large amount of debts. I wanted to keep the loans which I received at a very low minimum. I reasoned that if the Lord had called me to go do a work for him, then I wanted to be free (that is, financially free) to do that work. I did not want to have a mammoth debt hanging over my head while at the same time seeking to serve the Lord. The Lord honored this desire of mine. I left school with a relatively small debt. And during our engagement, my fiance and I saved up enough money to pay our loans off in full. We made the payment shortly before we were married. And in the ministry which we are in at this present time, it is good to be free from the pressure of unpaid school bills.

The Black community needs Christian young adults who are free to serve. Paul made himself a slave to others in order to win them to Christ. There is a dire need for the services of black people who are willing to become slaves of the black community for the sake of Christ. Our folks need to be won to the Lord. And I believe that it is going to take committed black Christians to do it. It will take black people who are willing to be themselves. We must learn to live what we are, and love what we are; black people created in God's image. To reach our community for Christ, it is going to take Christians who will be willing to make great sacrifices, and who are free to make those sacrifices.

I believe that the Lord is looking for black Christians who are free. He is looking for those whom he exclusively owns, so that he can use them in bringing black folks to himself; as well as use them in meeting the needs of black people. It seems to me that people will respond positively to those who are genuinely concerned about them and their welfare. If we as black Christians really become serious about holistically helping our people, I believe that we will see a favorable response. I believe also that the Lord will be pleased very much by our endeavors.[12]

C. *There is a restriction to liberty involved in fostering inter-personal relationships for the purpose of evangelizing.* In the passage of 1 Cor. 9:19-23, we observed the difference between Paul's relationship to the weak, and his relationship to the Jews, the proselytes, and the Gentiles. Paul became *as* a Jew, *as* a proselyte, and *as* a Gentile. But he became, not *as* weak, but he *became weak.* Paul was limited in how far he could go in becoming a Jew and proselyte, or a Gentile. We saw how in each of these cases there was an exception. That dual-exception had one side that related to God and the gospel, and another side that related to people and love.

This dual-exception is the restriction to liberty in fostering inter-personal relationships for the purpose of evangelizing. Never sacrifice justification by faith, and never sacrifice a sincere and obligatory love. We need to keep this in mind when we desire to "become all things to all men." Building bridges in order to witness is not quite as simple as "when in Rome do as the Romans do." As we relate to others, we must be careful to maintain our Christian integrity.

For a nitty gritty example of relating to people, we can turn to the lives of Jesus, and his forerunner, John the Baptizer. Jesus said, "To what then shall I compare the men of this generation, and what are they like? They are like children sitting in the market place and calling to one another, 'We piped to you, and you did not dance; we wailed, and you did not weep.' For John the Baptist has come eating no bread and drinking no wine; and you say, 'He has a demon.' The Son of man has come eating and drinking; and you say, 'Behold, a glutton and a drunkard, a friend of tax collectors and sinners!' Yet wisdom is justified by all her children" (Lk. 7:31-35).

John the Baptist came preaching a baptism of repentance. He was preparing the way for Jesus. He lived out in the wilderness. He ate locust and wild honey. He wore a garment of camel's hair, and a leather girdle around his waist. People from all around went out into the desert to see John and to hear what he had to say. Many of them were baptized, confessing their sins (Mt. 3:1-12; Mk. 1:1-8, Lk. 3:1-20).

John was a tough prophet. Jesus said so himself (Lk. 7:24ff.). One might say that John was not very sociable. He did not mingle much with the people. He ate no bread and drank no wine. He led a very austere life. Yet, the people eagerly heard his message. The common folks listened to his preaching, and responded to it (Mt. 21:28-32). He was effective in reaching them for the Lord. It was the Lord's will for John the Baptist to leave behind many of the blessings and comforts which life affords (cf. Lk. 1:13-17,80). This is how the Lord wanted John to live. And this is the way that John did live. And the Lord used him greatly in his ministry.

On the other hand, Jesus came on the scene heavily mingling with the people. Jesus was very sociable. Jesus was a "Friend" of tax-collectors and sinners. He went to their get-togethers. He talked their language. He was fed at the tables of people who were despised. He ate their bread. He even drank their wine (Mt. 11:16-19; Lk. 5:29-32; 7:36-50; 15:1-2).

Jesus' message was this: "Come to me, all who labour and are heavy laden, and I will give you rest. Take my yoke upon you, and learn from me; for I am gentle and lowly in heart, and you will find rest for your souls. For my yoke is easy, and my burden is light" (Mt. 11:28-30). And the common folks heard him gladly, and followed him (Mt. 9:9-13; Mk. 12:37).

Here we have an example of two different men—Jesus and John, two different lifestyles, and two different ministries. (I would not have made the comparison except that Jesus made it himself.) Both of them were heard by the common folks. Both of them were rejected by the religious leaders of their day. Both lived drastically different lifestyles, yet both related well to their people. Each one underwent tremendous sacrifices. They both yielded their rights (cf. 2 Cor. 8:9; Mt. 11:7-9,18; Mk. 6:17-29). They both lived radical lives, and God was able to use each one in his own way. What did Jesus and John have in common? I believe it was the heart of their message. Each one showed the people how to get right with God. Each one showed their love to the people. Other than these two things their lives split in opposite directions. This is one of the most vivid examples of "Christian liberty" within the Scriptures.

What does this teach us? This teaches us that we are free to live in such a way that will help us to foster inter-personal relationships for the purpose of bringing people to the Lord. When we respect the dual-exception, the rest of our lifestyle, whatever it may be, is to be worked out between ourselves and the Lord.[13]

D. *Self-discipline is a key to preserving one's liberty.* Paul gave witness to the Corinthians of how he subdued his own body (9:27). He brought his body into subjection through self-discipline.

Self-control is needed in order to preserve our Christian liberty. In

Gal. 5:13a, Paul says, "For you were called to freedom, brethren; only do not use your freedom as an opportunity for the flesh." It is possible for liberty to slip into license. Paul did not want the Corinthians to become flabby in their wills. He wanted them to always be in complete control of themselves.

Many people like to participate in the games at the food stores; like bingo, raffles, etc. But innocent games such as these can lead into a "love for money," and a desire for hard gambling. Self-control is required in order to prevent this from happening. It might be well to forego some of those "innocent" games in order to keep your resistance up.

Whenever a person is able to deny themselves things which are "good," you might say that such a person is self-controlled. I think that it is wise and healthy to send yourself through a personal test concerning self-discipline. For instance, miss a meal, or skip going to a good movie. Or limit your telephone conversations to a few minutes. Push yourself or pull yourself. You don't have to do this, but it could show you the amount of self-control which you possess.[14]

Paul said that in order for us to exercise our Christian liberty, we must have self-control in all things. And if we cannot control ourselves, we are strongly testifying that we are not free, but bound.

Summary & Conclusion

These then are the four things we have tried to learn from the passage of 1 Cor. 9:19-27. A. Christian liberty involves preserving one's freedom. B. Each Christian should preserve his liberty in order to freely give it to others. C. There is a restriction to liberty involved in fostering inter-personal relationships for the purpose of evangelizing. D. Self-discipline is a key to preserving one's liberty.

By examining Paul's two experiences of being a saving slave, and possessing subduing self-discipline, I have tried to illuminate the principle of preserving one's freedom (1 Cor. 6:12b). We have been able to study all three of Paul's experiences in 1 Cor. 9. This chapter, along with chapters four and five, have highlighted in detail the three principles of Christian liberty.

In the next chapter we will examine how Paul warned the Corinthians about properly understanding the activities in which they participate. We'll move on from here.

Understanding What Has Been Taught

1. Why did Paul give his service voluntarily?

2. Name the four groups of Paul's several relationships.

3. Name three ways in which Paul became as a Jew.

4. What was the significance of the name change from Saul to Paul in Acts 13:9, 13?

5. Could Paul have ever yielded his nationality? Why? Why not?

6. What was unique about Paul's relationship to the "weak"?

7. What is the dual-exception to liberty in fostering inter-personal relationships for the purpose of evangelizing?

8. What did Paul receive for his service in spreading the gospel?

9. What are the three aspects of subduing self-discipline?

10. From where did Paul draw his analogies about discipline?

11. What did Paul mean when he talked about being "disqualified"?

Responding To And Applying What Has Been Learned

Questions

1. What activities tend to have a binding effect upon your life?

2. Are you committed to serving the black community? Are you leaning in this way? Why? Why not?

3. What do you think about Christians who try to sacrifice their ethnicity in order to win others to the Lord? How can you help them to understand that this practice is not healthy?

4. In what areas do you need to improve your self-discipline?

5. What "laws" have the Lord led you to lay aside in order to win others to himself? Was it helpful?

Suggestions

Individual

1. Secure prayer and counsel from a friend about overcoming something which binds you.

2. Determine if your commitment to things, concepts, places, and programs surpasses your commitment to people.

Group

1. Plan to go to an "unChristian" place in order to spread the gospel. (e.g. a tavern, pool hall, etc.)

2. Plan a group-fast for special problems, understanding Christian liberty, and encouraging self-discipline.

KNOWING THE FACTS—Chapter 7

1 Corinthians 10:1-22

I want you to know, brethren, that our fathers were all under the cloud, and all passed through the sea, and all were baptized into Moses in the cloud and in the sea, and all ate the same supernatural[1] food and all drank the same supernatural[1] drink. For they drank from the supernatural[1] Rock which followed them, and the Rock was Christ. Nevertheless with most of them God was not pleased; for they were overthrown in the wilderness.

Now these things are warnings for us, not to desire evil as they did. Do not be idolaters as some of them were; as it is written, "The people sat down to eat and drink and rose up to dance." We must not indulge in immorality as some of them did, and twenty-three thousand fell in a single day. We must not put the Lord to the test, as some of them did and were destroyed by serpents; nor grumble, as some of them did and were destroyed by the Destroyer. Now these things happened to them as a warning, but they were written down for our instruction, upon whom the end of the ages has come. Therefore let any one who thinks that he stands take heed lest he fall. No temptation has overtaken you that is not common to man. God is faithful, and he will not let you be tempted beyond your strength, but with the temptation will also provide the way of escape, that you may be able to endure it.

Therefore, my beloved, shun the worship of idols. I speak as to sensible men; judge for yourselves what I say. The cup of blessing which we bless, is it not a participation[2] in the blood of Christ? The bread which we break, is it not a participation[2] in the body of Christ? Because there is one bread, we who are many are one body, for we all partake of the one bread. Consider the people of Israel; are not those who eat the sacrifices partners in the altar? What do I imply then? That food offered to idols is anything, or that an idol is anything? No, I imply that what pagans sacrifice they offer to demons and not to God. I do not want you to be partners with demons. You cannot drink the cup of the Lord and the cup of demons. You cannot partake of the table of the Lord and the table of demons. Shall we provoke the Lord to jealousy? Are we stronger than he?

A. The Precedent of Israel, 1-13
   1. Their Participation, 1-4
   2. Their Disqualification, 5-10
      a) Its Cause, 5-6
      b) Their Conduct, 7-10
         1) Idolatry, 7
         2) Immorality, 8
         3) Testing The Lord, 9
         4) Grumbling, 10
   3. Their Summation, 11-13
B. The Precaution Against Idolatry, 14-22
   1. The Prohibition, 14
   2. The Explanation, 15-18
   3. The Implications, 19-22

In our haste to use our Christian liberty, we can sometimes ignorantly participate in things which are definitely sinful. We do this because we do not know the facts about a given activity. Chapter three dealt with knowing the Scriptures. This chapter deals with, so to speak, knowing the world. The Lord would not have us to be ignorant about this world, or the age in which we live. He wants us to *know the facts.*

In dealing with the problems which we face in our day, it is often good to look back into the past in order to receive direction. This is what Paul does. He reaches back to the time of the liberation of Israel from Egypt, in order to give a warning to the Corinthians about a questionable issue. In their zeal for eating food offered to idols in the idol-temples, the Corinthians had ignorantly and unwaringly entered into practicing idolatry. Paul has to bring their sin to their attention. He warned them that just as the Israelites had been punished for their sins, so also they will be judged by the Lord if they do not forsake their idolatry.

Elucidation

As we look into 1 Cor. 10:1-22, we will be able to see how Paul helped the Corinthians to better understand what was happening in the practice of idolatry. There are two main sections to this passage: *A. The Precedent of Israel, verses 1-13, and B. The Precaution Against Idolatry, verses 14-22.* Let's see what each section teaches.

A. *The Precedent of Israel,* 1-13

In the last verse of chapter 9, Paul showed the Corinthians that it is possible to become "disqualified" as a Christian. To insure his continued approval before the Lord, Paul exercised complete self-control. He subdued his body (9:27). Now in the beginning verse of chapter ten, Paul gives a vivid example of what he is talking about in terms of disqualification. The subject of the example is Israel, or as he calls them, "our fathers" (10:1). The time in Israel's history from which Paul draws the example is the period of their exodus from the land of Egypt. After their liberation from bondage to Pharoah, the Israelites were (in the language of the Isthmian games), participating in a "foot race" to the promised land. All of them started the race, but most of them were disqualified. Let's see how Paul examined their experience. This examination has three parts: *1. Their Participation (1-4); 2. Their Disqualification (5-10); and 3. Their Summation (11-13).*

1. Paul begins verses 1-4 by associating the Corinthians, who were mostly gentiles, with the Israelites. He calls the Israelites, "our fathers" (1). Christians are related to the Israelites through Abraham on the basis of faith (Gal. 3:6-10). Paul wants to make sure that the example which he explains to the Corinthians is not shoved off on the grounds of disassociation. He wanted them to realize that if the *fathers* underwent this certain experience, that the *sons* might also undergo a similar experience.

From this point, Paul begins to explain two aspects of the Israelite's *participation experience* which aspects are the same experiences of the Corinthians. These two aspects are Baptism and Communion. When the Israelites left Egypt, Paul says that they were baptized in the cloud and in the sea. The cloud was the "pillar of cloud" by day and "pillar of fire" by night. It lead the Israelites along the way to the promised land. The sea was, of course, the Red Sea. It opened up to let the Israelites pass safely through on dry ground. But it closed on the Egyptian army and drowned them (Ex. 13:21-22; 14:22-29). Here, at this great event, Paul sees God as the baptizer, the Israelites as the candidates, the element as the cloud and the Red Sea, and the purpose of the baptism as showing the Israelites that Moses was God's chosen leader for them. He was their liberator (Acts 7:35-36).

As the Israelites journeyed from the Red Sea, Paul said that they took Communion. He said that they ate the same "spiritual food," and drank the same "spiritual drink" (3,4). The spiritual food which they ate was manna. When the people got hungry on their journey, the Lord sent them bread from heaven. The spiritual drink which they drank was water which the Lord miraculously provided for them (Ex. 16:4, 35; 17:6; Num. 20:10-11; Dt. 8:3; Ps. 78:15-16, 24-29). They received a blessing for eating the manna and drinking the water. For in taking the Lord's Supper, they were actually having fellowship with Christ. This is why Paul says, "they drank from the spiritual Rock which followed them, and the Rock was Christ" (4b). Christ was continually with the Israelites, and communed with them through the manna and the water.

So Paul says that *the Israelites participated in the Baptism and the Lord's Supper.* How extensive was this participation? Paul says it was a *total* participation. "All" were under the cloud, "all" passed through the sea. "All" were baptized. "All" ate. "All" drank. It was a total community affair. Each and everyone was baptized. Each and everyone took Communion. It is important to keep this in mind as we go into the next point.

2. Even though all the Israelites participated in the "foot race" to the promised land, most of them were *disqualified* before they made it (5-10). Paul said, "Nevertheless with most of them God was not pleased;

for they were overthrown in the wilderness" (5). How many is "most?" How many of the Israelites were "strewn" about the desert? All of them except two! That's right. All of the Israelites, twenty years old and upward, died on the way to the land of Canaan. All except two: Caleb and Joshua (Num. 14:13-38; Ps. 78:31; Heb. 3:16-19; Jude 5).

Why were most of the people destroyed in the wilderness? Paul tells the Corinthians that this happened because most of the Israelites displeased the Lord. "God was not pleased" with most of them because of their lack of faith (Heb. 3:19; 11:6). However, their lack of faith manifested itself in their affections. *They desired evil* (6). They lusted after evil things (6b; cf. Num. 11:4, 34; Ps. 106:14-15). Paul gives four examples in verses 7-10 of how the Israelites craved after evil things. *These four things were idolatry, immorality, testing the Lord, and grumbling.*

He told the Corinthians, "Do not be *idolaters* as some of them were; as it is written, 'The people sat down to eat and drink and rose up to dance'" (7; Emphasis mine.). This verse is in reference to the occasion in Ex. 32:1-6. During this incident Moses was up on Mt. Sinai receiving the Ten Commandments and other instructions from the Lord. The poeple became impatient when they saw that Moses was long in coming. So one day they asked Aaron to make them a golden calf (symbol of a Canaanite god) from their golden earrings. Aaron willingly assented to their request by making a golden calf and an altar for their sacrifices. The next day the people got up early in the morin', offered their sacrificies, and then celebrated their newly created "god." One might say that they had a "good time;" idolatry, sexual activities and all.

Since the Lord knew what was going on, he quickly sent Moses back down the mountain. When Moses returned to the camp he proceeded to deal with the sin of the people. At his command three thousand people were killed by the Levites. And then, the Lord sent a plague among them which probably led to some more deaths (Ex. 32:28, 35).

"We must not indulge in *immorality* as some of them did, and twenty-three thousand fell in a single day" (8; Emphasis mine.). This event is recorded in Num. 25:1-18. It happened after the occasion when Balak the king of Moab sought the help of Balaam, a hireling prophet, for the purpose of cursing the Israelites. Balak was fearful of the Israelites (Num. 22:1-4ff.). He therefore wanted to eliminate them. He reasoned that a curse would be helpful in destroying the Israelites. So he hired Balaam to pronounce the curse.

But when Balaam tried to curse the Israelites, the Lord caused him to bless them instead. And after four series of blessings, the Bible says that Balak and Balaam parted company. But sometime before the prophet Balaam went back home, he gave Balak some advice on overcoming the Israelites. He told Balak to get some Moabite girls to invite some of the Israelite men to one of their religious "get togethers." Well, Balak followed his advice. And when the Israelite men went to the pagan worship services, they participated in the Midianite sexual rights, and eventually they got into idolatry.

The Lord became very angry at the Israelites and commanded Moses to hang the leaders who had "yoked themselves to Baal of Peor." The Lord also sent a plague among the people. It was checked only after a righteous act by Phinehas. The total number of people who died that day were 24,000 (Num. 25:1-18; 31:16; Ps. 106:28-31; Rev. 2:14).

"We must not *put the Lord to the test,* as some of them did and were destroyed by serpents" (9; Emphasis mine.). In Num. 21:4-9 we can read about the time that the Israelites tested the Lord. It happened in about their thirty-eighth year of wandering in the desert. They were beginning to prepare to go into the promised land. And as they journeyed toward Canaan, they took a route which led them around the land of Edom. The Bible says that "the people became impatient on the way" (Num. 21:4). As a result of their impatience, they began to speak out against Moses. They thought that they were going to die from lack of water and food. God had been supplying them with manna all along, but they became tired of eating it.

Without asking any questions or engaging them in dialogue, the Bible says that the Lord sent fiery serpents among the people. (Actually, the Scripture says that the serpents were already in the desert (Dt. 8:15). The Lord had been graciously protecting the people day after day. He now withdrew his merciful hand.) As a result, many of the people were bitten by the snakes, and many of them died. They then confessed their sin to Moses. He prayed for the people and the Lord gave him an answer. Moses made a bronze serpent and set it upon a pole. If any of the people who had been bitten looked up at the serpent, they would become healed (cf. Jn. 3:14-16).

We must not *"grumble, as some of them did and were destroyed by the Destroyer"* (10; Emphasis mine.). The Israelites were known for their grumbling, their complaining. Therefore, it is hard to pinpoint this particular incident. This might have been the time after the spies had surveyed the promised land. When they returned, the majority of them expressed doubts to the people about going ahead with the conquest of the land. The people then complained against Moses and Aaron. All except two of the spies died in a plague (Num. 14:1-30; Ps. 106:24-27).

On the other hand, this time of grumbling might have been the occasion of Korah's rebellion. Korah and his company challenged the leadership of Moses and Aaron. As a result, the Lord split open the ground to swallow up the rebels and their families. The Israelites then murmured against Moses and Aaron for being the cause of Korah and his company's destruction. As a punishment for their complaining, the Lord sent a plague among the people. Many of them died before the plague was checked by Aaron (Num. 16).

There is a third incident which Paul might have had in mind. It stemmed from Korah's rebellion. Some of the Israelite leaders did not think that Aaron was the *only high priest for the people.* The Lord subsequently proved that Aaron was his main man by causing Aaron's Rod to bud when the other's rods did not bud. The challengers then became very frightened, realizing that because of their sin, they were doomed to die. They realized that if they even went near unto the tabernacle, that they would be faced with death (Num. 17:1-13).

No matter which incident Paul had in mind, the Corinthians probably knew what he was talking about since Paul was no doubt using a familiar example. And they knew that the consequences of complaining was death by the "Destroyer."

In these few verses, (7-10), Paul has used at least four occasions from Israel's history in order to show the Corinthians that the Israelites were disqualified from entering the promised land. Time after time the Lord had to punish the nation because of their sin. They could not control themselves. They *lusted* after evil things. As a result, they were judged time and time again within their forty years of wandering. Their disqualification was almost as complete as their participation in the Baptism and Communion. It was so complete that only two from the original group entered the land of Canaan. The rest of the people who went into the land of promise were a totally new generation.

3. Now that Paul has depicted the experience of the Israelites, he then goes on to *summarize* what that experience should mean to the Corinthians (11-13). First he says that "these things happened to them as a warning, but they were written down for our instruction, upon whom the end of the ages have come" (11, cf. 6). Paul wants the Corinthians to know that they should look at what happened to the Israelites as an example for themselves (cf. Rom. 15:4). They should consider these things a warning. A better translation of this verse would be, "Now these things happened to them as a warning example, and they were written down for our warning..." Both the historical happening and the sacred recording of the Israelites' experience served to precaution Christians not to sin against the Lord. This was especially important to the Corinthians because the days in which they were living were (literally) the "ends of the ages," the last days (cf. Gal. 4:4; Heb. 1:2).

From this point, Paul proceeded to give the meaning of this example for two groups among the Christians. Verse 12 is written to the overconfident or careless. These were the ones in Corinth who would think that they were very secure in eating meat offered to idols. Paul said to them, "Therefore let any one who thinks that he stands take heed lest he fall." Paul wanted this group of Christians to be careful lest they become disqualified as most of the Israelites had become disqualified. He wanted these Christians to continue to be approved unto God. He did not want their lives to be ruined because of a carefree attitude toward their Christian liberty.

The second group of people Paul addresses are the underconfident or fearful. These are the ones who may have been apprehensive about the use of their Christian liberty. They also may have been disturbed about the social environment of Corinth. They may have had fears about their own ability to live in such ways that were pleasing to the Lord. This would have especially been the case after they had been reminded by Paul that only two of the older generation Israelites made it into the promised land. Not even Moses had made it! (Num. 20:10-12; Dt. 34:1-8).

92

So how could they expect to continue to please the Lord! Paul says to this group, "No temptation has overtaken you that is not common to man. God is faithful, and he will not let you be tempted beyond your strength, but with the temptation will also provide the way of escape, that you may be able to endure it" (13).

Paul did not want this group to be fearful. He wanted them to trust the Lord in the midst of their testings. He taught them that their testings were not peculiar, but were in fact the same kind that men everywhere must face (cf. Heb. 2:14-18; 4:14-16). Moreover, He told them that God would not put any more on them than what they could bear. God would be faithful to screen all their trials. He also would be faithful to make a way of escape. He would show the Corinthians how to conquer their testings. They would be able to endure them.

Passage Summary

This passage, teaching about the Israelites' wilderness experience, serves as a precautioning precedent. Paul's mentioning of the Israelites' "participation" in the ordinances would have surely related to the Corinthians. They, too, were baptized and partook of Communion. By showing the different sins of the Israelites which led to their destruction, Paul would have rung a bell in the mind of the Corinthians. They, too, were prone to the sins of the Israelites by eating idol-food in a pagan temple. They could "crave evil" by eating idol-meat with a guilty conscience. They could have become "idolaters," by visiting with the many prostitutes who served in the temple. They could have even "tested" the Lord by dividing their allegiance between him and demons (cf. 10:21, 22). They could have "grumbled" at Paul. They could have spurned his authority and counsel regarding "food offered to idols." Paul, in a general way, has warned the Corinthians in verses 1-13. He has used these verses to set the tone for what he will say to them in verses 14-22. Now let's see what specific instruction he gives to them.

B. *The Precaution Against Idolatry, 14-22*

The particular activity which the Corinthians should examine in the light of the previous forewarning is *idolatry.* This is the sin which could possibly cause their "disqualification." This section can be divided into three parts. First, *Paul gives a Prohibition (14); second, he gives his Explanation (15-18); and third, he gives the Implications of his explanation (19-22).*

1. "Therefore, my beloved, shun the worship of idols" (14). This is Paul's burden. This is his *prohibition.* He has said all that he did in verses 1-13 in order to tell the Corinthians to "flee" from idolatry. The Corinthians had a hard time breaking away from their old way of life. Some of them were dragging their feet. Paul wanted them to get moving. He wanted them to make a clean cut with idolatry and with anything that would give occasion to it—like eating idol-meat in a pagan temple.

Paul also wanted the Corinthians to know that he loved them. The things which he said to them were for their own good. Some of the Corinthians might have thought that Paul's motives were not right. So Paul wanted them to know that they were his friends. Because he loved them, he did not want them to suffer the consequences of practicing idolatry.

2. In verses 15-18, Paul *explains* his reasons for teaching the Corinthians to flee from idolatry; that is, refusing to eat food offered to idols within a pagan temple. In verse 15 he expresses confidence that the Corinthians would draw the same conclusion as he himself has come to. He calls them "sensible men." He considered that they had enough practical wisdom in order to judge for themselves what he was saying (cf. 1 Thess. 5:19-22).

The burden of Paul's explanation has to do with properly understanding the Lord's Supper (cf. Mt. 26:26-29; Mk. 14:22-25; Lk. 22:14-20; 1 Cor. 11:23-26). Paul makes two points about the Lord's Supper. First, he let the Corinthians know that when they take the Lord's Supper that they are commonly participating or communing together in the blood and body of the Lord. By taking Communion, the Corinthians enter into fellowship with the Lord himself (16; cf. 10:4b). By partaking in faith, they therefore receive the benefits of the Lord's death and resurrection. They were remembering the Lord. And they were proclaiming "the Lord's death until he comes" (1 Cor. 11:26ff.; cf. Phil. 3:8-11).

Secondly, Paul wants the Corinthians to know that when they take Communion that their unity is being affirmed. He said, "Because there is one bread, we who are many are one body, for we all partake of the one bread" (17). Paul stresses their oneness so that they will realize that the entire body is affected by the actions of each individual member. Paul also wanted to get the Corinthians to properly share their meals, especially the *AGAPE,* "love feast" (which was eaten before the Lord's Supper) with one another. Since it was not good for the believers, not even the poor believers, to eat at the banquets in the idol-temples, then the church had to do right and take up the slack. (See 1 Cor. 11:17-22 for the problem in the church.)

Paul uses an analogy from the religious practices of Israel to press home his remarks. Paul asks, "...are not those who eat the sacrifices partners in the altar?" (18b). The law regarding sacrifices made provisions for the priest, and also the offerer, to eat a portion of that which was sacrificed (Lev. 7:11-34; 10:12-15; Deut. 12:11-28; 1 Sam. 9:10-24). The altar made the sacrifice which was laid upon it sacred (Mt. 23:19). Therefore, those who ate the sacrifices were partners in holiness, because they were partners in the altar. By using this analogy, Paul is reinforcing the fact that the Corinthians receive a blessing from partaking the Lord's Supper. They receive "blessings" from the Lord (16a).

3. From verses 19-22, we learn that Paul wanted to be sure that the Corinthians knew what he was getting at. He did not want them to have any doubts about his conclusions. What had Paul been *implying?* He had not been saying that "food offered to idols is anything, or that an idol is

anything." He had dealt with that issue before (cf. 1 Cor. 8:4-6). What then were his implications? He was saying that "what pagans sacrifice they offer to demons and not to God" (20a).

There is something worse than food offered to idols. There is something more erroneous than thinking that an idol has a real existence. There is a far graver sin than practicing idolatry. *That thing is to be partners with demons.* Paul knew what went on in idolatrous worship. He knew that demons were the reality behind idolatry. He knew that there was a "spell cast by demons over ther worshippers at idol-feasts which led actually to a compact with demons."[3] So when a person participated in idolatry he also became a communicant with demonical forces (Deut. 32:17; Ps. 106:34ff.; Rev. 9:20). Paul understood the implications of idolatry, but the Corinthians were ignorant of these implications.

Paul carries his argument about the implication of demonic worship one step further. He says, "You cannot drink the cup of the Lord and the cup of demons. You cannot partake of the table of the Lord and the table of demons" (21). Paul showed the Corinthians that there could be no dual allegiance between the Lord and demons. The Lord's kingdom is in direct opposition to Satan's kingdom (Eph. 6:10-20; 2 Cor. 4:4; Acts 26:16-18). And not only are the two kingdoms in direct opposition to one another, but even the results of the fellowship with demons and fellowship with the Lord are directly opposite. From fellowship with the Lord the Corinthians would become holy, pure, and clean. From fellowship with demons the Corinthians would become unholy, impure, and defiled. A commentary of Paul's thinking about this subject can be found in 2 Cor. 6:14-7:1.

> Do not be mismated with unbelievers. For what partnership have righteousness and iniquity? Or what fellowship has light with darkness? What accord has Christ with Belial? Or what has a believer in common with an unbeliever? What aggreement has the temple of God with idols? For we are the temple of the living God; as God said, "I will live in them and move among them, and I will be their God, and they shall be my people. Therefore come out from them, and be separate from them, says the Lord, and touch nothing unclean; then I will welcome you, and I will be a father to you, and you shall be my sons and daughters, says the Lord Almighty." Since we have these promises, beloved, let us cleanse ourselves from every defilement of body and spirit, and make holiness perfect in the fear of God.

Paul brought this passage to an end by warning the Corinthians that if they continue to participate in heathen banquets, they would then be in danger of experiencing the Lord's judgment. (Matter of fact, they were already experiencing the Lord's judgment because of a related sin (1 Cor. 11:27-30).) Paul said to them, "Shall we provke the Lord to jealousy? Are we stronger than he?" (22). Paul knew that the Lord was jealous over his people. And when his people would go astray from him, He then would judge them (Deut. 32:21). And even though some of the Christians in Corinth considered themselves "strong," (regarding eating idol-food in pagan temples), they nevertheless were not stronger than the Lord (cf. Eccl. 6:10; Is. 45:9).[4]

Passage Summary

This then ends the teaching of Paul on the subject of idolatry. We have seen the prohibition, the explanation, and the implications which he has taught to the Corinthians.

Looking back over this first part of the 10th chapter of 1 Corinthians, we have seen two things. First, in verses 1-13 Paul taught the Corinthians how the Israelites failed to reach the promised land because of their sin. They were so to speak, "disqualified" from their "foot race" to the promised land because of their lack of self-control in craving after evil things. Second, in verses 14-22, Paul warned the Corinthians that they were in danger of being judged by the Lord, (just as the Israelites were judged), because of their association with idolatry. This association with idolatry came about by their participating in the idol-feasts held in the pagan temples. Now we are in a position to see what we can learn from this chapter about Christian liberty.

Concretization

What can we learn from 1 Corinthians 10:1-22?

I believe that there are three important lessons about Christian liberty which we can learn from this passage. *First, when a Christian misuses his liberty, his past or continued participation in church ordinances does not provide him with protection from the Lord's judgment. Second, the Lord gives a specific warning and a specific encouragement to those who exercise their Christian liberty. And third, each Christian must have a good knowledge about the questionable activities in which he participates.*

A. *When a Christian misuses his liberty, his past or continued participation in church ordinances does not provide him with protection from the Lord's judgment.* In this chapter, we saw that in spite of their participation in the ordinances (Baptism and Communion) the Lord judged the Israelites and was on the verge of judging the Corinthians. What would make God judge them? He would judge them because they misused their liberty. And the Lord would not deal with Christians any differently in our day and time. He is no respecter of persons. If we misuse our liberty, he will judge us also. And he will judge us despite the fact that we have been baptized and take Communion.

There is a blessing in submitting to the church ordinances. When a person is baptized, he publicly identifies with Christ and his Church. And as a result of that identification he receives the blessings and the privileges of the Church. And as a person receives Communion he enters into fellowship with the Lord. And because of this fellowship with the Lord, he receives blessings.[5] But inspite of these blessings, a person should not think that the ordinances are some kind of "magic" or, for that matter, a safeguard against the Lord's judgment upon sin. The Bible says that "The Lord will judge his people" (Heb. 10:30b).

Christians must exercise self-control in their lives, and especially in the area of Christian liberty. The Israelites did not exercise self-control, and, therefore, were judged by the Lord. Christians can also be judged if they do not exercise self-control. Peter warns us not to use our "freedom as a pretext for evil" (1 Pet. 2:16a). Sometimes when we refuse to yield our liberty, we are indirectly giving an indication that we may have a sin problem. If we act in this way, then our liberty only serves to justify our sin. And some Christians further whitewash their justification by easing their conscience through taking Communion. Nevertheless, the Lord will judge sin.

One other thing needs to be stressed under this point. Each Christian needs to be sure of his own convictions in spite of what the majority does. Although all of the Israelites were baptized, yet only two of them entered the promised land. These two men held to their convictions (Num. 13:30; 14:6-9). They did not change, even in the face of opposition. When it comes to Christian liberty, we must stick to our own convictions. Just because everyone in your Christian group may be baptized members, it doesn't mean that they all *are* pleasing, or will *stay* pleasing to the Lord.

Every Christian must be sure of where he stands on questionable issues. He must please the Lord for himself.

B. We can learn from the passage we have studied that *the Lord gives a specific warning, and a specific encouragement to those who exercise their Christian liberty.* The *warning* is given in 1 Cor. 10:12: "Therefore let any one who thinks that he stands take heed lest he fall." The Lord cautions each Christian who is over-confident in the use of his liberty. The Lord does not desire for any Christian to be presumptuous. Christians ought to keep alert to the dangers which accompany the exercise of their liberty. Pride has a way of blinding a person to reality. The devil may set a trap or snare which will lead to the downfall of an over-confident Christian (1 Pet. 5:6-8). To fall out of fellowship with the Lord is a tremendous price to pay for a flippant attitude toward questionable issues. May the Lord help us to be on guard.

The *encouragement* which the Lord gives is found in 1 Cor. 10:13. "No temptation has overtaken you that is not common to man. God is faithful, and he will not let you be tempted beyond your strength, but with the temptation will also provide the way of escape, that you may be able to endure it." The Lord wants each Christian to be more than a conqueror. He is concerned that each Christian learns to endure. I suppose that there are some Christians who become very legalistic in their relationship to Christ. Maybe they were taught to live in this way. Or maybe they react against the ungodly lifestyles which they see everyday. But legalism is not Christian liberty, neither is it Christian. It should be avoided like the plague. The Lord doesn't cherish fellowship with automatons!

Under-confidence can be just as bad as over-confidence. The Lord can help the fearful. He lets them know that they can make it in the practice of Christian liberty by trusting in him. Fear of sinning ought not to drive us to legalism (or ascetism), but to trust in the Lord. He will make a way for us.

C. The third thing which we can learn from our study of 1 Cor. 10:1-22 is very important. It is this. *Each Christian must have a good knowledge about the questionable activities in which he participates.* Because Paul had knowledge that there were demonic forces behind idolatry, he could tell the Corinthians to stay clear of the idol-feasts. He had a good understanding about the questionable area of eating idol-meat in an idol's temple. And because of that knowledge, he was able to give some good instruction to the Corinthians.

A good question to ask ourselves is this: "How much do I know about my particular activities?" This deals with knowing the world. (It is in contrast to Searching the Bible, Chapter 3.) there are three ways in which we can learn the world. It is done either by instruction, observation, or experience. When it comes to learning the world, experience is a hard way to go. Granted, there are some things which can only be learned by experience. But the overwhelming majority of activities which are happening in this world tend to be sinful (cf. 1 Jn. 2:15-17). To learn these things by experience will often prove disastrous to anyone's life. Many black people have never fully "recovered" from the "street life." It is better to learn the world by instruction and observation. We should be quick to listen and learn from the mistakes and experiences of others. Even by taking some time to read, we can learn a lot about many different activities. Also, our parents can be helpful. Sometimes they know more than what we give them credit for knowing.[6]

In our day there is a vast exposure to horoscopes. Is it justifiable for a Christian to read and follow the horoscopes? The dictionary defines horoscope as "1. A diagram of the heaven for use in calculating nativities, etc.; 2. The art or practice of foretelling future events by observation of the stars and planets." Are horoscopes okay? Afterall, this is the age of Aquarius, isn't it? Everywhere we look we see people, black people, parading their signs and living by their horoscopes. It is a growing trend among youth. People even build their inter-personal relationships around their signs.

This manifestation of a drive for horoscopes is not limited to expression by non-believers either. Christian folks are also on the bandwagon. Recently I heard a radio announcer advertising a church program which was called a "Zodiac Extravagansa."

Little do many Christians realize the facts behind horoscopes, signs, and the zodiac. These things are part of the system of astrology. Astrology is "the observation of the sun, moon, planets, and stars for the purpose of determining the character of individuals and the course of events."[7] And the Bible does not have very much good to say about astrology. A study of these passages would prove very enlightening: Deut. 4:19; 17:2-7; 2 Kings 17:16; 23:4-5; Job 31:26ff.; Is. 47:13; Jer. 10:2; Dan. 2:27-28; 5:5ff.; Acts 7:42. The Bible has a clear condemnation for occultism, magic, and various forms of divination (Lev. 19:26, 31; 20:6-7, 27; Dt. 18:9-14).

It would be spiritually healthy for Christians to become more knowledgeable about the zodiac, signs, horoscopes, astrology, and occultism. There are greater implications to signs and horoscopes than what meets the eye. These things are not questionable. On the surface, a sign may appear to be social and harmless. But underneath, just like in idolatry, this is a part of Satan's system.

Christians must become knowledgeable of their activities. And they must be able to draw mutual exclusive implications, just as Paul did when teaching about idolatry (1 Cor. 10:21). If we do our homework of gaining information, knowing the facts, then we will know where to draw the line for ourselves.[8]

Another observation needs to be noted. There are a number of black Christians who are developing ties to the Black Muslims. What an ungodly alliance! It seems as though we don't know the facts about the Black Muslims. Or else, we have not drawn the necessary implications. Christians are followers of Jesus (Jn. 14:6), not followers of Muhammed. Welcoming Black Muslims into our fellowship should not be tolerated. The Lord will hold us accountable for our ignorance.

Knowing the facts not only has to do with the negative side of things, but also the positive. For a crucial for instance, there are many positives about black history and culture—our heritage—which young blacks need to understand and appreciate.

Of particular concern, in this broad area of understanding our heritage, is the Black Church. There has been a "falling away" from the Black Church by many young black students. Moreover, it has been noted by analysts that this "falling away," has to a large degree been precipitated by white Christian institutions who are "trustworthily educating" young black Christian minds.

Consequently, 1. the negative attitudes of white (and some black) instructors toward the Black Church are enstilled in the minds of unconscious blacks—2. who then play these attitudes against the faults of the Black Church (not considering that all Christians and churches possess faults)—and 3. being spurred with the catalysts of some black preachers and other people who have in speaking and writing, privately and publicly, narrow-mindedly, unsympathetically, and unhistorically castigated and desecrated the foremost institution of black people, the black church (which black church made them the good that they are, and which church they have opted out on for various ministries and white money)—then these black students with those baneful attitudes, against human faults, with instigating catalysts do indeed leave the Black Church. And they do this usually to their own detriment and to the forsaking of the many Black Church folk and their needs.

Young black Christians need to know the facts about our religo-cultural history and heritage. We need to understand our whooping preachers, our deacons, our mothers, our boards, our worship experiences, our Dr. Watts, our spirituals, our long prayers, our chants, our moanin', our mourner's bench, our emotion, our shoutin', our dancin', our conversion experiences, our public professions of faith, our testifying, our programs, our anniversaries, our dinners, our dressin' up, our business meetings, our revivals, our dynamics, our beliefs, and our much more, inside and also *outside* the Black Church.

Once again— *we need to know the facts about our religo-cultural history and heritage.* For when we understand this history and heritage, then we can appreciate what the Lord has done—foremost through the Black Church—in a unique and monumental way for our people.[9]

As we acquire this kind of understanding, then the changes in the Black Church which should be made in the realm of Christian liberty—and there *are* some changes to be made—can be made from *within the Black Church setting,* and be made from an attitude of respect and mercy both before the Lord and in deference to our forefathers and foremothers. Let us then be knowing the facts.

Summary & Conclusion

In review, we have learned three main things about Christian liberty from the passage of 1 Cor. 10:1-22. A. When a Christian misuses his liberty, his past or continued participation in church ordinances does not provide him with protection from the Lord's judgment. B. The Lord gives a specific warning and a specific encouragement to those who exercise their Christian liberty. C. Each Christian must have a good knowledge about the questionable activities in which he participates.

In this chapter we have studied the experience of the Israelites after they were delivered from Egypt, and the experience of the Corinthians in idolatry. Paul cautioned the Corinthians that they could become just like the Israelites and incur the Lord's judgment because of abusing their liberty. Their participation in the ordinances did not protect the Israelites from God's judgment upon their sin. The Corinthians were ignorant about the activity of eating idol-meat in a pagan temple. This activity not only involved idolatry, but it also involved demonical fellowship. And Paul taught the Christians that they were not able to maintain fellowship with the Lord and fellowship with demons simultaneously. To have fellowship with demons is sin.

Through understanding this passage, we have learned several lessons, the most important one being this: Christians must have knowledge about the activities in which they participate. Now we can move on to the next chapter which will stress implementing the principles and dealing with the unexpected in doing so. That chapter will also contain Paul's concluding remarks to all that he has said in 1 Corinthians 8:1-10:30.

Understanding What Has Been Taught

1. From what experience in Israel's history did Paul draw his example?

2. In what two "ordinances" did the Israelites participate?

3. Why were the Israelites "disqualified" from entering the promised land?

4. Give two instances in Israel's experience which caused the Lord to judge them?

5. In Paul's summary of Israel's experience, what did he say that this precedent meant to the Corinthians?

6. What did Paul command the Corinthians to do about idolatry?

7. What is the unseen reality behind idol worship?

8. Was attending idol-banquets and taking Communion mutually exclusive activities for the Corinthians? Why? Why not?

9. If the Corinthians had continued their practice of going to the pagan-temple banquets, what consequences would they have experienced?

Responding To And Applying What Has Been Learned

Questions

1. What is your attitude toward Baptism and Communion? Why do you feel this way?

2. Do you think that you need the warning or the encouragement which the Lord gives? Why?

3. Do you think that you know enough about the activities in which you participate? How can you learn more?

Suggestions

Individual

1. If you are saved, and have not as yet been baptized, I recommend that you talk with your pastor about taking on this ordinance. Also, regularly take Communion.

Group

1. Have an indepth study on Astrology.

2. Explain the meaning of Baptism and Communion to your group.

3. Begin to compile a group compendium of various elements of our religo-cultural heritage as reflected in the Black Church.

MAKING YOUR MOVE—Chapter 8

1 Corinthians 10:23-11:1

"All things are lawful," but not all things are helpful. "All things are lawful," but not all things build up. Let no one seek his own good, but the good of his neighbour. Eat whatever is sold in the meat market without raising any question on the ground of conscience. For "the earth is the Lord's, and everything in it." If one of the unbelievers invites you to dinner and you are disposed to go, eat whatever is set before you without raising any question on the ground of conscience. (But if some one says to you, "This has been offered in sacrifice," then out of consideration for the man who informed you, and for conscience' sake—I mean his conscience, not yours—do not eat it.) For why should my liberty be determined by another man's scruples? If I partake with thankfulness, why am I denounced because of that for which I give thanks?

So, whether you eat or drink, or whatever you do, do all to the glory of God. Give no offence to Jews or to Greeks or to the church of God, just as I try to please all men in everything I do, not seeking my own advantage, but that of many, that they may be saved. Be imitators of me, as I am of Christ.

A. A Practical Procedure, 10:23-30
  1. The Primary Consideration, 23-24
  2. The Particular Circumstances, 25-30
    a) In the Place of Marketing, 25-26
    b) At a Private Meal, 27-29a
    c) Conclusion, 29b-30
B. A Profound Pronouncement, 10:31-11:1
  1. The Praise to God, 10:31
  2. The Profit for Men, 10:32-33
  3. The Pattern of Paul, 11:1

On one occasion a young man decided to come to our Black Light Fellowship group that met on Monday evenings. We had become acquainted with him one Sunday afternoon when we were coming home from church. When we mentioned the Bible study to him, he took an immediate interest and decided to drop in on the group. During our 2½ hour meeting time we had a varied program.[1] One element of our program, which was structured primarily for high school age young people, was an activity and refreshment time. During the activity time for this night we were playing some table games. The new brother was late coming to the meeting, and so we were in the middle of our game time when he came in. As we sat around the table enjoying our refreshments and playing a game, a few of us (as we later conferred) began to sense that the new comer was not quite up to "playing table games." He considered that it was a waste of time. Nevertheless, he endured the activity time, after which we went on with the remainder of the meeting.

After everyone had gone home for the evening, I began to have a growing feeling that our brother was not very satisfied with a number of things which he had experienced that evening. The next morning the burden was still on my heart. So the Lord led me that day to seek the brother out so that we could talk about what had happened. One of the things which I squared away with the brother that afternoon was that we would be willing to dispense with our activity time, if he would be willing to come back to our meeting. I affirmed to him that we did not think that our table game activity was wrong. (We believe that it afforded an opportunity for healthy relaxation, an ice-breaker, and beneficial conversation.) But for his sake, we would yield our rights. As the leader of the group, I had conscientiously spoken on behalf of the group with the hope that the rest of the group would have taken similar steps. The confidence which I had in the group proved to be accurate. That night they expressed that they were willing to forego the table game activity for the edification of the brother. The burden was lifted from my heart. *I felt that we had made the right move.*

And so it is. It is not enough to know the principles of Christian liberty. We must put them into practice. And we must be prepared to put them into practice at a moment's notice. If our group had followed the leading of the Spirit in the first place, then our meeting might have been more advantageous to our brother.

Elucidation

In the passage to be considered for this chapter, Paul will give some directions based on what he has said in 1 Cor. 8:1-10:22. He will teach the Corinthians how to "make their move" in living Christian liberty. And then he will give a conclusion to this entire subject. I have entitled the first part of this passage, A Practical Procedure (10:23-30); and the second part, A Profound Pronouncement (10:31-11:1). Let's see what Paul has to say.

A. *A Practical Procedure,* 10:23-30

In these verses, Paul will show the Corinthians how to apply the principles of Christian liberty to two particular circumstances (25-30). But before he gives these instructions, he will teach them what ought to be their utmost concern in the entire matter (23-24). We will consider these two points.

1. Paul wanted the Corinthians to keep a *primary consideration* in their minds as they exercised their Christian liberty. This main and major thing was their *neighbors' good.* In the first part of verse 23 Paul restates the principle of helpfulness: " 'All things are lawful,' but not all things are helpful" (see 6:12). (We stressed this principle in chapter five.) In the second part of verse 23, he states for the first time the principle of edification. " 'All things are lawful,' but not all things build up." (The principle of edification was stressed in chapter four.)

Here we have two principles. One is for the welfare of one's self, and the other is for the welfare of others. Both are righteous, and both are needful. Yet, Paul would stress to the Corinthians that they should be more concerned about others than themselves. So he said in verse 24, "Let no one seek his own good, but the good of his neighbour." The primary consideration of a Christian should be (literally) "the things of others." Paul knew that there would be differences in people. He also knew that there would be occasions when a person would have to choose between the principle of helpfulness and the principle of edification. So he told them to earnestly seek to build up other people (cf. Phil. 2:4; 1 Cor. 13:5).

2. Now that Paul has taught the Corinthians to desire to help others above themselves, he then goes on to show them how to apply the principles which he has taught them. *He gives directions for two specific situations; first, In the Place of Marketing (25-26); and second, At a Private Meal (27-29a).* He then concludes his directions in verses 29b-30.

Only part of the meat which had been offered to idols in the pagan temples was consumed in the service. Some of the meat was eaten at a banquet in the idol's temple, (10:14, 19-22), or given to the worshipper to eat at home. Sometimes the remainder of the meat was sent to the "market-place" (*AGORA*) to be put on sale in the "meat market" (*MAKELLON*).[2]

Now when a Christian sister went shopping in the market for her food, a question would arise in her mind. Should she buy this meat which had been offered in sacrifice? (Not only had the meat been offered to an idol in the temple, but it also might have been consecrated by the butcher. Sometimes he would burn off the hair on the meat to the gods.) Should not the Christian sister ask where the meat had come from; especially, if she was a Jew since the Jews had food regulations?[3] Shouldn't she have become concerned about the meat? Paul gives his answer to this question in verses 25-26. "Eat whatever is sold in the meat market without raising any question on the ground of conscience. For 'the earth is the Lord's, and everything in it'."

Paul instructs the Christian sister, on the basis of the principles which he has previously stated, to eat whatever is put on sale in the meat market. Notice Paul's emphasis. He did not merely say "buy" what is sold in the market. He said "eat" what is sold. He had previously explained, in 1 Cor. 8:4-6ff., that it was permissible to eat meat which had been offered to idols. Now he has put the principle into practice.

And not only should Christians eat what is sold in the market, they must eat without asking any questions as to the origin of the meat. Paul does not prohibit the asking of questions in regard to the value of the meat. (For instance its freshness or choiceness.) But he does prohibit questions as they relate to whether or not the meat had been offered to an idol. Either to the butcher, at the kitchen table, or reminising over the fine meal, questions as to the "religious nature" of the meat, conscience questions, were strictly forbidden. And the reason for remaining ignorant is simple enough. Everything in the world belongs to the Lord, and, therefore, it is he who has given us all things to fully enjoy (Ps. 24:1; 1 Tim. 6:17).

To eat food offered to idols at a heathen banquet in a temple was strictly forbidden by Paul (10:14-22), but he did not prohibit the buying and eating of idol-food in one's own home. Each Christian is free to do this; and to do this without reserve. But, *what if an unbeliever should invite a Christian over to his home for a meal?* Afterall, this was a common occurrence in Corinth at the time (cf. 1 Cor. 5:9ff.). If so, then Paul says that it would be up to the Christian to accept or reject such an invitation. But if a Christian did accept the invitation, (just as his Lord Jesus had done, Lk. 5:29-32; 19:5-7), what should be his response to the meal which had been prepared for him? Should he, being in the presence of a non-Christian, make inquiry into the origin of the meal? What should he do? Paul gives the answer in verse 27. He says, "If one of the unbelievers invites you to dinner and you are disposed to go, eat whatever is set before you without raising any question on the ground of conscience."

The procedure which Paul instructs the Corinthians to follow when shopping, is the same procedure he wants them to follow when eating a private meal in an unbeliever's home. The principle is this: eat with a free conscience (cf. Lk. 10:7). They should not worry about what had happened beforehand to the meat; whether or not it had been sacrificed to idols. They should freely partake. One can hear in Paul's instructions our familiar saying, "What you don't know won't hurt you."

But, unlike in the circumstance of shopping, there is an exception to Paul's instructions when dining with a guest. The exception is given in verses 28-29a. In these verses, Paul says, "But if some one says to you, 'This has been offered in sacrifice,' then out of consideration for the man who informed you, and for conscience' sake—I mean his conscience, not yours—do not eat it."

It seems that Paul had in mind a third party who had also been invited to the meal; a "someone." This person might have been either a sympathetic unbeliever or, more probably, a "weak" Christian.[4] This Christian with a weak conscience would have done some inquiring about the meat. He would have found out that it had been sacrificed to idols. He would then have proceeded to (privately?) warn his Christian brother about the nature of the meat which was about to be served. In order not to offend the unbelieving host, he said that the meat was "sacrificed for sacred purposes," rather than offered to idols. In such a case, the "man of knowledge" should not eat the sacrificed meat. (He should yield his right because the weak brother may be led into sin. Review 8:7-13.) He should abstain out of respect and deference to the weak brother and his conscience (24). And Paul makes sure that the Corinthians know whose conscience he has in mind. It is the other person's conscience that he has in mind. The conscience of the "weak" brother.

Now that Paul has given the exception to the rule, he then proceeds to give the reasoning behind his instructions. This conclusion is expressed in verses 29b-30: "For why should my liberty be determined by another man's scruples? If I partake with thankfulness, why am I denounced because of that for which I give thanks?" In the first question, Paul is virtually saying that his liberty would cease to be of any good, if the exercising of that liberty is ruled by the criteria in another person's mind. In the second question, Paul gives his personal basis for exercising his liberty. Whatever he can do, being thankful and giving thanks, is legitimate for himself (cf. 1 Tim. 4:4). And it is wrong for another person to denounce, to "blaspheme," a brother who exercises his liberty in thankfulness. The truths implied in these questions will be useful in keeping the "man of knowledge," who yields his liberty for the sake of a "weak" brother, in his proper mind.

Passage Summary

In summarizing verses 23-30, we notice that Paul has taught two things. First, he has taught the Corinthians that their primary consideration should be the other person's well-being, not their own (23-24). Second, he has provided instructions for two different circumstances: when shopping at the meat market, and when invited to the home of an unbeliever for a meal (25-30). In both of these circumstances, the Christian should buy and eat whatever is made available without "checking out" whether or not the meat has been sacrificed. To this practical procedure there is but one exception. When someone at a dinner engagement makes it known that the prepared food has been offered in sacrifice, then the Christian should not eat the sacrificed meat. But he should only abstain for the benefit of the informant. And in doing so, he should hold fast to his own convictions. Paul wanted the Corinthians to keep these things in mind when making their move in exercising their liberty.

This then brings us to the second part of this passage which we are considering. It contains Paul's conclusion to all that he has said in 1 Cor. 8:1-10:30.

B. *A Profound Pronouncement,* 10:31-11:1

Throughout chapters 8-10 of 1 Corinthians, Paul has sought to explain and illuminate three principles of Christian liberty: edifying, helpfulness, and preserving freedom. At the beginning of these chapters, he gave an introduction to this subject in which he talked about "knowledge" and love. He then went on to deal with idols and the one God; with the "man of knowledge" and the "weak" brother, and stumbling blocks. He discussed his own personal practices, concerning support for his ministry, his evangelistic service, and his utmost self-discipline. He then warned the Corinthians about misusing their liberty by citing an example from Israel's history, and explaining the perils of banqueting in an idol-temple. Then he gave the Corinthians the ground rules for shopping in the market, and eating at the home of an unbeliever. Now Paul has come to his concluding remarks. He is going to "put on the gravy." In these four remaining verses he says what appears to be three very profound statements. The first has to do with God, the second with men, and the third with Paul himself. They are, *1. The Praise to God (10:31); 2. The Profit for Men (10:32-33); and 3. The Pattern of Paul (11:1).*

1. Paul begins his conclusion by saying, "So, whether you eat or drink, or whatever you do, do all to the glory of God" (31). Paul desired for the Corinthians to realize that they were to live a totally sacred, spiritual life. This holistic spiritual living would bring *praise to God.* This is profound. Nothing they do should be "secular," and nothing they do *needs* to be "secular." Whatever they do—eating, drinking, participating in the games, handling business affairs, shopping, attending public festivals, making art and architecture, being entertained at the amphitheater, etc.[6]—*whatever they do,* is able to be done to God's glory. When they apply these principles of Christian liberty to the many questionable issues of their lives, they will then begin to live in such a way as to bring praise to God. And undoubtedly they would also subsequently bring the Lord's blessing upon their lifestyle.

2. The second profound statement has to do with living for the *profit of men.* "Give no offence to Jews or to Greeks or to the church of God, just as I try to please all men in everything I do, not seeking my own advantage, but that of many, that they may be saved" (32-33). Paul did not want the Corinthians to unnecessarily offend anyone. (See 1 Cor. 1:22ff. for the offence of the cross.) Each Christian should live in such a way so that he will avoid becoming an offence to those outside as well as inside the church. Therefore Paul wants the Corinthians to *please all men in everything they do* so that some people can become saved.

Now it can be successfully argued that Paul did not fully succeed in pleasing everybody all of the time. But it can't be debated that he did not *try* to please everyone all of the time. And this is what is profound. He wants the Corinthians to try to please everybody in everything. They should not however try to please people for selfish motives, nor at the expense of godliness. For this would be wrong (cf. Gal. 1:10; 1 Thess. 2:3-4). But they should seek to be pleasing to people, not for their own profit, but for the profit of others. That is, so that others can be saved.

One might ask, "Can a person at the same time live both to the glory of God and the pleasing of men? Paul himself answers this question in Rom. 14:18. In this verse he says that the person who conscientiously and considerately exercises his liberty can be "acceptable to God and approved by men." These first two pronouncements by Paul are not mutually exclusive. And this is what further adds to their profundity.

3. The third of Paul's pronouncements, which ends his concluding remarks, is found in the first verse of chapter eleven (an unfortunate chapter division; this verse should be in the previous chapter). "Be imitators of me, as I am of Christ." Paul sets himself up as a *pattern,* an example to the Corinthians. What is striking about this teaching is that it comes under the discussion of Christian *liberty,* where each man is free to follow the dictates of his own conscience.

Paul is not encouraging the Corinthians to mimic his outward actions. (In order to do this, they would first have to become apostles!) But he is encouraging them to follow the principles which he has laid down for them; which principles he also used to order his own lifestyle. This is what the Corinthians should mimic.

But why should they imitate Paul? For two good reasons. First, Paul himself imitates Christ. Therefore Christ is the standard for governing one's actions in Christian liberty. And the punch in the Lord's example is found in this: he gave himself up for others. "Therefore be imitators of God, as beloved children. And walk in love, as Christ loved us and gave himself up for us, a fragrant offering and sacrifice to God" (Eph. 5:1-2). Someone else might ask, "Why should the Corinthians imitate *Paul*? Aren't there other Christians around who are likewise imitating Christ?" This is a valid point, but not for the Corinthians. For Paul had a special relationship to them. And this is the second reason why they should follow his example. He is their *father* in Christ. He said to them, "I do not write this to make you ashamed, but to admonish you as my beloved children. For though you have countless guides in Christ, you do not have many fathers. For I became your father in Christ Jesus through the gospel. I urge you, then, be imitators of me" (1 Cor. 4:14-16ff.).

As their father, Paul is wise enough to know that it would be easier for the Corinthians to follow his example (which was a pertinent model for them), than it would be for them to follow the example of Christ, from which they were somewhat removed in time. (On imitating, see Phil. 3:17; 1 Thess. 1:6; 2 Thess. 3:7-9; 1 Cor. 4:9-12.)[7]

Passage Summary

By way of summary, Paul has taught the Corinthians to order their lives to the praise of God, to the profit for men, and by the pattern of himself. These then are his concluding remarks to a passage which expresses A Practical Procedure for the Corinthians to follow, and A Profound Prouncement which should continually ring in their ears as they seek to live lives that are pleasing to God. After the teachings of this passage (10:23-11:1) I would suppose that Paul considered the Corinthian Christians ready to "make their move" to righteously practice their Christian liberty.

Concretization

What can you learn about "Making Your Move" from 1 Cor. 10:23-11:1?

I think that there are six things about Christian liberty which we can learn from this passage that will assist us in making our move. *First, in order for a person to righteously exercise Christian liberty he must have proper priorities. Second, the principle of edification does not demand that a person absolutely forsake a given action or activity for the sake of another. Third, each Christian should freely exercise his liberty unless someone expresses a "weak brother's" conviction. Fourth, the principles of Christian liberty have all-inclusive personal and all-inclusive public applications. Fifth, practicing these principles of Christian liberty can become an asset to Christians in helping others. And sixth, an example to follow can be very helpful when learning to apply the principles of Christian liberty.*

A. We should keep in mind that *in order for a person to righteously exercise Christian liberty he must have proper priorities.* What are these priorities? They are 1. pleasing God, 2. serving people, and 3. helping your *self.* These priorities are so simple and basic that we sometimes overlook them. But this is what Paul was trying to stress in 1 Cor. 10:23-24, and 10:31-33. And if we do not observe these priorities, then we will err in exercising our Christian liberty. For when it comes down to making decisions, we will become confused about what to do if our priorities are mixed up. So, then, let us learn well these priorities and continually remind ourselves of them.

B. *The principle of edification does not demand that a person absolutely forsake a given action or activity for the sake of another.* At the end of 1 Cor. 8 we found Paul saying, "if food is a cause of my brother's falling, I will never eat meat, lest I cause my brother to fall" (13). In chapter 10, we found him instructing the Christians to freely eat of idol-food in their own homes and also in the homes of others unless someone raises the issue of the religious nature of the meat (25-29a). Furthermore, he argues very strongly about the individuals right to do as his own conscience leads him (29b-30).

This leads me to conclude that the exercising of the principle of edification is relative to both people and places. In 1 Cor. 8:7 the words "being weak" indicate a lasting condition, not a momentary occurence. In 1 Cor. 8:10 Paul says *"if* his conscience is weak." In 1 Cor. 8:13 Paul gives a conditional statement, *"if* food..." There were probably cases where the eating of food offered to idols did not cause a brother to stumble. In 1 Cor. 10:25, Paul implies that whatever a person does in his own home is his own business. In 1 Cor. 10:30, Paul seems to suggest that the person who (literally) "continues to denounce" him because he exercises his liberty, ought to at some time or another come to a change. The principle of edification is relative.

In the first chapter, I spoke of my experience in shooting pool while in college. I also spoke of how this white young lady seemed to be offended by my activities. The Lord did not lead me to entirely give up playing pool. But he did lead me to play in privacy, in the evening time, when I did not think that this particular person would be around. Some might call this kind of action hypocritical. But it is only apparent hypocrisy. Underneath, there were some definite principles at work. A hypocrite is an unprincipled person.

Paul speaks about this thing of privacy in Rom. 14:22 where he says, "The faith that you have, *keep between yourself and God;* happy is he who has no reason to judge himself for what he approves." (Emphasis mine.) Sometimes it is unwise for a Christian to parade his liberty. At times, it is more advantageous to just quietly practice and enjoy your freedom along with those few who share similar convictions. And, of course, the Lord will enjoy your fellowship as well! Let us remember that edification is relative and that therefore "secrets" are necessary.

C. *Each Christian should freely exercise his liberty unless someone expresses a "weak brother's" conviction.* In the passage which we studied for this chapter we found out that Paul told the Christians to freely exercise their liberty wherever they were. And I believe that Paul would say the same thing to black Christians today. Black Christians are free to live in the way which they feel that the Lord would have them to live. And we are under no obligations to ask "questions of conscience." Neither should we allow ourselves to be scruntinized by the judgments of others. We are liberarted in the Lord!

As we exercise our liberty we will at times undoubtly be faced with situations where other Christians think that we should not do a particular thing. When we are faced with such situations, then the Lord expects us to yield our liberty. We should not, however, yield our liberty because of the way that others are "thinking." They must *express* their conviction, even as the weak brother verbally warned the "man of knowledge" at the home of the unbeliever (10:28). Now after a person expresses his conviction, and we feel obligated to yield our rights, we must let that person know that we are yielding our rights for his sake, and not our own. He must know, and know very well, that we are yielding not because we think a certain action is sinful. We yield because *he* thinks it is sinful, and we want to respect him and his conscience.

It seems that the kind of incident as described in 1 Cor. 10:28 should not happen twice. The "man of knowledge" should teach the weak brother about his own convictions. The Lord expects those who can freely exercise their liberty to be teachers of others. The "strong" should teach the "weak" in order to bring them to maturity. Nevertheless, the conscience of the weak brother should be respected, even while it is developing.

One day my wife and I decided to invite a brother (whom we had not known for very long) over for dinner. In the course of talking about the situation, my wife said that she felt that this brother might be a vegetarian. When I made the contact by phone, I asked him about his eating habits. And sure enough, he was a vegetarian. I did not discuss his convictions with him over the phone. But when he came for dinner (*our meatless dinner!*) we sort of felt him out. He expressed his convictions, which were in no way snobbish, and we expressed ours. He said that he didn't mind others eating meat in his presence. And we let him know that we were respecting his convictions by not having any meat at the meal. The occasion proved to be very satisfying.

There are some good activities which can be given a bad name because some "people of knowledge" refuse to yield their rights to those who are weak. Paul talks about this in Rom. 14:15-16. There he says, "If your brother is being injured by what you eat, you are no longer walking in love. Do not let what you eat cause the ruin of one for whom Christ died. *So do not let your good be spoken of as evil."* Let us not, in exercising our freedom, give a good thing a bad name.

D. *The principles of Christian liberty have all-inclusive personal and all-inclusive public applications.* We learned from 1 Cor. 10:31 that Paul desired for the Corinthians to live a *totally* spiritual life. In verses 32-33, he taught them that they should seek to please *all* men.

A Christian is not a person who has a compartmentalized life. I recently was talking with a person who was passionately suggesting to me that there is a point in a person's life where his religion ends and his personal business begins. To which talk I just as passionately said, "No way!" God should be glorified in everything that we do. And God *can* be glorified in everything that we do. And this is part of the joy of being a Christian. We, as developing black young men and black young women, can please God in everything that we do! The Bible says, "And whatever you do, in word or deed, do everything in the name of the Lord Jesus, giving thanks to God the Father through him" (Col. 3:17).

It is indeed enlightening that the early Christians took common things and sanctified them in the name of the Lord. For instance, the Word (*LOGOS*) of Jn. 1:1ff. was a Greek (and also a Hebrew) concept which the Christians infused with new meaning and used to describe Jesus. The "cross," a means of inflicting and describing a terrible mode of execution, (revived from the Phoenicians and used extensively by the Romans) is virtually glorified by Christians of all ages (cf. Gal. 6:14). Also, it would shock some Christians to realize that some of the hymns which we cherish find their origin through the joining of sanctified words and common bar tunes!

So much for the precedents. The challenge remains for black Christians to use and transform our culture—our total culture and social living—in the name of the Lord. As we individually do this, we will be living a totally sacred, spiritual life. This is the all-inclusive personal application of the principles of Christian liberty.

These principles also have an all-inclusive public application. When Paul said, "Give no offence to Jews or to Greeks or to the church of God" (32), he seemed to be talking about three aspects. Maybe the Jews would have been the cultural aspect, the Greeks the social aspect, and the church of God the Christian aspect. (Whatever the case, his remarks are comprehensive.) I believe that wherever we find ourselves as black people—in our churches, among our social contacts, or in a white cultural setting—we have some principles which we can lean on in order to live an authentic lifestyle of Christian liberty.

E. *Practicing these principles of Christian liberty can become an asset to Christians in helping others.* In the fourth chapter we learned that, dependent upon our actions, a person's spiritual well-being may be at stake. (See point D of Chapter four.) This application is the other side of the coin. By implementing these principles into our lives we can help others. We can seek the "advantage" of many. Some can be "saved" (33).

We already talked about the lifestyles of John the Baptizer and Jesus. (Mt. 11:16-19; 21:31-32; Lk. 7:24-35; Chapter six.) Because they freely practiced their "Christian liberty" they were able to help many people. The advice that Paul gave to the Corinthians when they were invited to dinner in the presence of an unbeliever (10:27) is the same thing Jesus told his disciples to do. In Lk. 10:7-9 we read; "And remain in the same house, *eating and drinking what they provide,* for the labourer deserves his wages; do not go from house to house. Whenever you enter a town and they receive you, *eat what is set before you;* heal the sick in it and say to them, 'The kingdom of God has come near to you'." (Emphasis mine.)

The above information leads me to say that we need to be understanding of those who try to win others to Christ. Sometimes Christians may frown at the actions of some who seek to evangelize others. Yet, the Lord may call upon a Christian to exercise his liberty in a way that tends to be "unpopular" so that he can effectively reach others. We must understand what God is doing in the lives of our fellow believers.

When proclaiming the gospel to others it is very important that the message of the gospel remains the focal point. The Lord Jesus did not want anything else but the Gospel to become an issue to those who should be saved. When we get hung up on anything that is "questionable" in presenting the gospel message, then we become less effective. But when people come to realize that we are interested in the crucial issues which they face, then our ministry becomes more prosperous. Let us then use the principles of Christian liberty as a means to the end of helping others.

F. *An example to follow can be very helpful when learning to apply the principles of Christian liberty.* Paul told the Corinthians to "Be imitators of me, as I am of Christ" (11:1). It is good to have a genuine Christian example to follow. And we should especially follow the example of our Christian leaders. We must look to our pastors and teachers for insights on living our Christian liberty. And inasmuch as they follow Christ we can follow them.

The Lord Jesus is our supreme example in all areas of living; the area of Christian liberty not being excepted. In the section of the book of Romans that deals with Christian liberty is found these words: "We who are strong ought to bear with the failings of the weak, and not to please ourselves; let each of us please his neighbour for his good, to edify him. For Christ did not please himself; but, as it is written, 'The reproaches of those who reproached thee feel on me'." (Rom. 15:1-3). The Lord Jesus sought to edify others above himself. Another passage depicting Jesus yielding his rights is found in Phil. 2:4-11:

> Let each of you look not only to his own interest, but also to the interests of others. Have this mind among yourselves, which is yours

in Christ Jesus, who, though he was in the form of God, did not count equality with God a thing to be grasped, but emptied himself, taking the form of a servant, being born in the likeness of men. And being found in human form he humbled himself and became obedient unto death, even death on a cross. Therefore God has highly exalted him and bestowed on him the name which is above every name, that at the name of Jesus every knee should bow, in heaven and on earth and under the earth, and every tongue confess that Jesus Christ is Lord, to the glory of God the Father.

(See also Col. 2:16-19, a passage touching on Christian liberty and encouraging the Christians to hold on to Christ.)

Jesus is our supreme example. And when we cannot see clearly how the Lord would respond to a given situation, let us then make haste to follow the example of our trusted Christian leaders. The lifestyle of Christian liberty will be "caught" more than it is "taught."

Summary & Conclusion

These are the six things which I think that we can learn about Christian liberty from the passage of 1 Cor. 10:23-11:1. Let me restate them. A. In order for a person to righteously exercise Christian liberty he must have proper priorities. B. The principle of edification does not demand that a person absolutely forsake a given action or activity for the sake of another. C. Each Christian should freely exercise his liberty unless someone expresses a "weak brother's" conviction. D. The principles of Christian liberty have all-inclusive personal and all-inclusive public applications. E. Practicing these principles of Christian liberty can become an asset to Christians in helping others. F. An example to follow can be very helpful when learning to apply the principles of Christian liberty.

Throughout this chapter I have tried to stress some things which you should keep in mind when "making your move" into Christian liberty. Within this chapter we have seen how Paul gave the Corinthians a practical procedure to follow in the affairs of their daily living. He then went on to close out his remarks on the subject of Christian liberty by giving a profound pronouncement. Now it is up to us to make our move. (Chapter 12 will be devoted to some very practical helps in implementing these principles into your life.)

This passage of 1 Corinthians 10:23-11:1 brings an end to our study of Christian liberty as far as the book of 1 Corinthians is concerned. We have discussed chapters 6,8,9, and 10 of this letter. Now we will turn to the letter of Romans (14:1-15:13) for the next two chapters.[8] In the coming chapter we will hit on unity, and in the chapter following on trusting the Lord. These are two very important aspects of Christian liberty. We trust that your continued reading will prove to become more enlightening on this important subject. Press on!

Understanding What Has Been Taught

1. What was to be the primary consideration of the Corinthians when exercising their liberty?

2. For what two circumstances did Paul give the Corinthians guidelines?

3. For what reason were the Corinthians instructed to eat anything without asking questions of conscience?

4. What unexpectedly might happen at the home of an unbeliever?

5. For whose conscience' sake must a "man of knowledge" yield his rights when informed about idol-meat being served at the home of an unbeliever?

6. What are the three aspects of Paul's profound pronouncement on the subject of meat offered to idols?

7. What did Paul mean when he told the Corinthians to do all that they did to God's glory?

8. Why did Paul set himself up as an example for the Corinthians?

Responding To And Applying What Has Been Learned

Questions

1. In what way, if any, have you ever been confused about what to do because of undefined priorities?

2. What questionable activities might it be wise for you to practice in private?

3. Is there another person in your life who forcefully persuades you in your attitudes toward Christian liberty? Is this good for you? Why? Why not?

4. Does the message of the gospel remain the focal point in your evangelism? Why? Why not?

5. Does knowing that you can live a totally spiritual life make any difference to you? Why? Why not?

6. Whose example do you follow in Christian liberty, and why do you follow this example?

Suggestions

Individual

1. Get together with a new Christian and teach to him, one on one, these principles.

2. Determine whose example you will follow when you are faced with dilemmas about certain questionable issues.

Group

1. Give out these six priority schemes to group members, and discuss the implications of each in the area of Christian liberty:

God	Others	You	God	Others	You
Others	God	Others	You	You	God
You	You	God	Others	God	Others

2. Study how the principles of Christian liberty were applied to marriage and worship services in 1 Corinthians 7, 12 & 14.

STRIVING FOR UNITY—Chapter 9

Romans 14:1-15:13

As for the man who is weak in faith, welcome him, but not for disputes over opinions. One believes he may eat anything, while the weak man eats only vegetables. Let not him who eats despise him who abstains, and let not him who abstains pass judgment on him who eats; for God has welcomed him. Who are you to pass judgment on the servant of another? It is before his own master that he stands or falls. And he will be upheld, for the master is able to make him stand.

One man esteems one day as better than another, while another man esteems all days alike. Let every one be fully convinced in his own mind. He who observes the day, observes it in honour of the Lord. He also who eats, eats in honour of the Lord, since he gives thanks to God; while he who abstains, abstains in honour of the Lord and gives thanks to God. None of us lives to himself, and none of us dies to himself. If we live, we live to the Lord, and if we die, we die to the Lord; so then, whether we live or whether we die, we are the Lord's. For to this end Christ died and lived again, that he might be Lord both of the dead and of the living.

Why do you pass judgment on your brother? Or you, why do you despise your brother? For we shall all stand before the judgment seat of God; for it is written, "As I live, says the Lord, every knee shall bow to me, and every tongue shall give praise to God." So each of us shall give account of himself to God.

Then let us no more pass judgment on one another, but rather decide never to put a stumbling block or hindrance in the way of a brother. I know and am persuaded in the Lord Jesus that nothing is unclean in itself; but it is unclean for any one who thinks it unclean. If your brother is being injured by what you eat, you are no longer walking in love. Do not let what you eat cause the ruin of one for whom Christ died. So do not let your good be spoken of as evil. For the kingdom of God is not food and drink but righteousness and peace and joy in the Holy Spirit; he who thus serves Christ is acceptable to God and approved by men. Let us then pursue what makes for peace and for mutual upbuilding. Do not, for the sake of food, destroy the work of God. Everything is indeed clean, but it is wrong for any one to make others fall by what he eats; it is right not to eat meat or drink wine or do anything that makes your brother stumble. The faith that you have, keep between yourself and God; happy is he who has no reason to judge himself for what he approves.

But he who has doubts is condemned, if he eats, because he does not act from faith; for whatever does not proceed from faith is sin.

15:1 We who are strong ought to bear with the failings of the weak, and not to please ourselves; let each of us please his neighbour for his good, to edify him. For Christ did not please himself; but, as it is written, "The reproaches of those who reproached thee fell on me." For whatever was written in former days was written for our instruction, that by steadfastness and by the encouragement of the Scriptures we might have hope. May the God of steadfastness and encouragement grant you to live in such harmony with one another, in accord with Christ Jesus, that together you may with one voice glorify the God and Father of our Lord Jesus Christ.

Welcome one another, therefore, as Christ has welcomed you, for the glory of God. For I tell you that Christ became a servant to the circumcised to show God's truthfulness, in order to confirm the promises given to the patriarchs, and in order that the Gentiles might glorify God for his mercy. As it is written, "Therefore I will praise thee among the Gentiles, and sing to thy name"; and again it is said, "Rejoice, O Gentiles, with his people"; and again, "Praise the Lord, all Gentiles, and let all the peoples praise him"; and further Isaiah says, "The root of Jesse shall come, he who rises to rule the Gentiles; in him shall the Gentiles hope." May the God of hope fill you with all joy and peace in believing, so that by the power of the Holy Spirit you may abound in hope.

A. The problem Among the Christians at Rome
   1. The Nature of the problem
      a) Two Groups
      b) Three Issues
   2. The Consequences of the Problem
      a) Attitudes
      b) Responses
      c) Spiritual Climate
B. The Solution to the Problem
   1. The Instructions of Paul
      a) Welcome
      b) Respect
      c) Be Sure
      d) Edify
   2. The Expectations of Paul
      a) Harmony
      b) Praise
      c) Hope

In Ephesians 4:3 Paul encourages the believers to be "eager to maintain the unity of the Spirit in the bond of peace." Fostering unity among our black people is a tremendous task. Down through the years we have allowed ourselves to be divided and splintered—a disunity we have been scarcely able to afford. It is not without some understanding that our divisions have carried over into our Christian circles. This hurts. But what hurts most of all is perceiving that "questionable areas" is a major ground for disunity among black Christians. This ground of disunity among black Christians makes myself, and many others, grieve very deeply. In this light, I've devoted this chapter to unity. I don't think that unity among us will come naturally. We must strive for it; hence the chapter title: Striving for Unity.

The apostle Paul had never visited the church of Rome. However, he did know (probably based on the information of his friends, cf. 16:1ff.) that there were some things which were lacking in their faith (Rom. 1:9-13; Rom. 16:25ff.). Among those things in which they needed strengthening[1] was a proper instruction concerning some "questionable areas" of living (14:1-15:13). Because the Christians at Rome did not know how to handle this problem, they became divided—primarily (but not exclusively) along the lines of Jews and Gentiles. Both of these groups comprised the church community.[2]

In this chapter we will examine the problem of the believers at Rome, and Paul's solution to their problem. Then we will attempt to draw a few applications for ourselves based on Paul's solutions.

Elucidation

A. *The Problem Among the Christians at Rome.*

In considering the problem manifested in this church, we will attempt to see its nature and its consequences.

1. We can notice two things about the *nature* of the problem. *It centered around two groups and three issues.*

First, the problem of this church centered around *two groups of people—Jews and Gentiles.* Notice these descriptions taken from Rom. 15:7-12: "circumcised," "patriarchs," "Gentiles," "his people," "all the peoples," "root of Jesse." In this passage there is definitely an emphasis on the Jews and the Gentiles. The church at Rome (as was said before) was made up of both groups. Unlike in Corinth, where there were mostly Gentiles and few Jews, the church in Rome probably had a substantial number of Jews among its numerous Gentiles. And because of these two very different people from two very different backgrounds, the problems which they had were magnified. The tone of this passage seems to infer that maybe the Jews were becoming troublesome to the Gentiles, which leads Paul to tell the Jews to "get off their (the Gentiles) case." This would not have been the first time that such an admonition was given to some troublesome Jews (cf. Acts 15:19, 24). Nevertheless, the division it seems (though it can't be pressed) did center around these two groups.

The second thing which we are able to say about the nature of this problem is that its focal point was at least *three issues: vegetarianism, (holy) days, and wine.* The city of Rome was cosmopolitan, so also the church. Consequently the people from various backgrounds and influences brought their different convictions and opinions concerning questionable things into the church.[3]

There were some in the church of Rome who did not eat meat. Notice these terms: "eat anything," "eats only vegetables," "eat," "food," "eat meat" (14:2,3,6b,15,17,20,21,23). There is not necessarily any indications that the problem of "meat offered to idols" was the issue.[4] It seems that some of the Christians refrained from eating merely meat while sustaining themselves on "garden herbs." Why they restricted their diet in this way is open to discussion. Some probably were vegetarian for Jewish reasons.[5] Others may have done it for reasons similar to those who do the same today; vegetarian principles. One thing we can say for sure is that there were definite religious overtones to this practice, as we will see shortly. These vegetarians began to have conflicts with those who were not, and vice versa. The conflicts might have brewed at church meals, in the home, at public meals, or in the market. Wherever the conflicts arose, they began to infect the church fellowship.

The second issue which became a focal point for division in the church was that of days (cf. 14:5 "day," "all days"). The days referred to might have been special Jewish holy days. That is, "a festival, or a new moon, or a sabbath," etc. (cf. Col. 2:16). It could have been that certain of the Christians wanted the church to give special recognition to such days; maybe in the form of worship services, and/or collective fasting. And the other Christians did not want such services, or fasting. So, for instance, when the day of Atonement, Passover, or the Feast of Tabernacles drew near, the tensions would began to rise among the church members.

The third focal point for controversy in the church was "wine." See the words "drink," and "drink wine," in verses 14:17, 21. Although drinking wine was a significant part of the first century cultures, there were evidently some Christians at Rome who abstained from drinking it. So whenever wine was served, for example during Communion, then the believers would began to become perturbed at one another.

These then are the three focal points of the problem at Rome: vegetarianism, (holy) days, and wine. Two general things should be mentioned about these three issues. One, Paul does not seek to specifically label who are the "weak" and who are the "strong." We do know that the weak ate only vegetables and the strong ate anything. And maybe it was the weak who observed special days and the strong who observed all days alike.[6] But the weak were not assigned to any particular group (Gentile or Jew), and neither were the strong. Actually, the persons who were "weak" in one area were probably "strong" in another. Or vice versa. Moreover, it might have also been the case that people on either side of the issues considered their opposites "weak" and themselves "strong."[7]

Two, Christians on either side of the issues did what they did in order to honor the Lord. Rom. 14:6 brings this out very well: "He who observes the day, observes it in honour of the Lord. He also who eats, eats in honour of the Lord, since he gives thanks to God; while he who abstains, abstains in honour of the Lord and gives thanks to God." Although some of the believers held convictions based on inadequate knowledge, it cannot be doubted that their motivations and zeal to please the Lord were dominant. They were seeking for righteousness, which on the one hand was to be commended, but on the other hand (in the face of their lack of wisdom) served only to aggravate the consequences of the problem.

2. As we consider the *consequences* of the problem of the church at Rome, we will be able to pinpoint *three areas: attitudes, responses, and the overall spiritual condition.*

There were *two main attitudes* which resulted from disagreement concerning the three focal issues mentioned above. They were "despising" and "judging" (14:3, 10). It was not enough that there were disagreements about whether or not one should eat meat, or whether or not every church member should be bound to honor the special holy days along with observing the rites of those days. There indeed were different convictions regarding these things. But the Christians at Rome did not respect one another's convictions. Instead they internalized negative attitudes toward each other. Some began to despise others. They thought that they were better than their brothers since they felt free to exercise their liberty, while their brothers did not. They thought of their brothers as "nothing." They made them of "no account." They treated them with contempt. They might have referred to them as "weaklings."

And yet, the abstainers were not free from their own negative attitudes either. For instance, those who ate only vegetables began to "judge" those who did not restrict themselves to such a diet. They possibly began to characterize the participators as "gluttons." They would say that the participators would eat *anything,* having no scruples, no self-control whatsoever! And if the participators continued in their actions, the abstainers were sure that the participators' relationship to the Lord would be wiped out; they would "fall" (14:4).

There was judging and despising. Both groups (in either of the three issues) thought they were right. Moreover, they thought that the Lord was on their side! (Even in the case of those who drank wine.) They judged one another (14:4,13) and felt that those who disagreed with them had failed (15:1).

There were *two basic responses* which resulted from the negative attitudes between the Christians at Rome. *These two responses were argumentation and ostracization.* Concerning argumentation, there were "disputes over opinions" (14:1). The Christians began to have heated disputes over these "questionable areas." They began to rake one another over the coals of their own individual reasonings. These issues, which were not germane to their faith, began to receive undo attention. The Christians began to openly express their doubts concerning the convictions of their brothers.

As argumentation often does, it led to ostracization. This was the other response among the Christians (14:1, 3; 15:7). One group would begin to shun those who held different convictions on these questionable issues. They did not "welcome" one another.

The *spiritual climate* of the church members at Rome was affected by their problem concerning questionable areas. What was becoming of their spiritual condition? Well, as a result of despising and judging, argumentation and ostracization, there was *spiritual degeneration.* The Christians were fast losing ground in the Lord.

To put it succinctly, their lives were being "messed up." Notice these terms (many of which we discussed in 1 Cor. 8, chapter four) which describe what was happening in their fellowship: there were "stumbling blocks" (14:13), "hindrances" (14:13); some were being "injured," "ruined," and "destroyed" (14:15,20), and some were made to "fall" and "stumble" (14:20,21). Another indication that their lives were being fouled up was the fact that they were losing the joy of their salvation. The word translated "injured" (*LUPEŌ*) in 14:15 signifies "to have pain of body or mind." It means "to be made sorry," "to be sorry, sorrowful." The Christians were becoming saddened over the things which were taking place. They were beginning to become discouraged and despondent. Furthermore, in the entire passage of Rom. 15:9-13, there is an emphasis on rejoicing. (Actually, this emphasis starts at verse 6 with the phrase "glorify the God and Father...") Notice the signs of rejoicing in these verses: "glorify," "praise," "sing," "rejoice," and "joy." The Christians were bickering so much over those questionable areas that it slipped their notice that they were losing their joy; that they were losing their freshness, their worship of the Lord. They began to lose the joy of their most precious possession—salvation. These things go to show that their spirituality was diminishing and degenerating.

Up to this point we have been considering the problem of the church at Rome: its nature and its consequences. Now we can see the kind of solution which Paul gives to these Christians.

B. *The Solution to the Problem*

As we consider how Paul handles this problem, we can focus on two main areas: the instructions and the expections of Paul.

1. Paul gives what seems to be *four basic instructions* to the Roman Christians. *He tells them to welcome, respect, be sure, and edify.*

First, Paul instructs the Christians to *welcome one another.* He says, "As for the man who is weak in faith, welcome him" (14:1, cf.3). And again he says, "Welcome one another, therefore, as Christ has welcomed you, for the glory of God" (15:7). Whether they eat meat or not; whether they honor holy days or not; whether they drink wine or not—wherever they fall as regards questionable areas—they should still welcome one another. To be sure, there are times when separation is necessary, even imperative (cf. Rom. 16:17-20). But differences over questionable issues are not to be a ground of separation. Therefore, the believers should not form "sanctified cliques" but instead receive each other into fellowship.

Second, Paul teaches the Christians to *respect one another's convictions.* He tells them not to argue over questionable matters. He desires for them to accept one another, "but not for disputes over opinions" (14:1). He subsequently even tells them to keep their own convictions to themselves. In 14:22a he says "The faith that you have, keep between yourself and God."

121

Paul also prohibits them from passing judgment on one another. His instructions are: "Let not him who eats despise him who abstains, and let not him who abstains pass judgment on him who eats" (14:3a). He gives three reasons why they should not judge each other: one, God has welcomed each believer (14:3); two, each Christian is God's household servant (14:4), therefore, the relationship between God and his servants is very personal and private; and three, God is the final judge (14:10-12) before whom one and all must give an account of themselves one day (cf. Jms. 4:11-12).

Third, Paul instructs the Christians to *be sure of their own personal convictions.* He tells them that "everyone [should] be *fully convinced* in his own mind" (14:5). He says of himself, *"I know and am persuaded* in the Lord Jesus that nothing is unclean in itself" (14:14a). He also said, "happy is he who has no reason to judge himself for what he *approves"* (14:22b). (All emphases mine.)

Paul wanted the Roman Christians to realize that if they desired their brothers to respect their convictions, then each one must first be sure of his own convictions. Paul would not allow for them to half-heartedly hold to some nebulous beliefs, while at the same time expecting others to relate to their unstable experience.

Fourth, Paul teaches the Roman Christians to *edify one another.* Notice these phrases: "decide never to put a stumbling block or hindrance in the way of a brother" (14:13b); "Do not let what you eat cause the ruin of one for whom Christ died" (14:15b); "Let us then pursue what makes for peace and for mutual upbuilding. Do not, for the sake of food, destroy the work of God. Everything is indeed clean, but it is wrong for any one to make others fall by what he eats; it is right not to eat meat or drink wine or do anything that makes your brother stumble" (14:19-21); "We who are strong ought to bear with the failings of the weak, and not to please ourselves; let each of us please his neighbour for his good, to edify him. For Christ did not please himself; but, as it is written, 'The reproaches of those who reproached thee fell on me'." (15:1-3).

In chapter 4, Building Your Neighbor, we discussed the principle of edification. Suffice it to say here that Paul stresses the same principle to the Romans as he did to the Corinthians. They were to build up one another. This was to be their utmost responsibility. In these two chapters of Romans, Paul has seemingly nothing to say about the principle of freedom, and he has very little to say about the principle of helpfulness. He hammers away on edifying.[8] He knew that if the believers at Rome would follow this principle, they woud then began to make progress toward resolving their problems.

2. Paul *expected* that several things would happen as a result of the Romans following his instructions. *He anticipated that there would be harmony, praise, and hope.*

His first expectation is that a *harmony would be fostered among their fellowship.* In 14:17-18 he says, "For the kingdom of God is not food and drink but righteousness and *peace* and joy in the Holy Spirit; he who thus serves Christ is acceptable to God and *approved by men."*

(Emphasis mine.) The peace referred to is not so much the tranquility of heart in the midst of adverse circumstances (Phil. 4:6-7) as it is the accord which believers have with one another in the Lord (Eph. 6:23; Phil. 2:1-2). The approval of men which Paul speaks about is the result of a Christian conscientiously using his liberty in the Christian community. The brothers appreciate this kind of living.

Paul expects that the negative attitudes of judging and despising will cease; that the argumentation and ostracization will come to an end; and that as a result the folks will get themselves together. In 15:5,6 he says to them, "May the God of steadfastness and encouragement grant you to live in such harmony with one another, in accord with Christ Jesus, that together you may with one voice glorify the God and Father of our Lord Jesus Christ."

This last verse leads us into the second desire of Paul. He anticipates that the Roman Christians will begin to *praise God for his salvation.* We already noticed from 14:17 that the kingdom of God is "joy in the Holy Spirit." Paul wants the believers to glorify God. Knowing that the joy of their salvation was being fast depleted, Paul wanted this state to be arrested and their joy restored.

When one carefully reads verses 7-13 in chapter 15, then he can easily see that these two first expectations of Paul, harmony and joy, are linked together with one another. Surely they are suitable companions!

The third expectation of Paul is that the believers in Rome will *have hope that the Lord can work things out.* This hope can be seen in 14:4b where Paul says, (probably in reference to the one who eats meat): "And he will be upheld, for the Master is able to make him stand." This is clearly an indication that Paul expects the Lord to be involved in a positive way concerning the problems which the Christians have encountered. And the emphasis on "steadfastness and encouragement" in 15:5,6 in a sure sign that Paul expects that the believers will wait on the Lord until they begin to see changes in their circumstances and lives.

The crowning point of this third anticipation of Paul seems to occur in verse 15:13 where he envisions that "the God of hope will fill [them] with all joy and peace in believing, so that by the power of the Holy Spirit [they] may abound in hope." In these verses Paul expresses faith that the Lord will—as the believers cooperate with Him—handle the situation. He will work things out all right.

Passage Summary

In looking back over the explanation of Rom. 14:1-15:13 we have covered the problem and the solution. The nature of the problem centered around two groups of people, Jews and Gentiles; and had as its focal point at least three main issues; vegetarianism, (holy) days, and wine. The Christians on either side of the issues did what they did in order to honor the Lord, though they both probably considered their opposites weak in the faith. The consequences of the problems were manifested in two main attitudes—despising and judging; and two basic responses—argumentation and ostracization. The overall spiritual climate was degenerating, for the lives of some of the members were being fouled-up, and a sadness was setting within the fellowship.

For a solution to the problem Paul gave several instructions. The believers were to welcome one another, respect each other's convictions, be sure of their own personal convictions, and edify one another. Paul expected, as a result of the believers following his instructions, that there would come to be a harmony among them, that there would be praise to God for his salvation, and that there would be a growing hope that the Lord would work things out.

Concretization

What are we able to learn from Rom. 14:1-15:13 about unity in Christian liberty?

From this passage in Romans, I think that we can learn three important lessons. *First, it takes a basic commitment to the principles of Christian liberty in order to foster a unity among Christians concerning questionable areas of living. Second, fostering a unity in Christian liberty liberates Christians to rejoice in their salvation. And third, in order to achieve a unity in Christian liberty, Christians must trust the Lord to work in the lives of their fellow believers.*

A. *It takes a basic commitment to the principles of Christian liberty in order to foster unity among Christians concerning questionable areas of living.* There can be no such thing as unity among Christians, in regards to questionable areas of living, if there is not a commitment to some "ground rules." Even the important prerequisite of commitment to one another is not enough in itself to foster a unity in questionable areas. There has to be some guidelines for a unity to be fostered. Or else, "every man will do what is right in his own eyes," resulting in further division and confusion.

Paul instructed the believers to do what was *right* (14:21). He told them to live in harmony, *in accord with Christ Jesus* (15:5). Paul did not envision a unity devoid of principles. Neither should we. He saw unity as the fruit of righteousness. So he said in verse 14:17, "For the kingdom of God is not in food and drink but *righteousness and peace and joy* in the Holy Spirit." (All emphasis mine.) *Righteousness leads to peace.* If the brothers and sisters live righteously—that is, observe the principles of Christian liberty—then they will foster a peace—a unity—among their Christian fellowship.

I feel that black Christians need to know that unity is not the same as uniformity. It is possible to do things uniformly and not be unified at all. It is likewise possible to be unified and not live uniform lives. Paul instructed the Romans to "pursue what makes for peace and for *mutual-upbuilding*" (14:9). (Emphasis mine.) The principles of Christian liberty allow for Christians to hold different convictions and still remain unified. For example, two Christians may choose to spend their holidays (holy days) in different ways. One may choose to attend church services, and the other may choose to visit relatives. They can be unified in that they are both seeking to honor the Lord. Unity is not necessarily the same as uniformity. If we learn this, and learn it well as black Christians, it will go a long way in uniting our people.

Unity is at the base of our relationships with one another. Diversity is on the surface. Therefore, as others observe our fellowship, they will come to notice that it is not in going to the same places, dressing in the same way, saying the same thing, participating in the same activities, etc., that make us get it together. The bonds of unity which tie black Christians together are much stronger than the strings of questionable areas. Our unity is more than in "food and drink" which are merely peripherals to the faith. What then binds us together? The ropes of Jesus' Lordship bind us together; for a kingdom implies a King! The things that make us one are our blackness, and such virtues as the quest for righteousness in our nation; for "Righteousness exalts a nation, but sin is a reproach to any people" (Prov. 14:34); or our desire for liberation for our people binds us together. These are the kinds of things which we must unify around. And the principles of Christian liberty will free us to do just that.[9]

B. *Fostering a unity in Christian liberty liberates Christians to rejoice in their salvation.* In our study we observed that the Christians in Rome were fast losing their joy because of internal conflicts. Paul set them back on the right track, and taught them to once again rejoice in the Lord. When we consider verse 14:17 again, we will notice that after righteousness and peace comes *joy.*

In Christian liberty, unity (peace) is not only the fruit of righteousness, but it is also the spring of joy. When Christians refuse to get hung-up on questionable issues, they are freed to praise the Lord for his salvation. I wonder how many black Christian groups are bound in spirit because they are stymied over inconsequential matters? Joy and unity go together. Joy without unity is a mockery to Christian fellowship. And unity without joy is like a concentration camp! Who wants it anyway?!

Probably the greatest indication of a joyless group is that there are no conversions taking place. Students are not getting saved. The relationship of people being saved to Christians rejoicing tends to be rather clear. For if no one is glorifying "God for his mercy" (15:9a), surely sinners will not be attracted to such a fellowship. When the grace of the Lord is relegated to second or third place behind questionable areas; when the "letter of the law" is being laid down for social standards; when there is arguing and dissension over peripherals rather than magnifying the God of our salvation; when these things happen, then sinners get turned off. They don't want to major in minors. And they sure don't want the law! They need *mercy.*

When our Christian groups begin to unify—not uniform—concerning Christian liberty, and begin to experience the resulting freedom to praise the Lord, then we can expect sinners to be attracted to the fellowship. We can also expect that some of them will get saved.

C. *In order to achieve a unity in Christian liberty, Christians must trust the Lord to work in the lives of their fellow believers.* Paul wanted the Christians at Rome to have "hope" (15:4). Moreover, he expected that they would "abound in hope" as a result of "believing" (15:13). Why did they need to believe? For one reason, even though Paul told them to respect each others convictions, he nevertheless knew that some of their convictions were unsound. Some thought that certain things were unclean (just as some of the Corinthians did, 1 Cor. 8:4-10), but these things were not unclean (14:14). Therefore, the Christians who possessed more sound convictions had to trust that the Lord would enlighten the minds of those who had less sound convicitions.

Another reason why they had to believe was merely because of the circumstances. When there are people in a fellowship who are different, have different lifestyles, and have different conceptions and views, only the Lord can put everything together. (As we so well know!) The Roman Christians had to honestly and earnestly ask the Lord to take over.

Today we have the same call to believe God. We must believe that the Lord can work in our own lives first. He must change our strange conceptions about questionable areas. He must help us to be sure of our own convictions. He must aid us in overcoming our prejudices. The Lord will assist us in loving our brothers and sisters, even though we have and live differences. The Lord can do it in our own lives, and also in the lives of others.

Sometimes we have blind spots as Christians. We have deficiences in our lives. We are blind to them, but others are not. This is why we need the prayers of others, and why we also need to pray for others. As we see our brothers and sisters becoming involved in things which might prove harmful to them, we must ask the Lord to deliver them. Much of the time prayer is the most suitable way of helping a brother or sister. This is especially so in questionable areas, where externals are not the sole ground for decisions, and where high emotions cause easy negative reactions. We must learn to believe God for one another.

And we must pray that the Lord will help our fellow believers to stand fast in their liberty. Some brothers and sisters are earnestly trying to please the Lord in questionable areas of living. This area is mostly to be learned by experience. And we do have our struggles! Rather than yield to the easy temptation of laying down the law (legalism) for, let's say, a new Christian, it would be better to consistently pray for him to make it. "And he will be upheld, for the Master is able to make him stand" (14:4b).

Sometimes our Christian fellowships are so entangled in a mess of questionable issues that even trying to discuss the problems serves only to aggravate the situation. Who can bring unity out of chaos? Who can help a group of headstrong black folks get it together? God can! Our God is a God of miracles. And we must believe him for the victory.

Summary & Conclusion

These are the three things which I believe are important in striving for unity in Christian liberty. A. It takes a basic commitment to the principles of Christian liberty in order to foster a unity among Christians concerning questionable areas of living. B. Fostering a unity in Christian liberty liberates Christians to rejoice in their salvation. C. In order to achieve a unity in Christian liberty, Christians must trust the Lord to work in the lives of their fellow believers.

This brings us to the close of another chapter. By this chapter I have tried to teach (by looking at the church in Rome and their problem) that unity is the fruit of righteousness and the spring of joy. We must strive for unity. Unity is not a luxury and it does not come naturally. If we fail to achieve it we are left with "discord among brothers." But if we secure it, it will be "good and pleasant" (cf. Ps. 133). Now we can turn to the next very important chapter which is on trusting the Lord.

Understanding What Has Been Taught

1. The problem of the church at Rome centered around what two groups of people? Was this a hard and fast division?

2. The problem of the church at Rome had what three issues as its focal point?

3. What were the two main attitudes which resulted from the problem of the Roman Christians?

4. What were the two main responses which resulted from the problem of the Roman Christians?

5. What was the spiritual climate of the church at Rome as a result of their problem? What were these Christians losing?

6. Explain three of Paul's instructions to help the Roman believers overcome their problem.

7. What did Paul expect would happen if the Roman believers followed his instructions?

Responding To And Applying What Has Been Learned

Questions

1. Have you been trying to achieve unity with fellow believers without any ground rules? Why? Why not?

2. Have you considered committing yourself to observing these principles of Christian liberty? Why? Why not?

3. In what way, if any, have you allowed questionable areas to usurp the joy of your salvation?

4. How much do you pray for your friends to grow in the area of Christian liberty? What kinds of changes has the Lord brought about in their lives?

Suggestions

Individual

1. Determine what issues may be hindering a unity between yourself and another brother, then purpose to talk it out.

Group

1. Discuss the possibility of your group becoming basically committed to these principles.

2. Structure a meeting around "Rejoicing In Your Salvation," and do nothing but praise the Lord.

TRUSTING THE LORD—Chapter 10

Romans 14:5-9

One man esteems one day as better than another, while another man esteems all days alike. Let every one be fully convinced in his own mind. He who observes the day, observes it in honour of the Lord. He also who eats, eats in honour of the Lord, since he gives thanks to God; while he who abstains, abstains in honour of the Lord and gives thanks to God. None of us lives to himself, and none of us dies to himself. If we live, we live to the Lord, and if we die, we die to the Lord; so then, whether we live or whether we die, we are the Lord's. For to this end Christ died and lived again, that he might be Lord both of the dead and of the living.

Romans 14:10-12

Why do you pass judgment on your brother? Or you, why do you despise your brother? For we shall all stand before the judgment seat of God; for it is written, "As I live, says the Lord, every knee shall bow to me, and every tongue shall give praise to God." So each of us shall give account of himself to God.

Romans 14:14a

I know and am persuaded in the Lord Jesus that nothing is unclean in itself;

In one of the plenary sessions during the annual meeting of the National Black Christian Students Conference[1] a discussion arose concerning some questionable issues. The topic of conversation centered around dancing in particular. During the open discussion, several people stood to the floor to speak their relevant remarks on the subject. It particularly impressed me what one brother had to say on the subject. What struck me about his comments were not so much his eloquency or profundity on the subject, but his honesty. The substance of his remarks were to this effect. He said that he himself had personally sought the Lord's will for himself about dancing. He went on to say that the Lord had told him that dancing was alright for himself, but that he had to remove a few "things" (moves) from his dances. As I listened to these comments, I remember saying to myself that this brother was liberated. I feel that he was free. Not necessarily because he was allowed to dance, but because he had sincerely asked the Lord to guide him; and the Lord had done just that. He had trusted the Lord to direct him, not merely in whether or not he should dance, but even direct him down to his nitty gritty style of dancing. "Trusting the Lord" had set him free to exercise his Christian liberty.

Trusting the Lord results in becoming liberated, holistically liberated. If black Christians are to become free in Christian liberty, then we must trust the Lord. Trusting Him is the sole basis for making Christian liberty an effective aspect of our lifestyles.

In Paul's solution to the problem of the Roman Christians, there is a resounding emphasis on the lordship of Jesus. I decided to cover this aspect of Christian liberty in this chapter, rather than in the previous one (but see point C of that chapter) because of its importance.

Concretization2

I think that there are three important things which we can learn from Rom. 14:5-12, 14a about the lordship of Jesus. *First, respect for the Lord should be the motivation for each Christian to either abstain or participate in questionable areas of living. Second, each Christian will be judged by the Lord for the way that he has used his Christian liberty. And third, the Lord is able to give each Christian some very strong convictions regarding questionable areas of living.* These lessons can help us in our Christian liberty.

A. From Rom. 14:5-9 we can learn that *respect for the Lord should be the motivation for each Christian to either abstain or participate in questionable areas of living.* We learned in the last chapter that the Christians who took a stand on either side of the questionable issues did so out of respect to the Lord. Both sides were trying to please the Lord in their everyday living. One man "esteemed" every day the same, while another man "esteemed" a particular day above all the others. Both did what they did to honour Jesus. One person ate meat, and gave "thanks to God," while another person did not eat meat, and he too gave "thanks to God." And both did what they did to honour the Lord.

We must have the same kind of respect for the Lord. Our participation in our abstention from certain questionable areas must be the result of our respect for the Lord. Someone then may ask, "If we either abstain or participate out of respect for the Lord, that leaves no other alternative responses, does it?" To which I reply, "Not so!" There is another alternative. It is given in verse 7. A person can do what he does in the area of Christian liberty, not so much out of respect to the Lord, but out of selfish motives. He can "live to himself," and even "die to himself."

The Scriptures clearly teach that each Christian must live in order to please the Lord, not himself. And we must please the Lord in everything, (Remember 1 Cor. 10:31-11:1?). Many of the problems which we face in Christian liberty are the result of selfish motives. Under the banner of "Christian liberty" many a thing can go on in the "name of the Lord" which he has nothing to do with at all. Somehow that third person, the one who lives to himself, always tries to get in on the action of Christian liberty. But true Christian liberty cannot be practiced by a person who lives selfishly. It can only be lived by those people who make it their aim to please the Lord.

Jesus died and was raised back to life so that he could be Lord of *everything* (14:8-9; Mt. 28:16-18ff.; Eph. 1:19ff.). And in this "everything" is included questionable areas of living. Some brothers and sisters do not honor the desires of Jesus in regard to Christian liberty. Instead they are bound and ruled by their peers, or their "unwritten" church rules, or the social climate, or their personal moods, or something else. They are, in other words, bound by themselves. Thus they become selfishly pragmatic in living. They tend to have no sure convictions. They drift. They are "double-souled" (cf. Jms. 1:8). Jesus desires to help these brothers and sisters in this important area of living. And he *can* help them, if they trust him. They can receive assistance if they realize that each Christian should either abstain or participate in a questionable area of living out of respect for the Lord, and not out of living to "himself."

B. We can learn from Rom. 14:10-12 that *each Christian will be judged by the Lord according to the way that he has used his Christian liberty.* In these verses Paul spoke to the Romans concerning the presumption and vanity of judging one another. He let them know that they *all* would "stand before the judgment seat of God;" and *"every knee* shall bow," and *"every tongue* shall give praise." *"Each* of us," he says, "shall give account *of himself* to God" (11-12). (All emphases mine.)

In the light of these comments, the vanity and presumptiousness of judging is manifested because of two reasons. First, the one who judges will himself be judged by the Lord. And when one remembers the words of Jesus, "Judge not, that you be not judged. For with the judgment you pronounce you will be judged, and the measure you give will be the measure you get" (Mt. 7:1-2; see also 7:3ff.),—when a person remembers these words—then he will become very reticent about sitting in judgment on others. This would be especially true regarding the area of Christian liberty. Second, it is vain and presumptuous to judge because we ourselves do not have the final say. The Lord is the final judge. Consider James 4:11-12, "Do not speak evil against one another, brethren. He that speaks evil against a brother or judges his brother, speaks evil against the law and judges the law. But if you judge the law, you are not a doer of the law but a judge. There is one lawgiver and judge, he who is able to save and to destroy. But who are you that you judge your neighbour?" One day we must all answer to the Lord. He is the one who will give us either a reward or retribution for our work. He himself has the authority to judge. And in the light of this, our judgments upon one another seem to be rather superfluous, to say the least.

But, let us not think that because we do not have any unwise Christians who are annoyingly keeping us uptight by their continual judgmental attitudes, that therefore the Lord is not keeping a record of our lifestyles. (Sometimes the judgmental attitudes of others remind us of the judgment that is to come.) To the contrary, in the words of the old Spiritual: "My Lord's A writin', My Lord's A writin', My Lord's A writin'. He's writin' all the time. He sees all you do and he hears all you say, My

Lord's A writin' all the time." The Lord is keeping a record. And all of us must appear before the judgment seat of God. And the way in which we have exercised our Christian liberty will be one of the subjects to be considered.

We need to learn to live in the fear of the Lord. The following passages can remind us that the Lord is to be feared. They speak of his coming judgment.

> For we must all appear before the judgment seat of Christ, so that each one may receive good or evil, according to what he has done in the body. Therefore, knowing the fear of the Lord, we persuade men (2 Cor. 5:10-11a).

> But with me it is a very small thing that I should be judged by you or by any human court. I do not even judge myself. I am not aware of anything against myself, but I am not thereby acquitted. It is the Lord who judges me. Therefore do not pronounce judgment before the time, before the Lord comes, who will bring to light the things now hidden in darkness and will disclose the purposes of the heart. Then every man will receive his commendation from God (1 Cor. 4:3-5).

> ...he [God] has fixed a day on which he will judge the world in righteousness by a man whom he has appointed, and of this he has given assurance to all men by raising him from the dead (Acts 17:31).

As we become knowledgeable of the reality of the Lord's judgment, it will begin to have a marked affect upon our living. When we really believe that one day the Lord will, so to speak, quote to us 1 Cor. 6:12 and 1 Cor. 10:23, and ask us, "How did you measure up?" then we will begin to take our Christian liberty seriously.

And yet, there is another side to the day of judgment. This day will not be a time of total somberness. It will also be a time of joy. In Rom. 14:11b Paul says that "every tongue shall give *praise* to God." (Emphasis mine.) The word translated *praise* (*EXOMOLOGEŌ*) means to "confess forth," that is, confess freely, confess openly. The day of the Lord's judgment will be a time of confession by celebrating and giving praise. Those who have been conscientious and considerate in the use of their liberty will have a "Hallelujah!" time. Their good deeds will finally catch up with them (Rev. 14:13), and they will receive rewards for their godly lifestyles. Their trust in the Lord, their faith which they have expressed in Him to guide them and direct them regarding questionable issues, will finally pay off. Their Christian liberty will bloom into a *glorious liberation* (Rom 8:21). So let us keep in mind that each Christian will be judged by the Lord for the way that he has used his Christian liberty.

C. We can learn from Rom. 14:14a that *the Lord is able to give each Christian some very strong convictions regarding questionable areas of living.* In the above mentioned reference Paul said "I know and am persuaded in the Lord Jesus that nothing is unclean in itself." An examination of this verse shows that Paul had some very strong convictions.

First, Paul refers to himself by the use of the first person singular pronoun "I." Second, the word which Paul uses for "know" (*OIDA*) suggests a "fulness of knowledge." Third, the word "persuade" shows that Paul had never been in a situation where he could have taken for granted what he now knew. He had to be convinced of the truthfulness of what he had learned. He had to make a change of mind. For when a person is persuaded, he is "prevailed upon by advice, urging, reasons, inducements, etc., to do something, or to believe something." Fourth, "in the Lord Jesus" suggests that Paul wanted his readers to understand that his beliefs came about as a consequence of his relationship to and fellowship with the Lord. Therefore, his convictions were righteous. And fifth, his personal conviction is absolute and comprehensive: "nothing is unclean in itself."

Paul received some very strong convictions concerning questionable areas of living. And these convictions, as was said above, came from Jesus himself (cf. Mk. 7:14-23). Paul is a pattern for us. For if we remain in union and communion with the Lord, he can give to us some very strong convictions also.

The means for receiving our strong convictions from the Lord seems to rest with our honesty. How much are we willing to open ourselves honestly before the Lord? I think that many of us harbor secret fears that if we begin to pray to the Lord about different questionable issues, that he will answer us a big "NO!". We sort of feel that the Lord is a "kill-joy." So we "hide" from him our inmost selves. We are not honest like the brother referred to at the beginning of this chapter. We are clandestine with God. As a result, we lose out anyway. "For whatever does not proceed from faith is sin" (Rom. 14:23b).

If we would honestly seek the Lord I believe that he would guide us. And I believe that one day we would find out that his will for our lives was not so bad after all. Moreover, we would become sure about our convictions. We would become settled and established in the faith (2 Thess. 3:3; 1 Pet. 5:10).

Do you have questions about certain things? Are there doubts in your mind about different activities? Could it be that you are not sure about various actions which you should take in special circumstances? Are you little in faith regarding your Christian liberty? Then why not try the Lord? He'll be your leader if you trust him. And he'll liberate your mind about questionable areas of living. He'll give you some very strong convictions.

Summary & Conclusion

By way of review, we have learned three things about trusting the Lord from Rom. 14:5-12, 14a. They are: A. Respect for the Lord should be the motivation for each Christian to either abstain or participate in questionable areas of living; B. Each Christian will be judged by the Lord for the way that he has used his Christian liberty; and C. The Lord is able to give each Christian some very strong convictions regarding questionable areas of living. By stressing these three things I have tried to show that trusting the Lord is the sole basis for making Christian liberty an effective aspect of our lifestyles.

With this chapter and the last one we have covered two main aspects of Christian liberty taken from Rom. 14:1-15:13. They are striving for unity, and trusting the Lord. We have also brought to an end our major explanations of the passages in 1 Corinthians and Romans that were pertinent to our subject. Now we can turn to the two final chapters which will respectively touch on envisioning some creative possibilities in Christian liberty, and helping others to understand and apply what has been written on these pages. Keep on pushin'!

Understanding What Has Been Taught

1. What was common in the experience of people who took a stand on either side of the issue of holy days?

2. Why did Christ die and rise again from the dead?

3. Whom did Paul say would be exempt from the Lord's judgment?

4. What will be the two moods on the day of judgment?

5. Name three reasons why we know that Paul held some very strong convictions.

Responding To And Applying What Has Been Learned

Questions

1. Do you know of any Christian who is living "to himself" under the banner of Christian liberty? If so how do you think he got this way?

2. If you had been called into judgment yesterday, what do you think the Lord would have said to you about Christian liberty?

3. How many people can you name that have very strong convictions about questionable issues? Can you think of some people who you believe would be better off if they had much stronger convictions?

Suggestions

Individual

1. Check out whether or not what you do or what you don't do is done "to the Lord."

2. Confess any sins of your past concerning Christian liberty.

Group

1. Let your group members prepare speeches about their strong personal convictions. Let them give the speeches in a supportive atmosphere.

2. Have a prayer meeting, and ask the Lord to help you all to deal with questionable areas of living.

CREATING A NEWNESS—
Chapter 11

Romans 15:14-17

I myself am satisfied about you, my brethren, that you yourselves are full of goodness, filled with all knowledge, and able to instruct one another. But on some points I have written to you very boldly by way of reminder, because of the grace given me by God to be a minister of Christ Jesus to the Gentiles in the priestly service of the gospel of God, *so that the offering of the Gentiles may be acceptable, sanctified by the Holy Spirit. In Christ Jesus, then, I have reason to be proud of my work for God.* (Emphasis mine.)

****

It must be borne in mind that the tragedy in life doesn't lie in not reaching your goal. The tragedy lies in having no goal to reach. It isn't a calamity to die with dreams unfulfilled, but it is a calamity not to dream. It is not a disaster to be unable to capture your ideal, but it is a disaster to have no ideal to capture. It is not a disgrace not to reach the stars, but it is a disgrace to have no stars to reach for. Not failure, but low aim is sin.[1]

****

A new commandment must echo through the dead minds and hearts of Black Christians especially. That commandment must be: Create! Create! Create! Create![2]

POSSESSING CREATIVITY

The above quotes seem to set well the tone for this chapter. Since we were made in the image of God, and God is Creator, then this means that we are also creators. And this creativity of ours can be brought into full bloom through our transforming relationship to Jesus Christ. The Lord wants us black Christians to be creative. And he is able to bring the creativity that is within us to full manifestation in our everyday living. Furthermore, he can bring our creativity into manifestation in the realm of Christian liberty.

NOVEL CREATIONS

The Lord desires for us to create "new" things. There are two meanings to the word new. "New" can mean either, 1. "recent origin or production, or having but lately come or been brought into being;" or 2. "now existing or appearing for the first time; novel." I believe that the Lord would not only have us to create recent things, but also to create novel things: things that are strikingly unique, unusual, and strange; things that are original, authentic, unimitated, underived, unprecedented, uncommon, and different. He wants us to become engaged in "creating a newness" in the area of Christian liberty.

Elucidation

Although the verses quoted at the beginning of this chapter serve as Paul's justification for having said all that he did in the previous 14½ chapters of the book of Romans, they nevertheless seem to provide us with an insight into Paul's aim in teaching the Roman Christians about liberty. Paul, as "a minister of Christ Jesus to the Gentiles (*ETHNOS*)" (15:16a) wanted to do his work well. He was "proud" (15:17) of the Gentiles whom he had helped to properly exercise their liberty. They were his "boast," his "glory" (cf. 1 Thess. 2:19-20; 3:8-9; Phil. 4:1). He worked very hard for the people to whom he ministered. He not only evangelized them, but he also built them up in the Lord (15:18ff.).

Paul was very straightforward with his "flock." He did not spare the rod, nor pull any punches (15:15). Why was he this way? In verse 16 he gives the answer. He said that he wanted the "offering of the Gentiles" to be *"acceptable"* to God. This word acceptable (*EUPROSDEKTOS*) signifies "a person or thing that has been regarded very favorably." It connotates a very desirable reception. Paul poured his life into the Gentiles because he wanted them to become pleasing to the Lord. He jealously instructed them in Christian liberty because he wanted their lives to make the Lord feel *reaeaealll goooood*!

But Paul's unfailing and unerring instruction to the believers was not enough in itself to ensure that his offering of the Gentiles would be acceptable to God. His "sacrifice" needed a special touch. His "flock" needed to become "sanctified by the Holy Spirit" (16b). Paul knew that the Spirit of the Lord had to put the finishing touches on his ministry in order that it would become "just right." The Holy Spirit would bring the teaching of Christian liberty into its own perfection in the lives of the Gentiles.

Concretization

It seems to me that it would be an injustice to the Lord, to his Word, and to the goal of Paul (his servant) if we did not seek to: 1. be "proud" of our ministry among black people; 2. endeavor to present black people as an "acceptable" offering to God; and 3. earnestly trust the Holy Spirit to "sanctify" our work among our people. And it would be a further injustice if we did not seek to do these three things with an emphasis on Christian liberty.

Paul's ministry to the Gentiles (to the *ETHNOS*), to the "nations," with his highest regard for their lives, sets a good pace for our ministry to black people. For this reason we must disciple black people in Christocentric Black-Ethnicism. And for this reason we must disciple black people in blackspirituality. Blackspirituality in questionable areas

137

of living is what we have been trying to accomplish with this study. We have been trying to learn how it is possible for black people to be totally spiritual in dealing with questionable areas of living. And through it all we have been trying to create a *newness:* a newness among black people in Christian liberty that is acceptable to God and sanctified by the Holy Spirit; a kind of newness among our people of which we can be proud.

TRANSFORMING THE BLACK CULTURE

In order to bring the above endeavor to fulfilment among our people, I believe that we must be willing to be leaders in creativity. As was said in the first chapter, I believe that the Lord wants black Christians to develop an intra-cultural, and through this an inter-cultural message. He wants us to develop a "Black Light." If we are to be co-workers with the Lord in accomplishing this task, then we must possess vision. We must ask the Lord to help us to "see" what kind of "new thing" he wants to bring to pass among our people. I am convinced that the Lord wants to liberate our culture so that it can bring good to us and bring glory to himself.

At this time you may be asking yourself what an intra- and inter-black cultural message has to do with Christian liberty. If so, I would invite you to recall the profound conclusion of Paul in 1 Cor. 10:31-11:1. In this passage Paul told the Corinthians to live a totally spiritual life. He said to them, "...*whatever* you do, *do all* to the glory of God" (31b). (Emphasis mine.) Paul knew that the principles of Christian liberty could be applied to many different areas of living (cf. chapter two, point C). And when he told the Corinthians to do "whatever" they did to God's glory, he knew full well everything which was encompassed in this "whatever." It encompassed their total culture.[3] So when we, as black Christians, begin to apply the "whatever" to our lives, then nothing less than an intra- and inter-black cultural liberation will result. The black culture will become transformed.

Culture can be defined as "the sum total of ways of living built up by a people in a designated area at a given time, which ways of living are transmitted from generation to generation." Culture involves art, architecture, speech, language, literature, music, drama, dance, religion, dress, learning, social intercourse, technologies, sciences, inventions, values, traditions, myths, lore, philosophies, government, laws, rites, et al.[4] Through the three principles of Christian liberty I believe that we can, and are challenged to, create a newness in our total culture. We are not bound to do the same old things. We can be novel.

Can we accomplish this task? I feel that only the Lord knows the answer to this question. A better question to ask ourselves is this: "Are we willing to express our creativity in this area?" If so, then the next few pages may be of assistance in stirring us to accept the challenge.

UNDERSTANDING THE TIMES

I believe that black Christians can learn an important lesson from observing the kinds of men who joined the army of David, king of Israel.

Of special significance are the qualities attributed to the men of Issachar. It is said of them that they were *"men who had understanding of the times, to know what Israel ought to do,"* (1 Chron. 12:32 emphasis mine).

Would to God that there were a cadre of young black men and young black women who had an understanding of the times of black people in white America, and who knew what black people ought to do in terms of struggling for our holistic liberation in the name of Jesus!

It is in this spirit that I have compiled a culturo-social profile of young Blackamericans. These comments give indications of the direction in which blacks should be headed in exercising Christian liberty. (These indications are given in addition to those suggested throughout the work.) These comments also express the kind of black culturo-social profile and direction we must always keep in mind while attempting to lead others in a comprehension of Christian liberty. For we must never forget that if our teaching is to be effective it must judiciously take into account the learner's living environment. Best teaching is never done in a vacuum.

A CULTRO-SOCIAL PROFILE OF YOUNG BLACKAMERICANS

The young Blackamericans who are being portrayed in this profile are those who, to a large degree, were born between 1948-1960, and are therefore between 18 and 30 years of age. This generation has been called a "new" generation, but also a "lost-found generation." And so being, it has been the cause of a "crisis in *our* history."[5]

They have grown up under extreme conditions of structural unemployment, inflation, deplorable housing, drug addiction, and fratricide.[5] This is said to be a generation experiencing "permanent Black depressions." Many of the lifestyles of this generation have emerged from what has been characterized as a "ghetcolony"; an atypical environment that is insensitive to their survival, disclaims their humanity, and makes them dependent on the inhumanity of their oppressor. Being capitalistically and colonially controlled, being politically, culturally, and educationally oppressive, and stemming from White racism, this environment produces in their lives fear, frustration, anxiety, despair, apathy, and death. It also forces this generation to define themselves in terms not conducive to producing a sense of self-worth, thus perpetuating self-defeating and self-destroying models.[8] This environment dictates those lifestyles which will be accepted, tolerated, suppressed, or destroyed, and therefore many Blacks are left to the reactions of general hostility, random aggressiveness, and fluctuation between self-depreciations and compensatory grandiosity and posturing.[12] Consequently, those lifestyles which are liberating to Black people give way to "plantation" mentalities.[8]

This generation is a generation of oppressed young Blacks, especially Black males, who are lost and locked into enforced idleness and the jails.[5] The mechanism which many have chosen to use in order to survive their problem has been termed the "Street Institution." In this institution, countless Black youth linger on street corners, in pool halls, and in taverns.[19] Their street instructors embody the coping, but depressing and defeating, lifestyles of pimps, prostitutes, hustlers, gang leaders, militants, and street men. Their language, or "verbal manipulation," is an indispensible functional means of communication that reflects their culture, is expressed aggressively, stabilizes threatening situations, and enables them to survive their overbearing environment.[8]

Blackamericans of this age group are those who have a keen "electronic sensibility."[5] They are a media generation—a generation where drug addiction is complemented or surpassed by T.V. and media addiction.[10] The movies and T.V., which project traditional stereotypes, unbelievable and unrealistic super-type Black men,[8] and negative images of frivolous and happy-go-lucky Blacks, has been the pastime of this generation.[11] An indication of this media problem can be detected by some of the questions which have been posed such as:

"First, are these new movies [those alleging to mirror some aspect of the Black experience] actually representative of the Black Experience or do they simply mimick white peoples' interpretation of our lives?

"Second, do these films serve a meaningful purpose to Black people or help to give us a clearer analysis of ourselves as a disenfranchised people?

"Third, are these films merely being produced as a tonic to pacify Black people and exploit the enthusiasms we have to see ourselves on screen?

"Fourth, do the images now being presented in Black movies provide us with something more positive than what we have been exposed to in the past?"[8]

This electronic media has "pacified and detached from reality" numerous Black youth who are neglecting their families, wasting their minds in the educational system, and who are developing undesirable, detrimental, and unwholesome beings. It is said that many of this generation survive off of "scientific made fact" that has increased institutional racism while mystifying and quieting them to their ethnic responsibilities.[5]

A "crippling narcissim" and "Meism" are terms that depict this young Black generation. Individualism, selfishness, and anxiousness about personal security has caused many youth and young adults to ignore the human needs of others—and thus they trouble their marriages, weaken the bonds of their family ties, and shy away from community commitments.[11]

This Blackamerican generation would rather live-in and shack-up instead of get married. They tend to be "swingers," expect to have more fun, and desire more leisure time. This generation has views about sex which tend to be exploitive of women and socially destructive. Many are trapped by new, and white, moral codes which they find distasteful but binding.[17] They have gone back into excessive partying and socializing which leaves many of them empty.[11]

They spend more than enough time and energy on fashions and

clothing styles while neglecting other important issues, interests, and abilities. They are preoccupied with looks and clothing, and maintain a high level of undue self-adoration. They are a strong economic supporter of both the fashion and music industries. Yet their music no longer reflects the healthy attraction to the Negro folk traditions of Blues, Jazz and the Spirituals, but they now move to the tunes of rock, soul, and rock-Jazz, changing uncritically and freely from Black artists to White artists. This kind of movement has been interpreted as having a drastic affect on the levels of their Black consciousness and identity.[5]

Being pragmatically and materialistically optimistic about the future, this generation seems to be oblivious to the dangerous omen of the extremely high underemployment that is plaguing them. Although there are those in this generation who would "prefer to develop and be responsible for their own business," yet, paradoxically, only a small number opt for "separate and self-sufficient Black communities."[20]

And yet, the young Blackamericans in this age bracket seem to be in far graver trouble than what is suggested above. For it has been noted that they have an "ambiguous orientation to the roots and archetypes of the Black experience;"[5] that they are guided by a "completely new institutional map,"[6] and a "new social formation" that is changing what it means to be Black in America. Although this generation is said to be experiencing a "massive unchaining of the Black unconscious," an "expansion of the Black psyche," and are individually more aggressive and militant than the previous generation, yet their racial expectations and attitudes have changed.[5]

In some of their minds the term "Black" has taken on negative connotations.[11] Many of their survival mechanisms are being collectively defused.[5] They tend to be devoid of "basic fundamental survival instincts."[7] They are analyzed to be lacking that "seventh racial sense" that has been typical of past Black leaders and therefore they don't possess that "exquisitely tuned anteanna that anticipates rejection or danger." This generation doesn't share the toughness, endurance, and determination—the backbone of their forefathers.[5] They are without a sense of collective Black militancy.[15]

And little wonder, for many of them feel that they have experienced less racism and discrimination than their parents. They tend to be ignorant of their Black history and culture, and therefore are less aware and proud of, among other things, civil rights and its leaders—whom they admire less than they admire entertainers. They are intellectually and emotionally removed from the struggles for equality by their elders. And greater numbers of this generation have much more social contact with Whites than do other Blacks. A good portion of them also favor total integration with White people through widespread marriage.[20]

The leadership of this young Black generation seems to be a contributing part of this Black regression. More and more their leaders are not identifying with the plight of the Black masses, nor are they living in the Black community. Although Black people in the U.S. have the greatest number of Black college graduates, many of them view the Black

141

struggle as a passing fad; they are not working actively and consciously for the liberation of Black people.[9] They are not connected with Black values.

Being trained in the White press, predominantly White colleges, and being dependent on White bar and medical associations etc., their main concern seems to be in "making it or not making it." They are obsessed with success American-style than with helping the rank and file of Black folks.[16] They want more financial prosperity, and desire to be "movin' on up." These leaders are said to be undergoing a de-educating process, and are being put into cosmetic and non-decision making positions. It has been pointed out that some of their brightest Black minds are an active part of the "liberation movements of White People."

The concept of self among many young Black leaders is not substantiated sufficiently to the point of acceptance, and thus they fail to move to higher levels of Black manhood or womanhood. Consequently there has been the rise of dominant white men and women in the lives of "educated" and "responsible" Black men and women who are thus neutralized and not accepted or respected.[9] Such issues as these are raised about this problem:

1. Why are there so many Black women alone and without men, who possibly as a result of this "abnormality," have adopted a very defeatist attittude towards life, self, others?

2. Where are the Black men?

3. Of the Black men who are visible—what are they about? What is their position in and what are their views on the family and Black Struggle and/or Life?

4. The current family situation as it now exists in the Black community—has it worked? Have we produced, from it, creative, aggressive, strong and determined children who will carry on the struggle for liberation and in effect build a better world for their people and others?

And concerning Black women without Black men:

1. They can continuously go *without* Black men which is unnatural and against life;

2. They begin to see and mate with white men and this is becoming the probable option mainly with the "educated" and professional Black women;

3. They share the men of other women and this is generally done secretively and without the third party's knowledge of it;

4. They move into prostitution which, in effect, means that the Black woman becomes the property of her pimp, which deals at *one* level with the sharing of a man; and

5. Black women begin to move heavily into lesbianism, that is homosexual relationships—an activity which has not been a traditional part part of our Black culture. (There is also the option of bisexuality which seems to be popular among young Black college trained women.)[9]

Religiously speaking, many of this generation have turned from Christianity, deeming it as the "White man's religion" because of the role White Christians played in slavery, discrimination, and segregation, and because this "White Christianity" pacified discontent and neutralized aggressiveness among Blacks.[8] Consequently, they are characterized as having little spiritual fiber, and are seduced by mysticism and astrology.[10] I see this generation, many of whom have not been adequately exposed to or have opted out of the traditional Black religion, as a *post-Christian generation*—relative to their parents and grandparents. There are a tremendous number of "unchurched" youth and young adults, though there are signs of them turning back to the Black Church.[18] There is also a rise, however, in those who participate in non-traditional institutions of religion. Considering this generation, an analyst remarked, "I wonder what is really going to happened to us?"[16]

What does this young Blackamerican generation need? To sum up several sources, they need a positive radical re-ordering of Black models. They need concerted power and mobilization of resources. They need self-determination and continuous unrelenting struggle for Black advocacy and human rights.[8] They need *Black values*, such as the following which are based on the customs and traditions of Afrikan societies, and have proven to be a "weapon, a shield, and a pillow of peace";

Nguzo Saba (Seven Principles)

Umoja (Unity)—to strive for and maintain unity in the family, community, nation and race.

Kujichagulia (Self-determination)—to define ourselves, name ourselves, and speak for ourselves, instead of being defined, and spoken for by others.

Ujima (Collective Work and Responsibility)—to build and maintain our community together and to make our brothers' and sisters' problems our problems and to solve them together.

Ujamaa (Cooperative Economics & Extended Family)—to build and maintain our stores, shops and other businesses, and to profit together from them.

Nia (Purpose)—to make as our collective vocation the building and developing of our community, in order to restore our people to their traditional greatness.

Kuumba (Creativity)—to do always as much as we can, in the way that we can in order to leave our community more beautiful and beneficial than when we inherited it.

Imani (Faith)—to believe with all our heart in our parents, our teachers, our leaders, our people and the righteousness and victory of our struggle.[13]

What does this Black generation need? They need alternative instituions to link Black generations together. And they need the older generation to teach them the "accumulated lore of the past," and to ease their culturo-social transition from one phase of maturation to another.[5]

Thus, in ending this profile, they need more institutions like those which promote principles of Black art for creativity and liberation such as:

1. We are an Afrikan people, bound together as a worldwide Afrikan family by race, ancestry, culture and common oppression.

2. Black art and Black life are inseparable. Our art is not fantasy and must be rooted in the historic experiences of Afrikan people. It is the recreation and interpretation of Black life.

3. Black art must be functional. To entertain is not enough. It must teach some valuable lessons or leave some important messages with its readers, listeners or viewers which help to:
   a. heighten their consciousness of themselves and the world about them,
   b. inspire them to improve their condition,
   c. heighten their understanding of the political, economic and social forces shaping their lives.

4. Black art must deal honestly and fully with every aspect of the Black condition, past and present. Our existence stretches thousands of years from the beginning of civilization in Afrika to our current presence in almost every nation in the world. Our art should not dwell narrowly or excessively on any single subject, but illuminate every variation, context, mood, attitude, period and lifestyle of the Black experience.

5. Black art must present positive images of Afrikan people, and if not, say something relevant to them about their condition while presenting negative images. At no time should it ever reinforce self-hatred or white-inflicted stereotypes of ourselves.

6. Black art must clearly show the social, political, economic and cultural contexts of any realities it treats. It is not enough simply to show a particular Black reality. Our art must also tell why it exists, its effects, and offer necessary alternatives.

7. Black art must relate to all Black people, not just the middle class or intellectuals. One of the huge distortions of Western civilization is its presumption that art should be the exclusive preserve of the rich, powerful or influential classes. Kuumba believes that Black art must be returned to its Afrikan tradition as part of the lifestyle and culture of all the people.

8. We reject, totally and eternally, the sterile Western concept of "art for art's sake." There is no such thing, and never has been. "All art reflects the value system from which it comes," says Ron Karenga.

9. There is a direct and lasting relationship between Black art and politics. Black artists have fundamental and permanent responsibility to be involved in and contribute significantly to the liberation struggle. Any Black artist who does not see political implications in his work is naive and probably irrelevant.

Political is used in the broad sense, referring to any issue or circumstances relating to or likely to affect the lives and destinies of Afrikan people. In this sense politics obviously becomes something vastly different and more important than electing Democrats, Republicans, or Socialists or Communists.

Further, we thoroughly reject any links with or reliance on the government or its agents, except in those rare cases where these links may facilitate the fullest and freest artistic expression and personal fulfillment of Afrikan people.

10. Black artists not only owe an equitable portion of their time and talent to the Black community, but also their earnings.

11. Black art and artists must be fully supported and judged by Black people, the only ones to whom our artists must be held accountable. We reject any attempt by whites to control or influence the principles, exhibition, direction, or subject matter of Black art. We must be the only judges of its relevance or irrelevance.

12. Black artists must be rooted in the Black community and totally involved in its activities and struggles.[14]

Now that our consciousness of the culturo-social experience of young Blackamericans has been heightened, we can now offer the following proposition on exercising our Christian liberty in such a context.

A PROVOKING PROPOSITION

WHEN THERE ARE BLACK CHRISTIAN STUDENTS WHO TAKE SERIOUSLY THE

> *Criterion*—a standard of judgment or criticism; an established rule or principle for testing anything.
> *Characteristics*—pertaining to, constituting, or indicating the character or peculiar quality; typical; distinctive; a distinguishing feature or quality.
> *Measure*—any standard of comparison, estimation, or judgment.
> *Standard*—anything taken by general consent as a basis of comparison; an approved model.
> *Principles*—general and fundamental truths which may be used in deciding conduct or choice.

and

> *Working Rules*—a guiding and serving principle or regulation governing conduct, action, procedure, arrangement, etc.

OF CHRISTIAN LIBERTY; AND THESE BLACK CHRISTIAN STUDENTS ARE WILLING, WITH THE HELP OF THE LIBERATOR, TO

> *Envision*—to picture mentally, especially some future event or events.
> *Imagine*—to form a mental image of (something not actually present to the senses), to think, believe or fancy.
> *Picture*—to form a mental picture or image of; imagine.
> *Conceive*— to form a (notion, opinion, purpose, etc.), to apprehend in the mind; understand. to relate ideas or feelings to one another in a pattern.

and have

> *Ideas*—any conceptions existing in the mind as the result of mental apprehension or activity, thoughts, conceptions, or notions; impressions; opinions, views, or beliefs.

145

Impressions—strong effects produced on the intellect, feelings, or conscience.

Notions—more or less general, vague, or imperfect conceptions or ideas of something.

Opinions—what is thought on any matter or subject; judgment or belief resting on grounds insufficient to produce certainty.

and

Conceptions—general notions; the predicate of (possible) judgments; a complex of characters; the immediate objects of thought in simple apprehension.

WITHIN

Arrangement—the manner in which things are prepared or planned.

Form—something that gives or determines shape; a mold.

Shape—the quality of a thing depending on its outline or external surface; the form of a particular thing, person, or being.

and

Structure—mode of building, construction, or organization; arrangement of parts, elements, or constituents.

ABOUT THE CREATION OF

Models—standards for imitation or comparison; patterns.

Patterns—style or type in general; an original or model proposed for or deserving of imitation; anything fashioned or designed to serve as a model or guide for something to be made.

Paradigms—a pattern; an example.

Paragons—a model or pattern of excellence, or of a particular excellence.

Types—a kind, class, or group as distinguished by a particular character.

Archetypes—a model or first form; the original pattern or model after which a thing is made.

Antitypes—that which is foreshadowed by a type or symbol, as a New Testament event prefigured by the Old Testament.

Prototypes—the original or model after which anything is formed.

Images—likeness or similitude of a person, animal, or thing.

and

Ideals—a conception of something in its highest perfection; a standard of perfection or excellence; a person or thing regarded as realizing such a conception or conforming to such a standard and taken as a model for imitation; an ultimate object or aim of endeavor, especially one of high or noble character.

ACCORDING TO THE

Customs—habitual practices; the usual way of acting in given circumstances; habits or usages collectively; convention; a long-continued habit which is so established that it has the force of law.

146

Habits—a disposition or tendency, constantly shown, to act in a certain way; a particular practice, custom, or usage.

Practices—habitual or customary performances.

and

Ways of living

OF BLACK PEOPLE;
THEN WE WILL BECOME BLESSED WITH THE

Kinds—nature or character as determining likenesses or differences between things; persons or things as being of a particular character or class.

and

Sorts—a particular kind, species, variety class, group or description, as distinguished by the character or nature.

of

Modes—customary or conventional usage in manners, dress, etc., especially as observed by persons of fashion; a prevailing style or fashion.

Manners—ways of doing, being done, or happening, mode of action, occurrence, etc. characteristic or customary ways of doing.

Means—an agency, instrumentality, method, etc., used to attain an end.

Methods—modes of procedure, especially an orderly or systematic mode; the ways of doing something, especially in accordance with a definite plan.

Procedures—the acts or manners of proceeding in any action or process; conduct; particular courses or modes of action.

Prescriptions—laying down, in writing or otherwise, rules or courses to be followed; appointments, ordinances, or enjoiners.

Fashions—prevailing customs or styles of dress, etiquette, procedures, etc. manners; ways; modes.

Styles—particular, distinctive, or characteristic modes of action; particular kinds, sorts, or types, as with reference to forms, appearance, or character.

Vogues—fashions, as at a particular time; popular currency, acceptance, or favor.

Rituals—forms or systems of religious or other rites.

Ceremonies—the formalities observed on some solemn or important and public or state occasions; formal religious or sacred observances; solemn rite.

and

Festivals—a periodic religious or other feast; any time or day of feasting; an anniversary for festive celebration; any course of festive activities.

THAT WILL GIVE DIRECTION TO, AND EXPRESS IN

Signs—actions, conditions, qualities, occurrences, or visible objects that point to a fact or conveys a meaning.

Emblems—objects, or representations of them, symbolizing a quality, state, class of persons, etc.; a symbol; an allegorical drawing or picture, often with explanatory writing.

and

Symbols—something used or regarded as standing for or representing something else; a material object representing something inmaterial; an emblem, token, or sign.

OUR COMPOSITE CULTURAL LIBERATION! AMEN!

Now I'll state the proposition in compact form.

"When there are black Christian students who take seriously the *principles* of Christian liberty; and these black Christian students are willing, with the help of the Liberator, to *envision* and have *impressions* within *form* about the creation of *paragons* according to the *ways of living* of black people; then we will become blessed with the *kinds* of *manners* that will give direction to, and express in *symbols* our composite cultural liberation! Amen!"[21]

If somehow these few meaningful words and thoughts have motivated you to, at least, *consider expressing* your Christian creativity within the black culturo-social context, then they have served their purpose.[22]

The principles of Christian liberty can have a dramatic impact upon a culture. There is evidence that these principles, as laid down by the Church in Acts 15:20,29, had a lasting impact upon different cultures.[23] They can work. Our part is to actualize them, and to insure that the coming generation is free to apply them (in the way that *they* see fit) to their own changing circumstances.

Summary & Conclusion

Within this chapter I have tried to stress five things. A. We possess creativity. B. The Lord wants us to create novel things. C. The Lord wants to transform our black culture. D. Understanding The Times. And E. A Provoking Proposition.

In stressing these things I have not suggested any specific novel creations. I trust that *you* will do that. I have basically tried to set forth an adequate working context for those who desire to create. And I hope that your faith will reach up and out to the best that the Lord has for you in this calling to create. In the process, you may not have all of your desires fulfilled. But—just like the people of faith in Hebrews 11 who saw and greeted the promises, but who died in faith without receiving what was promised—you too will be *approved* for your faith (Heb. 11:2,13,39).

Let us start "creating a newness" with the assurance that one day our Lord and Liberator will "make all things new" (Rev. 21:5).

Understanding What Has Been Taught

1. How do we know that we are creative?

2. What are two meanings of the word "new?"

3. What three things did Paul say about/strive for in regard to his "offering" of the Gentiles?

4. What does an intra- and inter-black cultural message have to do with Christian liberty?

5. What is culture, and what kinds of things compose it?

Responding To And Applying What Has Been Learned

Questions

1. What do you think about being "proud" of your ministry to black people?

2. Do you wish that you were more creative? Why? Why not?

3. Is your "vision" to meager? Why? Why not?

4. Do you agree or disagree with the provoking proposition? Why?

5. In what ways do you think that you can improve your understanding of the times in which blacks are living? (Dying!)

Suggestions
Individual

1. Subscribe to some black literature in order to receive a better and broader understanding of what blacks are thinking.

2. Consistently read black works in order to gain a deeper impression of our history and heritage.

3. Take every opportunity you can to write essays, term papers, etc. on the black experience.

4. Choose your own propostion from the given context and use it for self-motivation.

5. If you have the chance, purchase or create some black art and clothing. See what kind of effect it has upon your self-conception.

Group

1. Take a comparative survey of black non-Christians and black Christians in order to see where the minds of each group are focussed in relation to crucial black issues.

2. Start a Black Studies collection for your group.

3. Discuss the proposition, and talk about vision. This is for consciousness raising.

4. Plan a meeting of brainstorming on creative social alternatives. Follow through, and see if you can carry out some of the suggestions.

ASSISTING THE LEARNER—
Chapter 12

Romans 15:14

I myself am satisfied about you, my brethren, that you yourselves are full of goodness, filled with all knowledge, and able to instruct one another.

INSTRUCTING ONE ANOTHER

Paul was persuaded of three things about the Christians at Rome. He was persuaded about their abundant goodness, their complete knowledge, and their ability to instruct one another. This chapter centers on the last of those three things: *the ability to instruct one another.* Hence the title, "Assisting the Learner." Whereas the previous chapter focussed on the future, this chapter focuses on the present. It hopefully will aid us in instructing our black brothers and sisters.

To be able to adequately teach others, we must first possess a desire to teach them. Being "full of goodness" will give us this desire. Second, we must have a good apprehension of the subject to be taught. We must be filled with "all knowledge." These are two prerequisites to teaching others. (The person being taught also plays an important part in learning, for he must be *willing* to learn. And he must be open to continually learning, for education is a continuous process.)

CHECKING IT OUT FOR YOURSELF

Those who teach others must also be continually learning. For knowledge is not static but dynamic. Truth is alive. Therefore, we must continuously be in tune to freshly experiencing all the different manifestations of truth. In this spirit, I would commend to you 1 Thess. 5:19-22 as a guideline for evaluating all that is written on the pages of this volume. I do not ask you to uncritically or naively accept what I have written. The Lord would not desire for you to do this either. He would have you to "check it out" for yourself. Here are the guidelines as given by Paul:

1. Do not quench the Spirit,
2. do not despise prophesying,
3. but test everything; [by the Word]
4. hold fast what is good,
5. abstain from every form of evil.

(Compare these guidelines with Paul's estimate of the Bereans in Acts 17:11-12. It is strikingly similar parallel.) I trust that your testing of everything that has been said will prove beneficial. I'm sure that you may still have some questions after having read through this study. This should not be reason for despair but for trust. As you trust the Lord, he will most likely give to you some personal soul-satisfying insights that you could receive from no one else. I hope this will become your experience.

A WORD ON FORGIVENESS AND MERCY

In the course of reading this book you may have had your "toes stepped on." The Lord might have convicted you that you weren't quite measuring up to his standard of holiness. This conviction may have been cause for concern, remorse, despondency, fear, anger, apathy, longing, or tears. Whatever your response to the Lord's working in your life, I want to let you know that "the Lord will not cast off for ever, but, though he cause grief, he will have compassion according to the abundance of his steadfast love; for he does not willingly afflict or grieve the sons of men" (Lam. 3:31-33). And I would further remind you that you should "not regard lightly the discipline of the Lord, nor lose courage when you are punished by him. For the Lord disciplines him whom he loves, and chastises every son whom he receives" (Heb. 12:5b-6).

The Lord disciplines us because he loves us. And if he has convicted us of our shortcomings, he has done it so that we can confess them. For he has said, "If we say we have no sin, we deceive ourselves, and the truth is not in us. If we confess our sins, he is faithful and just, and will forgive our sins and cleanse us from all unrighteousness" (1 Jn. 1:8-9). The Lord will forgive us if we "agree" with him about our sins. And if we do this, he will not only forgive us, but he will also cleanse us from all our unrighteousness. He will become involved in conquering the sin that is hindering our lives. Forgiveness is a matter of moment, but cleansing takes time. But however long it takes, the Lord will stick by us until the work is complete, "For he has said, 'I will never fail you nor forsake you'" (Heb. 13:5b).

The Lord knows that we need mercy. This is why he had to give up his life on our behalf. If at this time you sense a need for his mercy, I am sure that you will find plenty of it at the throne of grace (Heb. 4:14-16). A talk with the Lord about your needs in the area of Christian liberty can begin a dramatic change in your life. Why not pause to talk with him at this time? (Here are some passages to ponder on the mercy of the Lord: Ps. 25; Ps. 103; Ps. 130; Heb. 8:8-12; Heb. 13:20-21.)

Before we attempt to teach others, it is very important that our own consciences and lives be free from guilt and oppression in the area of Christian liberty. Jesus himself was the one who said, "Why do you see the speck that is in your brother's eye, but do not notice the log that is in your own eye? Or how can you say to your brother, 'Let me take the speck out of your eye,' when there is the log in your own eye? You hypocrite, first take the log out of your own eye, and then you will see clearly to take the speck out of you brother's eye" (Mt. 7:3-5). Let us then start our teaching by ministering to our own needs of forgiveness and mercy.

REVIEW OF LESSONS LEARNED

Following is a listing of all the major lessons that we have tried to learn through this study. They are given chapter by chapter. This listing is useful for receiving a general overview of the subject that we have studied. Study lessons and sessions can be easily built around internalizing these principles.

Chapter 1—Pressing The Need

A. There is a great need for principles of guidance, in questionable areas of living, for those Christians who are concerned about being made whole in the name of Jesus Christ.
B. The need is threefold: Christian, cultural, and social

1. *Christian*
   —Christians are principled
   —Unchanging principles
   —Concentrating on germane matters
   —Evangelism

2. *Cultural*
   —Unique black indentity and culture
   —Christocentric Black-Ethnicism—Christ's desire
   —Transforming the black culture
   —Encroachment and inadequacy of white Christianity
   —"Black Light"

3. *Social*
   —Critiquing black social diversity
   —Uniting black Christians
   —Creative social alternatives

Chapter 2—Employing Three Principles

A. In our unique context, we have the same kinds of problems in our lives (regarding questionable issues) which the first-century Christians had in their lives.
B. The teaching of Christian liberty is a genuine Christian teaching.
C. There are three principles which must modify our Christian liberty.
1. Is it helpful?
2. Is my freedom being preserved?
3. Does it build my neighbor?
D. The principles of Christian liberty have multiple applications within their own limitation.

Chapter 3—Searching The Bible

A. We are prone to have tendencies of license.
B. There may be Bible passages which have a bearing upon a particular supposed questionable area of living.

Chapter 4—Building Your Neighbor

A. We must be open to accepting the counsel of others concerning questionable areas of living.

B. Christian liberty involves edifying.

C. When dealing with questionable areas, it is equally important to properly understand both God and people.

D. A person's spiritual progress may be at stake dependent upon how we deal with questionable areas of living.

E. Our own lives may be at stake if we unnecessarily offend others in the area of Christian liberty.

F. Each Christian must come to definite resolves concerning edifying.

Chapter 5—Helping Your Self

A. Christian liberty involves doing what is beneficial.

B. Each Christian should understand the extent of his own rights and be prepared to defend those rights.

C. Each Christian should be prepared to yield his rights for the sake of expedience.

D. Each Christian must be able to distinguish between an area of liberty and an area of no-liberty.

Chapter 6—Preserving Your Freedom

A. Christian liberty involves preserving one's freedom.

B. Each Christian should preserve his liberty in order to freely give it to others.

C. There is a restriction to liberty involved in fostering inter-personal relationships for the purpose of evangelizing.

D. Self-discipline is a key to preserving one's liberty.

Chapter 7—Knowing The Facts

A. When a Christian misuses his liberty, his past or continued participation in church ordinances does not provide him with protection from the Lord's judgment.

B. The Lord gives a specific warning and a specific encouragement to those who exercise their Christian liberty.

C. Each Christian must have a good knowledge about the questionable activities in which he participates.

Chapter 8—Making Your Move

A. In order for a person to righteously exercise Christian liberty he must have proper priorities.

B. The principle of edification does not demand that a person absolutely forsake a given action or activity for the sake of another.

C. Each Christian should freely exercise his liberty unless someone expresses a "weak brother's" conviction.

D. The principles of Christian liberty have all-inclusive personal and all-inclusive public applications.

E. Practicing these principles of Christian liberty can become an asset to Christians in helping others.

F. An example to follow can be very helpful when learning to apply the principles of Christian liberty.

Chapter 9—*Striving For Unity*

A. It takes a basic commitment to the principles of Christian liberty in order to foster a unity among Christians concerning questionable areas of living.

B. Fostering a unity in Christian liberty liberates Christians to rejoice in their salvation.

C. In order to achieve a unity in Christian liberty, Christians must trust the Lord to work in the lives of their fellow believers.

Chapter 10—*Trusting The Lord*

A. Respect for the Lord should be the motivation for each Christian to either abstain or participate in questionable areas of living.

B. Each Christian will be judged by the Lord for the way that he has used his Christian liberty.

C. The Lord is able to give each Christian some very strong convictions regarding questionable areas of living.

Chapter 11—*Creating A Newness*

A. We possess creativity.

B. The Lord wants us to create novel things.

C. The Lord wants to transform our black culture.

D. Understanding The Times

E. A Provoking Proposition

The Process Of Implementation

Following are a sequence of questions which one can use as a guideline in working his way through a particular questionable issue. The chapter from which each question is drawn should be consulted if there is a need for further information and intensification of a particular point. This consultation is recommended inasmuch as this sequence of questions is mainly a starting point, and also inasmuch as remembrance and repetition are indispensable elements in the learning and reinforcement of learning processes.

1. What is the questionable issue? (Chapter 1)
2. What is the black cultural context of the questionable issue? (Chapter 1)
3. What is the black social context of the questionable issue? (Chapter 1)

155

4. What is the cross-cultural context of the questionable issue? (Chapter 1)
5. What is the Christian community context of the questionable issue? (Chapter 1)
6. Have you determined to put your confidence in and be guided by the foundational Scriptural teaching on the subject of Christian liberty? (Chapter 2)
7. Has the Bible been thoroughly searched and studied in order to determine if this questionable issue fits under the category of Christian liberty? (Chapter 3)
8. Have you done thorough research in order to learn as much as you can about this particular questionable issue? (Chapter 7)
9. Can, does and will this questionable issue build your neighbor? (Chapter 4)
10. Can, does and will this questionable issue help your *self*? (Chapter 5)
11. Can, does and will this questionable issue preserve your freedom? (Chapter 6)
12. How will this questionable issue be done with an attitude of trust in the Lord? (Chapter 10)
13. What things will you keep in mind when and if you make your move to do this questionable issue? (Chapter 8)
14. How can you use this questionable issue as a springboard in order to strive for unity among your group by fostering a basic commitment to the principles of Christian liberty? (Chapter 9)
15. In what way is this questionable issue provoking you to exercise more broadly your God-given creativity in an exciting, new, black way? (Chapter 11)
16. In what way are you prepared to pass along what you have learned about this questionable issue to your other black brothers and sisters? (Chapter 12)

QUESTIONS & SUGGESTIONS

As you have noticed, there are a number of questions and suggestions following each chapter. It is my desire that they will not be skimmed over, but used as an aid to utilizing this study.

Those items under the heading of *Understanding What Has Been Taught* are questions which should be useful for remembering the teaching of the various chapters. They deal mainly with apprehending the facts, and are therefore objective in nature. Their answers can usually (but not always) be found under the heading of *Elucidation.*

Those items under the heading of *Responding To And Applying What Has Been Learned* are questions and suggestions—leading the learner to foster a good attitude toward the discussion at hand, as well as prompting him to implement into his lifestyle, as best as he can, what he understands. The questions are mainly subjective and reflect to a large degree the *Concretization* of each chapter.

Both groups of questions can be easily used in the form of a test, and the suggestions can be taken on as weekly projects by individuals and groups. Neither of these sections should be viewed as exhaustive. For undoubtedly you may think of items of your own which will aid you and yours in understanding and living what this study has to offer.

SOME OVERALL SUGGESTIONS

1. Outline the book.
2. Compose a comprehensive definition of Christian liberty including the following elements:
   A. Our Christianity
   B. Our Ethnicity
   C. Our Intra-black cultural message
   D. Our Inter-black cultural message
   E. Questionable Areas
   F. Searching The Bible
   G. Liberty
   H. Edification
   I. Expedience
   J. Preservation of Freedom
   K. Knowing The Facts
   L. Making Your Move
   M. Striving For Unity
   N. Trusting The Lord
   O. Creating A Newness
   P. (Whatever you feel ought to belong!)
3. Compose diagrams and charts as aids to teaching this material.
4. Conduct a workshop or a retreat around this subject.
5. Reread the book.

Doing the above should sharpen your effectiveness as you seek to communicate and manifest to others what you have learned.

Summary & Conclusion

In this last chapter we have covered several areas that should prove useful to you in *assisting the learner.* These areas are: A. Instructing One Another; B. Checking It Out For Yourself; C. A Word On Forgiveness And Mercy; D. Review Of Lessons Learned; E. The Process Of Implementation; F. Questions & Suggestions; and G. Some Overall Suggestions.

Now in closing, to all those blessed Black Believers who have faithfully read these pages seeking Black Christian cultural and social freedom, let me exhortingly and genuinely say:

"—you then who teach others, will you not teach yourself?"
(Rom. 2:21a).

"Do your best to present yourself to God as one approved, a workman who has no need to be ashamed, rightly handling the word of truth" (2 Tim. 2:15).

"Pray for us, for we are sure that we have a clear conscience, desiring to act honourably in all things" (Heb. 13:18).

In the name of Jesus Christ, our Lord and Liberator, Amen!

The Lord Bless You!

Understanding What Has Been Taught

1. What are two prerequisites to instructing one another?

2. What are the five points of the guideline for evaluating Christian teachings?

3. Why does the Lord discipline his children?

4. How is the Lord's mercy expressed to us in view of our short-comings?

5. What is the nature of the questions and suggestions behind each chapter, and how can they be used?

6. What should be done if one needs a greater understanding when applying the "Process of Implementation"?

Responding To And Applying What Has Been Learned

Questions

1. In what ways do you consider yourself capable of instructing others?

2. Would you consider your conscience clear regarding questionable areas of living? Why? Why not?

3. In what areas and in what ways do you need to concentrate in order that you may gain a clear conscience?

4. Of all the principles, which ones stick out most in your mind? Why do you supposed these impressed you more than others?

5. Which of the principles do you think you should take more care to remember and observe? Why is this important for you to do?

Suggestions

Individual

1. Use the five principles under "Checking It Out For Yourself" as a basis for clearing up any confusion and questions that are on your mind as a result of reading this study.

2. Make yourself a schedule for reviewing one or more of the principles each week.

3. Follow the "Process of Implementation" to determine your response to a particular questionable issue.

Group

1. Conduct a group meeting around training teachers how to effectively teach Christian liberty to black students.

2. Plan a time for your group to present a creative presentation (drama? play? musical?) to another group (younger? older?) on the subject of Christian liberty.

APPENDIX 1

BLACK LIGHT
by Walter & Thelma McCray

I. We are "black..."
A. We were born this way!
B. We were created this way by God!
C. We appreciate our blackness!
   —We say, along with the woman of Shulem, "I am black and beautiful!" (Song of Solomon 1:5a; TEV Margin).

II. We are "...light"
—Jesus said, "As long as I am in the world, I am the light of the world" (Jn. 9:5).
—Jesus said, "I have come as light into the world, that whoever believes in me may not remain in darkness" (Jn. 12:46).
—Jesus said, "I am the light of the world; he who follows me will not walk in darkness, but will have the light of life" (Jn. 8:12).
A. We willingly and joyfully choose to follow Jesus who is our light, our life (Jn. 1:4).
B. And since we do follow him, he says to us, "You are the light of the world" (Mt. 5:14a).

Since we are a black light, then...
III. We are very visible
—Jesus said, "A city set on a hill cannot be hid" (Mt. 5:14b).
A. Our presence as black Christians cannot be hid because we are set on a hill by the Lord.
B. Our presence as black Christians is felt because of the white society in which we live.

IV. We are very unique and useful
A black light exposes and reveals things which are not ordinarily seen by a white light. We have a similar purpose as black Christians.
—Jesus said, "Nor do men light a lamp and put it under a bushel, but on a stand, and it gives light to all in the house" (Mt. 5:15).
A. The Lord has lit us, and put us as black Christians on a stand.
B. The Lord desires to use us to expose the sin—untruthfulness, wrongness and badness—that is not ordinarily seen by others.
C. The Lord desires to use us to reveal the righteousness—truthfulness, rightness, and goodness—that is not ordinarily seen by others.

V. We are determined to be an illustrious black light
—Jesus said, "Let your light *so shine* before men, that they may see your good works and give glory to your Father who is in heaven" (Mt. 5:16).
A. We must let our black light shine in such a way before others, that they will observe our lifestyle, our model, our "black light," and give God our Father the praise!

160

APPENDIX 2

OUTLINE OF 1 CORINTHIANS

I. Introduction 1:1-9
   A. Greeting 1-3
   B. Thanksgiving 4-9

II. The Report from Corinth 1:10-6:20
   A. Factionalism 1:10-4:21
   B. Incest 5:1-13
   C. Lawsuits 6:1-12a
   D. Fornication 6:12b-20

III. The Letter from Corinth 7:1-16:12
   A. Marrying & Marriage 7:1-24
   B. Virgins 7:25-40
   C. Food Offered to Idols 8:1-11:1
   D. The Church Meetings 11:2-34
   E. Spiritual Gifts 12:1-14:40
   F. The Resurrection 15:1-58
   G. The Collection & Paul's Plans 16:1-11
   H. Brother Apollos 16:12

IV. Conclusion 16:13-24
   A. Exhortations 13-18
   B. Greetings 19-22
   C. Benediction 23-24

1. A Perfect Preface 8:1-3
   a. The Emptiness of "knowledge" 1a, 2
   b. The Effects of Love 1b, 3

2. A Proper Perspective 8:4-13
   a. The Reality of God 4-6
      1) An Idol is Nothing 4a,5
      2) God is Everything 4b,6
   b. The Reasoning of People 7-13
      1) They Hold Differing Convictions 7-8
      2) They Draw Depthless and Damaging Conclusions 9-13

3. A Personal Policy 9:1-27
   a. The Sacrificed Support 1-18
      1) The Basis & Nature of the Support 1-6
      2) The Defense for & Denial of the Support 7-15
      3) The Restriction & Reward of Sacrifice 16-18
   b. The Saving Slave 19-23
      1) His Self-imposed Service 19
      2) His Several Relationships 20-22
      3) His Share in the Gospel 23
   c. The Subduing Self-discipline 24-27
      1) Its Motivation 24
      2) Its Preparation 25
      3) Its Concentration 26-27

4. A Precautioning Precedent 10:1-22
   a. The Precedent of Israel 1-13
      1) Their Participation 1-4
      2) Their Disqualification 5-10
      3) Their Summation 11-13
   b. The Precaution Against Idolatry 14-22
      1) The Prohibition 14
      2) The Explanation 15-18
      3) The Implications 19-22

5. A Practical Procedure 10:23-30
   a. The Primary Consideration 23-24
   b. The Particular Circumstances 25-30
      1) In the Place of Marketing 25-26
      2) At a Private Meal 27-30

6. A Profound Pronouncement 10:31-11:1
   a. The Praise to God 10:31
   b. The Profit for Men 10:32-33
   c. The Pattern of Paul 11:1

APPENDIX 3

OUTLINE OF ROMANS

I. Introduction 1:1-17
   A. Greeting 1:1-7
   B. Prayer & Desire 1:8-15
   C. Theme 1:16-17

II. Salvation Through the Gospel 1:18-11:36
   A. The Salvation of All People in General 1:18-8:39
   B. The Salvation of the Israelites in Particular 9:1-11:36

III. The Lifestyle of the Righteous 12:1-15:13
   A. A Living Sacrifice 12:1-2
   B. Personal Living: Gifts & Godliness 12:3-21
   C. Community Living: Government & Neighbors 13:1-14
   D. Church Living: Liberty, Edification, & Unity 14:1-15:13

IV. Conclusion 15:14-16:27
   A. Paul's Ministry 15:14-33
   B. Sister Phoebe 16:1-2
   C. Greetings to Paul's Friends 16:3-16
   D. Exhortations 16:17-20
   E. Greetings from Paul's Companions 16:21-23, (24)
   F. Doxology 16:25-27

APPENDIX 4

BACKGROUND TO THE BOOK OF 1 CORINTHIANS

Corinth was a city of ancient Greece. It was located at the southern end of Greece on the Isthmus of Corinth—a narrow strip of land bordered by the gulf of Corinth on the west and by the Saronic gulf on the east. It had two seaports, Cenchrea on the east and Lechaeum on the west, and being thus situated, it was in control of the land route between north and south, and the sea route between east and west—the Aegean and Ionian seas. At times the city suffered devasting earthquakes.

The Corinth of the N.T. was a relatively new city, having been totally destroyed and prohibited from being rebuilt, by the Roman general L. Mummius Achaicus. It was not rebuilt until 46 B.C. by Julius Caesar, who founded it as a Roman colony. In 27 B.C. it became the capital of the Roman province of Achaia (that is, Greece), and the seat of the governor.

The population of Corinth, approximately 500,000, was truly cosmopolitan. Its inhabitants, who came from all levels of society, included *Romans*—who were freedmen from Italy, and government officials and businessmen (these were the only actual "citizens" of the city); *Greeks*—who came to the city from the surrounding province; *Orientals*—which group included a large number of *Jews,* those who came to the city in order to make money, and those who were banished from Rome by the antiJewish legislation of Claudius; and many many *transients* from all over.

Corinth has been called the "first and worst" city of southern Greece. It was famed for its luxury, wealth, materialism, commerce, trade, art, vice, immorality, and notorious corruption. To "Corinthianize" was a euphemism for "to practice immorality." The temple of the Greek goddess Aphrodite, located on a plateau of the 1,857 foot high Acrocorinth of the old city, was known at one time to have 1,000 prostitutes called "sacred slaves." And this immoral atmosphere was definitely prevalent in the new city. Often the Greek plays portrayed the Corinthians as drunkards. The city was known throughout the world for its many taverns, houses of prostitutions, and gambling places. For a nitty gritty description of Corinth, one can read Rom. 1:18-32. Paul wrote these verses after spending about two years experiencing the city.

Corinth made much of its wealth from its strategic location. The city was able to charge tolls on both land and sea merchandise. Sometimes small ships were transported across the Isthmus on a tramway with wooden rails. And the goods on those ships, and others, were taken from one side to the other by ox-cart. This provided the city with a good revenue. Also, the many travelers who frequented the city provided a steady market for the goods which they manufactured and sold.

Although Corinth was known for its lack of literary creativity, it did produce several statesmen, and archaeology has confirmed that the city was a master in art and architecture. This included bronze work, sculpture, paintings, columns and pillars. Their art and architecture were inspired by athletics, religion, and Greek life.

Some of Corinth's major trades were shipping and shipbuilding, metallurgy, pottery, farming, shopkeeping, construction, and leatherwork.

The city itself had numerous public buildings and a comparable administration. It was the seat of the proconsul Gallio before whom Paul was tried. Its courts were strict but just. Corinth also presided over the famed Isthmian games, which games were second only to the Olympics. The games were held every two years in a stadium located near the city, and they were dedicated to the god Poseidon. They were very well attended, and the athletes prepared far in advance for their respective events. Those events included beast fighting, boxing, discus throwing, foot racing, and wrestling. There were also some other contests of lesser importance.

Among some of the ruins which have been located in Corinth are the *AGORA* or "market place", the site of the public assembly, where the people went shopping in the "meat market" (*MAKELLON*), and which also served as the place of the proconsul's judgment seat, the *BĒMA*. The temple of Apollo has been uncovered, and there is also a sanctuary of Asclepius, the god of healing. A few famous fountains which supplied the city with water have been located, as well as the amphitheater (which seated 18,000) and the Odeon or music hall. Several basilicas have also been uncovered.

The religious environment of Corinth at the time of Paul included Graeco-Oriental religions, the Graeco-Roman Pantheon, religious philosophies, and emperor worship.

Such was the city to which Paul brought the Gospel.

The primary information about Paul's dealing with the church of Corinth can be found in Acts 18. During Paul's second missionary tour he decided to stop at Corinth (c. 50 A.D.) after preaching the Gospel in Berea and Athens (Acts 17:10ff.). While in the city he provided for his own expenses through his trade of tentmaking, along with Aquila and Priscilla, while he stayed with them (Acts 18:2-3). He carried on his preaching ministry in the synagogue and was subsequently strengthened in that work with the arrival of Silas and Timothy (Acts 18:4,5). After facing much Jewish opposition to his message, he separated from the synagogue and began teaching in the home of Titus Justus. Many people were saved through this ministry, including the synagogue ruler Crispus (Acts 18:6-8). Through a vision the Lord encouraged Paul to continue his ministry. This assurance evidently led him to stay in Corinth for the period of over 18 months (Acts 18:9-11,18).

When Gallio became proconsul, the troublesome Jews mounted a united attack against Paul. But Gallio threw the case out of court. Paul then continued to stay in the city until he set sail for Ephesus after stopping in Cenchrae (Acts 18:12ff.).

The membership of the church which Paul founded in Corinth was quite large (Acts 18:8). Many of the members took on some of the characteristics of the city itself (cf. 1 Cor. 1:26-27; 1 Cor. 6:9-11). As a result of their ungodly lifestyles, Paul had to deal with a number of different problems which arose in the church. And in dealing with those problems, his relationship to this church at times became very strained. During the period after his founding of the church (between 52 A.D. and 57 A.D.) there is evidence of at least two other visits which Paul paid to them. There is also evidence of four letters which he wrote to them. We have two of the four letters. We have the second letter, our 1 Corinthians, and the fourth letter, our 2 Corinthians.

Our study on the subject of Christian liberty concerns us with 1 Corinthians. The circumstances which prompted Paul to write this letter seem to have been two-fold. First, Paul had heard from some of the members of a Chloe's household that there were some serious divisions within the church (1 Cor. 1:10ff.). Factions were being built around the church leaders. And second, the Corinthians desired to question Paul about some instructions which he had written to them in his first letter (cf. 1 Cor. 5:9ff.). So they wrote Paul a letter in response to his first letter, and sent it to him (while he was in Ephesus, 1 Cor. 16:8-9) by a few brothers; probably by Stephanas, Fortunatus and Achaicus (1 Cor. 16:17). In their letter they asked Paul to clarify himself (cf. 1 Cor. 7:1; 8:1; etc.). The three messengers who brought the letter to Paul also informed him about the outrageous immorality and ungodly legal proceedings that were taking place at the church (1 Cor. 5-6). Therefore Paul wrote First Corinthians to straighten out the divisions, correct the special problems, and clarify his previous instructions. (See Appendix 2 for a glimpse of the contents of the book.) One of the situations which Paul addressed in this letter was "food offered to idols" (8:1ff.). His dealing with this subject is a primary basis for the study in this book.

It is sad to say, but by the end of the first century (97 A.D.) there is evidence that the church at Corinth was still plagued by many of the same problems which Paul had sought to correct. In forty years time they had not sincerely heeded the voice of God speaking through Paul. They had not become "spiritual" (1 Cor. 3:1).[1]

APPENDIX 5

BIBLE STUDY GUIDE SHEET
by Walter & Thelma McCray

I. *Relating to the Lord & Liberator Involves:*
   A. Understanding Him
   B. Worshiping Him
   C. Obeying Him
   D. Trusting Him
   E. Thanking Him

II. *A Good Example to Follow is Given in Ezra 7:10:*
   Ezra the scribe *prepared his heart*
   A. *To seek* the law of the Lord
   B. *To do* it, and
   C. *To teach* it . . .

III. *These are Five Ways In Which We Can Come to Understand the Word:*
   A. Hearing it—Jms. 1:19-20; Rom. 10:17; Mt. 11:15
   B. Reading it—Rev. 1:3; Deut. 17:18-19; 1 Tim. 4:13
   C. Studying it—Acts 17:11; 2 Tim. 2:15
   D. Memorizing it—Ps. 119:9,11; Prov. 7:1-3
   E. Meditating on it—Ps. 1:2; Josh. 1:8; 1 Tim. 4:15

IV. *Some Key Questions for Probing a Passage of Scripture are:*
   A. What does it say? (Facts: people, place, events, actions, ideas, etc.)
   B. What does it mean? (What was the writer trying to get across to his readers?)
   C. What does it teach? (about Jesus, liberation, justice, oppression, identity, unity, etc.)
   D. How can I apply this to my life?
      1. What are its implications for me as a black person?
      2. What are its implications for black people?
      3. Etc.

V. *Here is the Needful Background Information for a Bible Book Study:*
   A. The Author
   B. The Readers
   C. The Origin (Place where it was written from.)
   D. The Destination (Place where it was to be received.)
   E. The Circumstances that prompted the writing.
   F. The Purpose of the Book.
   G. The Kind of Literature (history, poetry, gospel, epistle, apocalyptic, etc.)
   H. An Outline of the Book.

VI. *Some Basic Bible Study Tools are:*
   A. Other Bible translations
   B. A Concordance
   C. A Bible Dictionary
   D. A Regular Dictionary
   E. A Bible Handbook
   F. A Bible Atlas
   G. A Bible Commentary

VII. *A Notebook is useful for:*
   A. Recording the fruits of your study.
   B. Recording what the Lord leads you to do.

VIII. *Praying about what you have learned involves:*
   A. Confession & Repentance
   B. Praise & Thanksgiving
   C. Worship & Adoration
   D. Intercession & Petition
   E. Meditation & Consecration

APPENDIX 6

OUR FINANCIAL POLICY

I. Our goal is to ultimately become financially self-supporting in our ministry. We would like to accomplish this goal by earning part of our living expenses through both:

   A. Direct ministries to primarily black churches, Christian groups, and organizations. (This would involve preaching, teaching, speaking, and assisting.)

and

   B. Indirect ministries to black individuals, churches, groups, and organizations. (This would involve developing and producing black Christian educational materials.)

II. While we are at this time seeking the attainment of our goal, and since our ministry is primarily within and for the black community, we are open to accepting gifts from both:

   A. Black Christians

and

   B. Black Christian churches, organizations, and groups inclusively.

Adopted by Walter & Thelma McCray on 12/30/76; revised 12/30/77

APPENDIX 7

A COMPARISON OF
1 CORINTHIANS 9:19-23 AND 1 CORINTHIANS 10:31-33

1 Corinthians 9:19-23	1 Corinthians 10:31-33
For though I am free from all men, I have made myself a slave to all,	So, whether you eat or drink, or whatever you do,
that I might win the more.	do all to the glory of God.
. . .I became. . .	Give no offense
To the Jews. . .as a Jew, in order to win Jews;	to Jews
to those under the law. . as one under the law. . . that I might win those under the law.	
To those outside the law. . .as one outside the law. . .that I might win those outside the law.	or to Greeks
To the weak. . .weak, that I might win the weak.	or to the church of God,
I have become all things to all men,	just as I try to please all men in everything I do,
that I might by all means save some.	not seeking my own advantage,
I do it all for the sake of the gospel, that I may share in its blessings.	but that of the many, that they may be saved.

APPENDIX 8

HOW WE PREFER TO VIEW OUR MINISTRY

Our ministry is one which is primarily within and for the black community. We believe that the Gospel is universal in its scope and blessings. We also believe (in accord with the command of our Lord to proclaim this universal message, Mt. 28:18-20) that the Lord has called us to the work of showing the pertinence and implications of the Gospel to the black community in particular.

We realize that we have not "arrived" as far as totally comprehending the entire Bible message. Neither have we "arrived" in fully understanding our own black people. But we are committed to, and expectant that the Lord will give us, a deeper awareness of Himself and black people, so that we will be better able to do our own part in achieving our total liberation in the name of Jesus Christ the Lord.

Therefore, in our ministry we endeavor as much as we can to address the needs, desires, and goals of black people, using the Word of God as our trusted foundation. We desire to joyfully serve in this capacity, and trust that our ministry will redound to the glory of God.

Adopted by Walter & Thelma McCray 5/3/77

APPENDIX 9

BACKGROUND TO THE BOOK OF ROMANS

It was to the church in the well-known city, said to be founded in 753 B.C. by the Etruscans, on the left bank of the Liber river, 16 miles from the Tyrrhenian Sea in west central Italy; in the city which became a republic (510 B.C.) and later, the capital of a world empire—an empire that was the creation of a self-governing people over an extended period of many centuries—; in the city of the Emperor, the Senate, the Forum, the Governors, and the Provinces; in the city which in Paul's time had a cosmopolitan population of approximately 1,200,000 people of which about half were slaves, and the majority of the rest were paupers supported in idleness by the free distribution of food; in the city whose efficient administration, military control, and system of roads made the spread of Christianity swift and safe; in the city which was known for its numerous laws and religious confusion; in the city of wealth, vice, extortion, opportunity and entertainment; in the city of great baths, columns, arches, and the Colosseum; in the city of architecture, temples, a famous library and shrine; in the city of the cruel inequalities upon the poor, of the underpriviledged, and of the inhumane; in the city which had dangers of fire, dangers of traffic, and dangers of assault and battery; in the city of over-crowded huge slum tenement houses, and mansions of senators, aristocrats, and "knights" who were businessmen and tax farmers; in the city of taxes, and publicans who exploited the people and the government; in the city of magnificense and squalor; in the city that became an image of carnal organized paganism; and in the city of much more—; it was to the church in this city, the city of Rome, to which Paul wrote one of his most profound letters, the book of Romans.

Paul wrote the book of Romans from Corinth in the period of 56-57 A.D. He wrote it at the end of his third missionary campaign during a three month stay in Greece (Acts 20:1-3). During this time Gaius was his host, Tertius was his secretary and Phoebe was most likely his messenger (Rom. 16:1-2, 22-23; 1 Cor. 1:14). Unlike the church at Corinth, the church at Rome was not founded by Paul. Matter of fact, even though Paul held Roman citizenship he had never been to the capital city (Rom. 1:15). The question which then arises is this: How did the church at Rome get started?

There are several explanations offered on the origin of the Roman church. First, some have suggested that the Jewish "visitors from Rome" on the day of Pentecost were the one's who took the Gospel back to the capital city (Acts 2:10,41). While this explanation is possible it does not account for the fact that the Roman church was composed of mostly Gentiles, and that this church had its own community life apart from the Jewish community in Rome. Second, some have suggested that Peter was the founder of the church at Rome, but there is no Bible evidence to support the explanation that Peter made a visit at an earlier date (earlier than the time that he was martyred) to that city. Furthermore, although Paul sees fit to note two men who are held in high esteem as apostles, he does not mention Peter at all (Rom. 16:7). And it would have been odd for him not to have mentioned Peter if Peter had founded the church. It would have also been strange for Paul to break his policy of not building on "another man's foundation" (Rom. 15:20) if indeed Peter was the founder of the church. It seems to me that the best explanation as to how the church at Rome got started is this. It got going from the witness of people from Rome whom Paul had met (cf. Acts 18:2,3) or converted on his missionary campaigns. A reading of Romans 16 will quickly reveal that Paul personally knew a number of the people in this church; he also knew of at least five different church groups; he had converted some of the people in this church (16:5); and he had recommended some people to this church (16:1-2; Acts 18:18). This evidence seems to point to the validity of this third explanation for the origin of the church at Rome.

When Paul wrote to this church it was fairly well an established body. Their faith was known throughout all the world (Rom. 1:8), and their obedience was similarly known (Rom. 16:19). And although they had some problem areas (Rom. 12:1-15:13; 16:17-18) they were still mature enough to instruct one another (Rom. 15:14). The church was cosmopolitan in membership, just like Rome itself, but there were evidently more Gentiles than Jews in the fellowship (Rom. 1:13; 15:16). Some of the members were kinsmen and past workers of Paul (Rom. 16:3,7). This church carried on its own existence apart from the well established Jewish colony at Rome, and most of the members were not Romans or were either just recently enfranchised (cf. Rom. 13:1ff.— these taxes and powers were exercised over non-Romans in particular).

There are several reasons that can be suggested as indications of why Paul wrote this letter. First, Paul did not have room for any more work in the areas where he had already been evangelizing. Therefore he wanted to go to Spain to continue his work (Rom. 15:19, 23-24). He most likely wanted the church at Rome to be his base of operation (just as the church at Antioch of Syria had been his base on his previous missionary endeavors (cf. Acts 13:1ff.; 14:26)). He wanted the church at Rome to support him in his work (Rom. 15:24, 28, 32). Second, Paul wanted to lay before the church at Rome the Gospel which he had been preaching. In previous years there had been some speculation and suspicions about Paul's ministry to the Gentiles. Paul therefore wanted the church at Rome to have a well-rounded view of his Gospel. Hence, there is a heavy emphasis in this letter on several major doctrines (Rom. 1-11). (He may also have wanted the Church in the capital city to have a good understanding of his message so that the church's influence might become more effective.) In the meantime, before coming to Rome, he was going to Jerusalem. It was at Jerusalem that he had at first received a vision from the Lord to go and preach to the Gentiles (Acts 22:17-21). He would now go to Jerusalem in order to present his "offering" of the Gentiles to the Lord. He would give an account of his ministry to the

Lord (Rom. 15:15-16). He would also have a second offering to give at Jerusalem. This offering was some financial assistance from the Gentiles to the "poor among the saints at Jerusalem" (Rom. 15:26). The third reason why Paul wrote this letter is this. He had heard (probably from some of his numerous contacts in this church) that the Roman Christians were experiencing some practical problems. Thus, they were in need of "some spiritual gift" to strengthen them (Rom. 1:11; 16:25). Hence, Paul gives them some very practical instruction on several issues (12:1-15:13). (See Appendix 3 for a glimpse of these issues.) Among Paul's instructions to them was some teaching on the subject of Christian liberty (14:1-15:13); which teaching has been used as a basis for this study.

Paul had intended to make only a "passing" visit to the church at Rome (15:24), but he ended up making a long visit. He was escorted to Rome (in about 61 A.D.) as a political prisoner (Acts 25:1-12; 28:14bff.). During this time in Rome Paul had the freedom to preach the Gospel openly (Acts 28:30-31). This evidently strengthened the church in this city very much.

In later years the church in Rome became a thriving church. Matter of fact, it became so thriving that its nature as a separate institution ordained by the Lord was co-opted into the Roman empire. It became a tool of the state and a propagator of some grave doctrinal errors. The letter (or treatise) by Paul to this church, if it had been cherished, could have been instrumental in keeping this church on the right course.[2]

NOTES

1. "Adiaphora" comes from a Greek word meaning "indifferent."
   "Adiaphorous" means that something is "morally neutral or indifferent;
   neither right nor wrong; doing neither good nor harm."
   "Adiaphorism" generally means "the tolerance by the Church of actions
   not specifically prohibited by the Scriptures."

   The adiaphora issue has occurred quite frequently in the history of
   Christianity. One occasion was in the sixteenth century in Germany
   where there was a major dispute over this subject. It involved some
   concessions which a theologian, a Philip Melanchthon, made to Rome
   under the concept of adiaphora. This happened when Charles V was
   king of France. Melanchthon and his followers, who were known as
   the "adiaphorists" were opposed by a Matthias Flacius and his
   followers for making these concessions which they deemed were not in
   accord with Reformation teachings. It is said that this Flacius saved
   the Reformation because of his actions.

   Below are two similar conceptions of the adiaphora:

   A. "It can concern actions that are indifferent (neither bad nor good,
   being neither commanded nor forbidden by God), ceremonies (neither
   forbidden nor commanded so they may be used or discarded), and
   doctrines (although taught in the Word of God, they are of such minor
   importance that they may be disbelieved without injury to the faith)."
   The New International Dictionary of the Christian Church, (1974),
   s.v. "Adiaphorist," by Robert G. Clouse.

   B. "Adiaphorists may teach: (1) that certain actions are indifferent
   because they are neither commanded nor forbidden by God and can
   be done or not at pleasure; (2) that certain rites and ceremonies may
   be admitted to the church or not for the same reason; (3) that certain
   doctrines are of minor importance and may be taught or denied
   without injuring the foundations of faith."
   Baker's Dictionary of Theology, (1960), s.v. "Adiaphora," by
   Alexander M.Renwick.

2. *The American College Dictionary*, (1966) s.v. "Principle." Given this
   general meaning, "principle" as used in this study will specifically
   refer to:
   A. "A fundamental, primary, or general truth on which other truths
   depend."
   B. "Right rules of conduct."
   C. "The method of formation, operation, or procedure exhibited in a
   given case."

3. On "survival" see (38) NBCSC, and (50) Williams in bibliography.

4. Reference (10) Bentley in bibliography.

5. "Christocentric Black-Ethnicism" comes from the exegesis and application of Mt. 28:19 to Black people. It means a "Christ-centered Black Nation." I first used it in an essay written by myself for the National Black Christian Students Conference. See (37) in bibliography.

6. See a developing philosophy on being Black and Christian—"Black Light"—by my wife and Me, in Appendix 1.

Chapter 2

1. Frederick Douglass said in an 1852 Independence Day speech: "Go where you may, search where you will, roam through all the monarchies and despotisms of the Old World, travel through South America, search out every abuse and when you have found the last, lay your facts by the side of the everyday practices of this nation, and you will say with me that, for revolting barbarity and shameless hypocrisy, America reigns without a rival."

   Frederick Douglass, "What To The Slaves Is The Fourth Of July?: Frederick Douglass' Independence Day Address (1852)," in *The Negro Almanac,* comp. and ed. by Harry A. Ploski and Roscoe C. Brown Jr. (New York: Bellwether Publishing Co. Inc., 1967), p. 90.

   And consider this comment:

   "Any people who could endure all of that brutalization and keep together, who could undergo such dismemberment and resuscitate itself, and endure until it could take the initiative in achieving its own freedom is obviously more than the sum of its brutalization. Seen in this perspective, theirs has been one of the great human experiences and one of the great triumphs of the human spirit in modern times, in fact, in the history of the world."

   Ralph Ellison, as quoted in Lerone Bennett Jr., *The Shaping of Black America* (Chicago: Johnson Publishing Company, Inc., 1975), p. 166.

2. Reference (11) Bentley in bibliography.

3. On the subject of black liberation see: *Toward A Holistic Liberation Of Black People: Its Meaning As Expressed In The Objectives Of The National Black Christian Students Conference.* See (37) McCray in bibliography.

4. See Appendices 2 & 3 for outlines of the books of 1 Corinthians and Romans.

5. There are several other verses on this subject of Christian liberty. Some of these are: Gal. 4:8-11; 5:1, 13-15; Col. 2:16-18, 20-23; Acts 15:20, 29; Rev. 2:14ff., 20ff.; Mk. 7:14-23; 1 Tim. 4:1ff.

There is a marked difference in Paul's (and John's) tone and manner of dealing with this subject in some of the above passages, and Paul's tone and manner of dealing with the problem as expressed in 1 Corinthians and Romans. When looking at these passages, it would be well to keep their historical context in mind. In *Galatians,* Paul was combating, in the person of the Judiazers, the false doctrine of legalism; that is, being subject to the law as a means of gaining perfection. The Judiazers tied questionable areas of living to a Christian's sanctification. They were binding the believers in legalistic actions. They were enslaving them in bondage to the "elemental spirits of the universe" (4:2). Since this teaching was contrary to the faith, Paul's refutation of it (and the questionable areas also, because of their close association with this teaching) is done with severity. Interpreting Paul's remarks in this light is helpful. A similar problem to that of the Galatian's was manifested in the book of *Acts chapter 15.* There the Judiazers were denying that a Gentile could become a Christian, unless he first became a Jew. Paul fought against this erroneous teaching also. And when it was finally decided by the Church that the Gentiles were justified by faith, and not by the works of the law, just as the Jews were justified, then Paul encouraged his Gentile converts (the ones of Antioch, Syria, and Celicia) to observe Jewish regulations when in Asia Minor. These regulations dealt with Jewish food laws and marriage laws. This was not a compromise by Paul, but a means of dealing with questionable areas (as we will see through this study). *In Colossians* Paul was fighting against another false doctrine, "the Colossian heresy." This doctrine had gnosticising tendencies which resulted in a dualistic approach to life. The spiritual was good and the material was evil. Some of the Christians became ascetics, thus abstaining from participating in many questionable issues altogether. This heresy also led to a degrading of Christ's pre-eminence. The people began to worship angels. Paul sought to root out this false teaching, and in doing so dealt with questionable issues in what may be perceived as a more or less laxed manner. *In Revelation* John the apostle is dealing with the Imperial cult of Rome, and also dealing with visiting pagan temples for feasts and possibly trade-guild affairs, which affairs ended up in licentiousness. During this time the Christians were being tempted to deny Jesus and to confess Caesar. The people were also being tempted to commit fornication with the pagan-temple prostitutes. Therefore in both contexts of Rev. 2, immorality is mentioned alongside the questionable issue of eating meat that had been offered to idols. It was sin for the Christians to participate in such activities as mentioned above. Therefore, Jesus, through John, absolutely forbids these actions and warns the Christians of impending judgment.

6. See articles in:

> *The Zondervan Pictorial Encyclopedia of the Bible,* (1975), s.v. "Gnosticism," by A.F. Walls. (Hereafter referred to as *ZPEB.*)

> *The New Bible Dictionary,* 1st ed. (1962), s.v. "Gnosticism," by A.F. Walls. (Hereafter referred to as *NBD.*)

7. Greek: *EXOUSIA* "authority," "right." (translated "liberty" in 8:9)

> *ELEUTHERIA* "freedom," "liberty."
> *ELEUTHEROS* "free," "free person," "independent."
> *EXESTI* "proper," "permitted," "lawful."

8. Greek: "helpful" from the word *SUMPHERŌ* "to bring together."

> "mastered" from the word *EXOUSIAZŌ* "to exercise authority."
> "build up" from the word *OIKODOMEŌ* "to build a house."

9. The author is grateful for beginning to comprehend the application (in the book of 1 Corinthians) of these three principles through the:

> *Corinthian Correspondence,* course with Dr. Gilbert Bilezikian, Trinity College, Deerfield, Illinois, 2nd Semester, 1973-74.

10. See Appendix 4 for the background to the book of 1 Corinthians.

Chapter 3

1. The Corinthians could have looked to the Jews as an example. For during this time period the Jews had a legal system of their own, and they would not go to the Gentiles in order to obtain justice. There were also Greek and Roman social groups who tried their own cases. See:

> G.G. Findlay, *St. Paul's First Epistle to The Corinthians,* vol. 2 of *The Expositor's Greek Testament,* ed. W. Robertson Nicoll, 5 vols. (Grand Rapids: Eerdmans Publishing Co., 1970), p. 81. (Hereafter referred to as *First Corinthians.*)

> C.K. Barrett, *The First Epistle To The Corinthians* (New York: Harper & Row, 1968), p. 137-138. (Hereafter referred to as *First Corinthians.*)

2. Concerning this point, there is a definite relationship between these words:

> "wrong" *ADIKEŌ* verses 7 and 8

> "unrighteous" *ADIKOS* verse 9 (and also verse 1).

3. Corinth had many public buildings and a good administration. It was the seat of the Governor and the Proconsul. The court was held in the *AGORA* or "market place," and this is where Gallio (the Roman Proconsul) had his *BĒMA* or "judgment seat." There were special days

for court business, and the proceedings were very strict, though just. A Roman citizen had the right to be heard before a Roman court, and he also had the right to appeal to Caesar.

ZPEB, s.v. "Courts, Judicial," by G. L. Archer.

4. It should be noted that Paul is not talking about a case between a Christian and a non-Christian. This is a different matter. It may indeed be beneficial at times for a Christian to use the civil court system (put in existence by God for the purpose of protecting unbelievers from oppressing one another, and from oppressing Christians) when in dispute with an unbeliever. Cf. Paul's defense in Acts 24:10-25:12.

5. "The temple of Aphrodite on Acrocorinth [a hill that overlooked the city] was unique in Greece. Its priestesses were more than a thousand HIERODOULOI, 'sacred slaves,' who engaged in prostitution." "To live as a Corinthian" meant to live in "luxury and immorality." "To Corinthianize" meant to "practice fornication." "A Corinthian girl" was a prostitute. Corinth was far worse than its contemporary large cities. Rom. 1:21-32 was written from Corinth by Paul after living in the city for over 1½ years. See:

ZPEB, s.v. "Corinth," by A. Rupprecht.

6. W.E. Vine, *An Expository Dictionary of New Testament Words*, (1966), s.v. "Know."

7. See Appendix 5 for a Bible Study Guide Sheet.

Chapter 4

1. *SKANDALIZŌ*, "to ensnare," "to offend." (See Note 5 below.)

2. This would not have been the case with every Christian in Corinth. For instance, the Jews, who were a part of this church, would not have been "accustomed" to idols. Idolatry was just as heinous to Jewish beliefs as it was to Christian beliefs.

3. Below is a common invitation to a banquet which was given in the city of Corinth: "Chaeremon invites you to dinner at the table of the lord Serapis (the name of the deity) in the Serapeum tomorrow the 15th at 9 o'clock."

Deissman, *Light From The Ancient East*, p. 351, as quoted in the *NBD*, s.v. "Idols, Meats Offered To," by R.P. Martin.

The International Standard Bible Encyclopedia, (1939), s.v. "Table," by Burton Scott Easton. (Hereafter referred to as *ISBE*.)

4. *OIKODOMEŌ* "to build a house," hence, to build anything.

5. "Destroyed"   *APOLLUMI*   "to destroy utterly,"
                              "to ruin," "a loss of
                              well being."
   "Sin"   *HAMARTANŌ* "to miss the mark."
   "Wound"   *TUPTŌ*   "a blow," "to smite,
                              strike, or beat."
   "Fall"   *SKANDALIZŌ* "to put a snare or trap
                              or stumbling block in
                              the way."

6. One should notice how Paul goes from the specific to the general.
   "Food offered   *EIDŌLOTHUTON*   verses 1,4,7, and 10
   to idols"
   "food"   *BRŌMA*   verses 8, 13
   "meat"   *KREAS*   verse 13

7. This is shown by the use of the double negative *OUMĒ*, expressing an emphatic prohibition or denial.

8. See articles, "The Black Christian Student and Interracial Male-Female Relationships," "Interracial Dating," and "Understanding and Resolving Black Man-Black Woman Conflicts," (Chaps. 7-9) in the *Handbook For Black Christian Students*. See Bentley (9) in bibliography.

Chapter 5

1. The Greek for this phrase is *ADELPHĒN GUNAIKA* meaning, "a sister as a wife." That is, a Christian wife.

2. *EXOUSIA* "authority"

3. See note 1.

4. On the meaning of the gospel and commitment to it see, Mk. 8:34-38; 10:29-30; Acts 4:12; Rom. 1:13-17, and 2 Cor. 4:13-15.

5. Martin Weston, "Conquering Razor Bumps," *Ebony*, March 1976, p. 54.

6. See Acts 22:22-29 for another example of Paul using his rights as a Roman citizen. He probably expressed his rights in advance of this beating because it was far graver than the other beatings which he had experienced (at the hands of Jews and Romans). This beating might have taken his life, or even crippled him for life.
   F.F. Bruce, *The Book Of The Acts* (Grand Rapids:Eerdmans Publishing Co., 1971), p. 445. (Hereafter referred to as *Acts.*)

7. On this point consider the following quote:
   "That this idea [the "3/5th compromise"] has never completely died out is seen both in the way in which enfranchisement of the Negro in the South (and in certain locations in the North) has been stedfastly resisted even to the use of illegal strategems designed to circumvent the declared statements of the Constitution and the Bill of Rights, and in the even more striking fact that today, over one hundred years after the Emancipation Proclamation, and the subsequent passage of the 13th, 14th, and 15th amendments, at least up to and through the 1960's, Congress is still having to pass laws which, on the premise that black Americans were entitled to the same rights and privileges as all others, should be regarded as superfluous!"

   William H. Bentley, "The Meaning Of History For Black Americans," an unpublished paper.

8. *Webster's New World Dictionary,* College ed. (1968), s.v. "Opportunism."

9. See Appendix 6 for our Financial Policy Statement.

10. These "wild parties" are the kinds of affairs where there is heavy drinking, sex, licentiousness, and lusts. These things and more are suggested by the following words in 1 Pet. 4:3-4:

"licentiousness"	*ASELGEIAI*	"lasciviousness, excesses, open outrages against decency."
"passions"	*EPITHUMIA*	"lusts, passions."
"drunkenness"	*OINOPHLUGIAI*	"overflowings of wine, occasions of debauchery."
"revels"	*KOMŌS*	"revellings."
"carousing"	*POTOI*	"drinking parties."
"wild profligacy"	*ASŌTIA*	"an overflowing or pouring out of prodigality or wastefulness."

Chapter 6

1. It is very unfortunate (and not without mutual understanding) that the concept and term "slave"—which acutely expresses the meaning of the Greek word *DOULOŌ* in verse 9:19—has become so reprehensible to black folks, and this is because of the inhumane and ungodly oppressiveness of whites upon blacks (here and abroad). It

is my hope that the use of this title will not be a deterrence to understanding this passage. We share mutual empathy.

2. *NBD*, s.v. "Proselyte," by R.A. Stewart.

3. Actually, Paul goes one step further in his analysis in this verse. He does not so much make a distinction between the nationality and the religion, as he does between the signs of the religion (manifested in the culture) and the true religion itself (manifested in the heart).

4. See the similar problem of the Christians addressed in the book of Hebrews, who were apparently lapsing back into Judaism, Heb. 10:26ff.; 12:18ff.

5. See Appendix 7 for an interesting comparison of 1 Cor. 9:19-23 and 1 Cor. 10:31-33.

6. There were 4 kinds of Greek games; Pythian, Nemean, Isthmian, and Olympian. The Isthmian games, held on the Isthmus of Corinth, were second in importance only to the Olympics. The city of Corinth presided over these games.

7. Some events that took place at the Isthmian games were, beast fighting, boxing, footracing, discus throwing and wrestling.
   ISBE, s.v. "Games," by William Taylor Smith.

8. The words "receive" and "obtain" in verse 9:24 are represented by similar Greek words:
   "receive"   *LAMBANŌ*
   "obtain"   *KATALAMBANŌ*   (a strengthened form of the above meaning; it is intensified.)

9. Paul's use of the word "preached" (*KERUSSŌ*) may suggest that he has the herald (*KĒRUX*) at the Isthmian games in mind. The herald "proclaimed the rules of the contest and (called) the competitors together." It would then be a shame if the herald himself were "disqualified" (*ADOKIMOS*).

10. A Black Christian brother has written a book in which every aspect of black dating is treated and critiqued. For contact information see (2) Porter in special note, bibliography.

11. Consider the purpose of the Israelites being set free from Egypt: "Let my son go that he may serve me" Ex. 4:23; cf. 7:16; 8:1,20; 9:1,13; 10:3,7-8, 11, 24, 26; 12:31.

12. See Appendix 8 for a statement about our ministry.

13. There is an implied exception to liberty in 1 Cor. 9:20ff. We touched on this point earlier. It is this: A Christian cannot sacrifice who he is, that is his ethnicity, for the purpose of evangelizing. Some people tend to think that the above verses teach us that Paul sacrificed his ethnicity. But, (as was shown before) this was not the case. Paul did not yield his identity. He could yield any thing, save the

dual-exception and his identity. There was no such person as a "faceless" Paul. This implied exception is of utmost importance for black people to learn. In our haste to relate to others, we can uncritically begin to lay aside so much that we will come to find out that we have "defaced" and rawed ourselves. Our ethnicity as a people has never adequately been redeemed and restored since our traumatic slavery experience. And yet, we still possess strong proclivities toward integration and assimilation for (what we deem is) the sake of the gospel; and, at the expense of the little ethnicity which we have. It is my prayer that the Lord will enlighten us and tighten us up in this area.

14. This manner of behavior follows the pattern of the voluntary vows mentioned in the O.T. These vows were imposed for the purpose of "self discipline for the achievement of character, and self dedication for the attainment of goals." Examples of this kind of vow can be found in Num. 6:1-8ff; and Ps. 132:2-5.

Chapter 7

1. Greek is *PNEUMATIKOS*, "spiritual" RSV margin. Used in this chapter.

2. Greek is *KOINŌNIA*, "or 'communion' " RSV margin. Used in this chapter.

3. *NBD*, s.v. "Idols, Meats Offered To," by R.P. Martin.

4. In Rev. 2:12-17 and Rev. 2:18-27 are two instances of some "strong" people who encouraged the Christians to eat food offered to idols (in pagan temples) and to practice immorality. Notice the Lord's judgment upon these enticers.

5. The ordinances, or sacraments, of the church are "an outward and visible sign, ordained by Christ, setting forth and pledging, an inward spiritual blessing." (A definition following the teaching and language of St. Augustine (354-430 A.D.) Bishop of Hippo in North Africa.)
   The New International Dictionary of the Christian Church, (1974), s.v. "Sacrament," by Ronald S. Wallace.
   NBD, s.v. "Sacraments," by R.J. Coates.

6. But even though our parents may not be aware of the contemporary scene (as may be in the case of parents who are up in years), it would be wrong for us to take advantage of their lack of knowledge. It would be very unkind to lean on them for the permission to do certain things of which we know they would not approve if they knew the facts about those activities.

7. *ZPEB*, s.v. "Astrology," by W.L. Liefeld.

8. Under this principle, and the general heading of this chapter, we must be seriously precautioned to study both the Order of Free Masons (also, other Fraternal Orders) and the carnival of Mardi gras. Moreover, the new forms of non-traditional institutions of religion which have the doctrine of "universalism" as their underlying tenet of faith should also be critically examined according to the major principle of this chapter.

9. For an upcoming history on the Black Church see (1) Bentley in special note bibliography. Being written by one of our prominent Black Christian ethnic-historical analysts, this history looks to be a major contribution to black folks and to the Church.

Chapter 8

1. Our meeting time was composed of:

Devotion	15 Minutes
Black Time	30 Minutes
Activity/Refreshment Time	45 Minutes
Discovery Time	45 Minutes
Consecration	15 Minutes

2. There is a picture in an illustrated N.T. which shows "Ruins of the shops on the northwest side of the market place in ancient Corinth. This market place was over 500 ft. long and was decorated with a colonnade of 7 Doric columns and an inner row of 34. It had 33 shops, each of which had a storeroom and a supply of cool water." This is the agora and the meat market.

The New Testament, KJV With Pictures (New York: American Bible Society, 1961), p. 182.

Probably other foods, such as fish, fruit, and bread, were also sold in the meat market (shops).

3. "Such food was prohibited to Jews, on three grounds: (a) it was tainted with idolatry; (b) it could not be supposed that the heathen had paid tithes on it; (c) if it was meat, it could not be supposed that it had been slaughtered in the proper way."

Barrett, *First Corinthians,* p. 188.

"Jewish rule was uncompromisingly strict upon this point."

Findlay, *First Corinthians,* p. 838.

4. Norman Hillyer, *1 and 2 Corinthians,* in *The New Bible Commentary,* ed. D. Guthrie et al. 3rd., rev. (Grand Rapids: Eerdmans Publishing Co., 1970), p. 1065.

Barrett, *First Corinthians,* p. 188.

5. A Jew or a Christian would most likely use the term *EIDŌLOTHUTOS* "sacrificed to idols" 8:1,4,7,10; 10:19. An unbeliever or a Christian who was a former idolater might use the term *HIEROTHUTOS* "sacrificed for sacred purposes" 10:28. In 10:19 (twice) the word *THUŌ* is used. It means to "sacrifice by slaying a victim."

6. See Appendix 4, Background to the Book of 1 Corinthians.

7. See Appendix 7, Comparison of 1 Cor. 9:19-23 & 1 Cor. 10:31-33.

8. See Appendix 9 for the Background of the Book of Romans.

Chapter 9

1. See Appendix 3, Outline of Romans.

2. See Appendix 9 for the Background to the Book of Romans.

3. John Murray, *The Epistle to the Romans*, 2 vols. (Grand Rapids: Eerdmans Publishing Co., 1968), vol. 2: p. 174.

4. This could however have been a problem with the Roman Christians. For meat that had been sacrificed to idols could have been bought in Rome just as in Corinth. But, the problem Paul is addressing seems to have been one of a more general nature.

5. See note 3 of chapter 8.

6. Maybe the "weak" needed special occasions in order to keep their lives focused on the Lord.

7. Consider the following:
1. There is no indication of one person being a relatively new Christian, as was probably the case in 1 Cor. 8:7ff.
2. In Romans there is an appeal for *mutual* edification, 14:19.
3. The one who ate anything probably referred to the vegetarian as a "weakling." And the vegetarian probably referred to the one who ate anything as a "glutton."
4. There is an appeal in Romans for both groups to stop judging one another, (14:10).

8. The reason why Paul emphasizes edification may be the fact that the Romans were already knowledgeable of the other two principles. They were evidently more mature than the Corinthians, who needed instruction about the other two principles because of their tendencies to do things which were detrimental to themselves.

9. For an excellent concept on unity, which stresses "unity in diversity without forced conformity," one should consult (12) Bentley in bibliography, for an explanation of the "NBEA Umbrella Concept." This is a very unique, comprehensive, definitive, articulate statement...as well as a model, having been, and being fleshed out in experience.

Chapter 10

1. The National Black Christian Students Conference has been in existence since 1974. Its parent body is the National Black Evangelical

Association.** It is an exclusively black conference in attendance and membership. Its chairperson is Dr. Ruth Lewis Bentley, and its co-chairperson is Sis. Wyn Wright Potter. The conferences are most beneficial. It is a must for every black college student. Contact can be made at this address: National Black Christian Students Conference, P.O. Box 4311, Chicago, Ill. 60680.

    **The National Black Evangelical Association is an organization providing fellowship among believers, and mutual edification through exposure to diversified ministries geared toward black people. For the history of the Association see (12) Bentley in the bibliography. To be revised 1978-79.

2. See the previous chapter, under elucidation, for the problem. The applications given here are built on the explanation given there.

Chapter 11

1. Benjamine E. Mays as quoted in *News From CRAFT* ed. Hezekiah Brady Jr. (Hopkins Park, Illinois: By The Center for Re-creation And Family Training Inc., P.O. Box 231, 60944), December 1977.

2. Position Paper to NBCSC, "Black Art: Content Of Black Survival Mechanisms," from Dr. Hycel B. Taylor (Chicago, Illinois: by the National Black Christian Students Conference, P.O. Box 4311, 60680, October 30-November 2, 1975), p. 3.

3. See Chapter 8 under "The Praise To God," 1 Cor. 10:31.

4. On culture, see (6), (22), (32), (35), (42) in bibliography.

5. Lerone Bennett Jr., "The Lost-Found Generation," *Ebony,* Special Issue: 'The New Generation', August 1978, pp. 35-42.

6. Dr. Charles V. Willie of Harvard University, as quoted in Lerone Bennett Jr., "The Lost-Found Generation," p. 36.

7. Thomas N. Todd, Attorney, Chicago Activist and Former V.P. of PUSH, as quoted in Lerone Bennett Jr., "The Lost-Found Generation," p. 38.

8. Eugene Perkins, *Home Is A Dirty Street: The Social Oppression Of Black Children* (Chicago: Third World Press, 1975), pp. 183, 182, 128, 85-86, 75-76, 92, 91, 43, 30-32, 35-36. (Hereafter reffered to as *Home Is A Dirty Street.*)

9. Haki R. Madhubuti (Don L. Lee), *Enemies: The Clash Of Races* (Chicago: Third World Press, 1978), pp. 199, 226-227, 140, 142, 184, 148-149, 136-137.

10. Michael A. Lomax, A young Black Atlanta Politician, as quoted in Lerone Bennett Jr., "The Lost-Found Generation," p. 40.

11. Alvin F. Poussaint, "What Makes Them Tick," *Ebony*, Special Issue: 'The New Generation', August 1978, p. 80.

12. Harlem Youth Opportunities Unlimited, Inc., *Youth In The Ghetto*, as quoted in Eugene Perkins, *Home Is A Dirty Street*, p. 76.

13. Maulana Ron Karenga, A Black Nationalist, *The Nguzo Saba* (A Black Value System), as quoted in Eugene Perkins, *Home Is A Dirty Street*, pp. 175, 184.

14. Val Gray Ward, Founder/Director KUUMBA, *Principles For Creativity and Liberation*, Chicago, 1971. (A Black Community Workshop "dedicated to contributing to the Black liberation struggle through creative expression".)

15. Lerone Bennett Jr., "The Lost-Found Generation," p. 38. The situation as conceived by analysts: political scientist Charles Hamilton of Columbia, economist Barbara Jones of Clark College, and Sociologist Anna Grant of Morehouse College.

16. Dr. Daniel C. Thompson, Vice President of Dilliard University; a leading authority on Black Leadership patterns, as quoted in Lerone Bennett Jr., "The Lost-Found Generation," p. 38.

17. Dr. Anna Grant, Chairman of the Dept. of Sociology at Morehouse, as quoted in Lerone Bennett Jr., "The Lost-Found Generation," p. 40.

18. Gwendolyn Bonner, A young Black Baptist Church woman of Memphis, Tenn., as quoted in Bill Berry, "Beyond The Here And Now," *Ebony*, Special Issue: 'The New Generation', August 1978, p. 96.

19. Paulette Jones, An unpublished paper, Chicago, 1974, as quoted in Eugene Perkins, *Home Is A Dirty Street*, pp. 181-182.

20. Roper Organization, Inc. as quoted in "The New Generation: A Statistical Study," *Ebony*, Special Issue: 'The New Generation,' August 1978.

21. After composing the "Provoking Proposition" the Lord brought to my attention what I consider to be a very exciting and confirming parallel in Acts 7:44-47. (The Bible verses are in all capitals.)

Acts 7:44-47	Parallel
OUR FATHERS HAD	"When there are black Christian students who take seriously the principles of Christian liberty;
THE TENT OF WITNESS	
IN THE WILDERNESS,	and these black Christian students are willing,
EVEN AS HE WHO SPOKE	
TO MOSES DIRECTED HIM	with the help of the Liberator,
TO MAKE IT,	
ACCORDING TO THE PATTERN	to envision and have impressions
THAT HE HAD SEEN.	within form
OUR FATHERS IN TURN BROUGHT IT IN WITH JOSHUA WHEN THEY DISPOSSESSED THE NATIONS WHICH GOD THRUST OUT BEFORE OUR FATHERS.	about the creation of paragons
	according to the ways of living of black people;
	then we will become blessed with
SO IT WAS UNTIL THE DAYS OF DAVID, WHO FOUND FAVOR IN THE SIGHT OF GOD AND ASKED LEAVE TO FIND A HABITATION FOR THE GOD OF JACOB. BUT IT WAS SOLOMON WHO BUILT A HOUSE FOR HIM.	the kinds of manners that will give direction to,
	and express in symbols
	our composite cultural liberation! Amen!"

22. The National Black Christian Students Conference had as its 1977 theme: "Action Models For The Black Community." This is a definite move toward Creating A Newness. See (38) NBCSC in bibliography.

23.   F.F. Bruce, *The Epistle of Paul To The Romans* (Grand Rapids: Eerdmans Publishing Co., 1963), p. 248, and note.
Bruce, *Acts,* p. 315, and note.

Appendices

1. Information for this section was supplemented by bibliographical sources: 2, 4, 18, 19, 24, 26, 27, 28, 39, 44, 51.

2. Information for this section was supplemented by bibliographical sources: 2, 17, 20, 27, 36, 39, 44, 51.

SELECTED BIBLIOGRAPHY

1. Aland, Kurt., et al. eds. *The Greek New Testament.* 2nd ed. United Bible Societies, 1968.

2. *The American College Dictionary.* (1966).

3. *Baker's Dictionary Of Theology.* (1960), s.v. "Adiaphora." By Alexander M. Renwick.

4. Barrett, C. K. *The First Epistle To The Corinthians.* New York: Harper & Row, 1968.

5. Bennett, Lerone Jr. *Before The Mayflower: A History Of The Negro In America 1619-1964.* Revised Edition. Chicago: Johnson Publishing Company, Penguin Books, 1961.

6. _____. *The Challenge Of Blackness.* Chicago: Johnson Publishing Company, 1972.

7. _____. "The Lost-Found Generation" *Ebony,* Special Issue: 'The New Generation,' August 1978.

8. _____. *The Shaping Of Black America.* Chicago: Johnson Publishing Company, Inc., 1975.

9. Bentley, Ruth Lewis, ed. *Handbook For Black Christian Students or How To Remain Sane And Grow In A White College Setting.* 2nd ed. Chicago, Illinois: By NBCSC, P.O. Box 4311, 60680, 1975.

10. _____. "Psychological Implications Of A Black Christian Students Movement." Adapted from a speech given at Wilberforce University, Wilberforce, Ohio, June 17, 1976. A paper distributed at the National Planning Committee meeting of NBCSC, Chicago, January 1977.

11. Bentley, William H. "The Meaning Of History For Black Americans." Unpublished paper, 1977.

12. _____. *The National Black Evangelical Association: Reflections On The Evolution Of A Concept Of Ministry.* Chicago, 1974. (Revised 1979.)

13. Berry, Bill. "Beyond The Here And Now." *Ebony,* Special Issue: 'The New Generation,' August 1978.

14. The Holy Bible. Revised Standard Version, (1946, 1952, © 1971, 1973).

15. Brady, Hezekiah Jr., ed. *News From CRAFT.* Hopkins Park, Illinois: By the Center for Re-creation And Family Training, Inc., P.O. Box 231, 60944, December 1977.

16. Bruce, F.F. *The Book Of The Acts.* Grand Rapids: Eerdmans Publishing Co., 1971.

17. _____. *The Epistle Of Paul To The Romans.* Grand Rapids: Eerdmans Publishing Co., 1963.

18. *The Corinthian Correspondence,* course with Dr. Gilbert Bilezikian, Trinity College, Deerfield, Illinois. 2nd Semester, 1973-74.

19. *The Corinthian Correspondence,* course with Dr. Murray J. Harris, Trinity Evangelical Divinity School, Deerfield, Illinois, Fall 1974.

20. Davidson, F. and Martin, Ralph P. *Romans,* in *The New Bible Commentary,* edited by D. Guthrie et al. 3rd. rev. Grand Rapids: Eerdmans Publishing Co., 1970.

21. Douglass, Frederick. "What To The Slaves Is The Fourth Of July?: Frederick Douglass' Independence Day Address (1852)," in *The Negro Almanac,* comp. and ed. by Harry A. Ploski and Roscoe C. Brown Jr. New York: Bellwether Publishing Co. Inc., 1967.

22. DuBois, W.E.B. *The Souls Of Black Folks.* New York: New American Library, A Signet Classic, 1969.

23. Dunston, Bishop Alfred G. Jr. *The Black Man In The Old Testament And Its World.* Philadelphia: Dorrance & Company, 1974.

24. Findlay, G. G. *St. Paul's First Epistle To The Corinthians,* vol. 2 of *The Expositor's Greek Testament,* edited by W. Robertson Nicoll. 5 vols. Grand Rapids: Eerdmans Publishing Co., 1970.

25. Franklin, John Hope. *From Slavery To Freedom: A History Of Negro Americans.* Third Edition. New York: Random House, Vintage Books, 1969.

26. Grosheide, F. W. *Commentary On The First Epistle To The Corinthians.* Grand Rapids: Eerdmans Publishing Co., 1953.

27. Guthrie, Donald. *New Testament Introduction.* Downers Grove: Intervarsity Press, 1971.

28. Hillyer, Norman. *1 and 2 Corinthians.* in *The New Bible Commentary,* edited by D. Guthrie et al. 3rd. rev. Grand Rapids: Eerdmans Publishing Co., 1970.

29. *The International Standard Bible Encyclopedia.* (1939). Consulted various articles for background information.

30. Latourette, Kenneth Scott. *A History Of Christianity.* Revised Edition, 2 vols. New York: Harper & Row, 1975.

31. Lemieux, Melba. "Third Annual Collegiate Poll: Black Students On White Campuses—Is There A Chance Of Survival?" *The Black Collegian,* March/April 1978.

32. Levine, Lawrence W. *Black Culture And Black Consciousness.* New York: Oxford University Press. 1977.

33. Madhubuti, Haki R. (Don L. Lee). *Enemies: The Clash Of Races.* Chicago: Third World Press, 1978.

34. Metzger, Bruce M. *A Textual Commentary On The Greek New Testament.* London: United Bible Societies, 1971.

35. Murray, Albert. *The Omni-Americans: New Perspectives on Black Experience and American Culture.* New York: Outerbridge & Dienstfrey, 1970.

36. Murray, John. *The Epistle To The Romans.* 2 vols. Grand Rapids: Eerdmans Publishing Co., 1968.

37. McCray, Walter A. *TOWARD A HOLISTIC LIBERATION OF BLACK PEOPLE: Its Meaning As Expressed In The Objectives Of The National Black Christian Students Conference.* Edited by Ruth Lewis Bentley. Chicago, Illinois: By NBCSC, P.O.Box 4311, Chicago, 60680, 1977.

38. National Black Christian Students Conference, Position Papers and Tapes: "Black Christian Identity, Unity, Community—LIBERATION!" (74); "Exploring Dimensions In Black Survival" (75); "Free to Be..." (76); "Action Models for the Black Community" (77). Chicago, Illinois: By NBCSC, P.O. Box 4311, 60680.

39. *The New Bible Dictionary.* 1st ed. (1962). Consulted various articles for background information.

40. *The New International Dictionary of the Christian Church.* (1974), s.v. "Sacrament," by Ronald S. Wallace; "Adiaphorists," by Robert G. Clouse.

41. *The New Testament.* KJV With Pictures, New York: American Bible Society, 1961.

42. Neibuhr, H. Richard. *Christ And Culture.* New York: Harper & Row Publishers, 1951.

43. Perkins, Eugene. *Home Is A Dirty Street: The Social Oppression Of Black Children.* Chicago: Third World Press, 1975.

44. Pfeiffer, Charles F. *Baker's Bible Atlas.* Revised Edition. Grand Rapids: Baker Book House, 1973.

45. Poussaint, Alvin F. "What Makes Them Tick." *Ebony,* Special Issue: 'The New Generation', August 1978.

46. Taylor, Hycel B. "Black Art: Content Of Black Survival Mechanism." Position Paper to NBCSC. Chicago, Illinois: By the National Black Christian Students Conference, P.O.Box 4311, 60680, October 30-November 2, 1975.

47. *Webster's New World Dictionary.* College ed. (1968).

48. Vine, W.E. *An Expository Dictionary Of New Testament Words.* (1966).

49. Weston, Martin. "Conquering Razor Bumps." *Ebony,* March 1976.

50. Williams, Chancellor. *The Destruction Of Black Civilization: Great Issues Of A Race From 4500 B.C. To 2000 A.D.* Chicago: Third World Press, 1976. Revised edition.

51. *The Zondervan Pictorial Encyclopedia of the Bible.* (1975), Consulted various articles for background information.

Books by Rev. Walter Arthur McCray

Black Folks and Christian Liberty (1979, 1987)
Be Christian. Be Black. Be Culturally and Socially Free!
$10.00 ISBN: 0-933176-08-2

Toward a Wholistic Liberation of Black People (1979)
Its Meaning as Explored in the Objectives of the National Black Christia
Students Conference
$3.00

Solid! (1981)
Nine Vital Lessons on Saving, Settling and Solidifying The Black Marriag
$5.00 ISBN: 0-933176-05-8

How To Stick Together During Times of Tension (1983)
Directives for Christian Black Unity
$7.50 ISBN: 0-933176-03-1

A Rationale for Black Christian Literature (1985)
$3.50

Reaching and Teaching Black Young Adults (1986)
$5.95 ISBN: 0-933176-07-4

Order publications from:

Black Light Fellowship, Post Office Box 5369, Chicago, IL 60680

Payment must accompany orders.
Include at least $2.00 for postage and handling.

Office:

Black Light Fellowship
2859 W. Wilox
Chicago, IL 60612
(312) 722-1441

Bookstores and wholesalers may inquire for a special discount.